COMPOSERS OF OPERETTA

COMPOSERS
OF OPERETTA

BY

GERVASE HUGHES

M.A., B.MUS.(OXON.)

GREENWOOD PRESS, PUBLISHERS
WESTPORT, CONNECTICUT

Library of Congress Cataloging in Publication Data

Hughes, Gervase.
    Composers of operetta.

    Reprint of the 1962 ed. published by Macmillan,
London; St. Martin's Press, New York.
    Bibliography: p.
    1. Composers--Biography. I. Title.
[ML390.H887C6 1974]   782.8'1'0922 [B]   74-9604
ISBN 0-8371-7612-3

This book is dedicated to Gwyneth Edwards.
But for her tolerance and forbearance
it would never have been completed.

CONTENTS

§

ROUND THE CONTINENT

§

BRITISH OPERETTA

§

FINALE

ILLUSTRATIONS

* Radio Times Hulton Picture Library
† Victoria and Albert Museum

'La opereta a cuyo brillante nacimiento asístimos en París con Jacques Offenbach y en Viena con Johann Strauss, género, que con los años trato de acercarse a su hermana mayor, la ópera, bien merece que le dediquemos una página aparte, sin poder abordar todas sus múltiples manifestaciones, sus creadores y creaciones pintorescas y sus triunfos deslumbrantes y mundiales.'

Kurt Pahlen,
Historia gráfica universal de música (Buenos Aires, 1944).

I
BRIEF OVERTURE

THE word Operetta, though Italian in origin, is a recognised part of the English vocabulary ; in French *opérette* and in German *Operette* convey the same meaning. This international acceptance makes it a more convenient term than 'light opera', which is vague, or 'comic opera', which is often inappropriate and always liable to confuse foreigners, since *opéra comique* and *komische Oper* mean something else. I see no valid reason why the multiformity of traditional nomenclature should not be sacrificed, and shall therefore count as operettas many compositions which were not so labelled by their creators. What is to be the qualifying characteristic ? It would be misleading to claim that operetta is a form of entertainment derived from opera but designed to amuse an audience rather than to stir its emotion : one of the best operas ever written, Verdi's *Falstaff*, is 'low comedy' almost throughout, whereas humour is noticeably absent from Messager's charming operetta *Madame Chrysanthème*. Nor is the calibre of the music a safe criterion. Operas can be commonplace or trivial (many are) ; operettas can be scholarly and distinguished, though anything *pretentious* involves disqualification, and it would be fair to stipulate that the composer's approach should be light-handed. Precise definition is elusive, but should we hesitate before making up our minds whether or not a particular work is an operetta we can rely on literal translation and ask ourselves if it can reasonably be called a little opera (using 'little' in the sense of 'unassuming' rather than 'small').

In nine cases out of ten there will be a swift and unequivocal reply, but occasionally stylistic considerations may delay the resolution of doubt ; if so, the word 'little' can be brought into play once more, this time as a mere measure of quantity. Saint-Saëns' *Princesse jaune* is discussed in these pages because it is a *miniature*, and on the same basis I have felt justified in admitting Puccini's *Gianni Schicchi* ; had either been expanded to fill a whole evening there would have been a rise in status which might have lifted it beyond our present scope. Because operetta is an off-shoot of opera we shall inevitably meet other border-line cases ; they will not necessarily be shrugged aside, but (unless a contrast needs to be pointed) our terms of reference will preclude detailed consideration of any work which cannot be described as an 'unassuming little opera'. They will also be subject to a chronological restriction : Pergolesi's *Serva padrona* (1733), Arne's *Thomas and Sally* (1760), Grétry's *Richard Cœur de Lion* (1784), Mozart's *Schauspieldirektor* (1786) and their fellows will come under notice only as progenitors, for the term operetta acquired neither widespread linguistic currency nor historical significance until about 1840, and I do not propose to apply it retrospectively except to a few tentative essays dating from the previous decade or so. The authentic genre is now almost defunct. Composers of Operetta (not all of whom, incidentally, were 'unassuming little men') were therefore virtually a product of the nineteenth-century.

Of those who achieved fame — fame which was often transient — the vast majority were specialists ; some had little or no musical training and possessed few qualifications beyond an aptitude for tickling the public ear, but others — including such important figures as Offenbach, Lecocq and Lehár — were sound craftsmen who for one reason or another decided to concentrate mainly on light music, if not on operetta exclusively. A large minority group comprised men of talent and versatility who did not always recognise their limitations and whose operettas — though perhaps but a small part of their total output — often showed them to better advantage than did their more ambitious works. Sullivan is the classic example, but Lortzing, Adam, Massé and possibly Heuberger belonged to the same fraternity. Next on the list come a few eminent composers who distinguished themselves in more lofty regions but occasionally threw off an operetta when they felt in the mood — Massenet, for instance, and Stanford. *Hors concours* stands one great master, Dvořák, who demonstrated his genius as readily in operetta as in every other branch of composition.

The origin and development of the various European schools will be separately traced. A chapter will be reserved for the North American continent and a few of today's 'musicals' will be allowed to creep into the picture ; they can justly claim lineal descent even though many were born out of wedlock. Biographical sketches of the outstanding exponents must suffice to establish the environments in which both they and their contemporaries lived and worked, for despite its title this book deals with an art-form rather than a race of artists, my purpose being to assess the musical worth of over a thousand operettas written by about two hundred and twenty composers. I hope that the ghosts of two hundred and twenty authors will forgive me if I do not follow any of *their* mortal careers, summarise their plots or compare their achievements. Yet since the libretto of an operetta has often played an essential part in the determination of success or failure, it is only fair that when its originator has been decisively on the side of the angels he should be named — and by implication commended. More often than not, however, librettists will herein remain (significantly) anonymous.

Operettas written in French, German, Italian or Spanish will be accorded their original titles unless an English equivalent is in everyday use, *e.g. The Merry Widow* ; where languages are encountered with which few of us are familiar, it would be unwise to enforce that principle. At the risk of offending the purists, I have therefore transcribed *Hin Ondes snaror* and *Dvě vdovy* in the Queen's English ; but the Index of Operettas, page 259, incorporates all the original titles (except those in Russian, which are based on a different alphabet), and when necessary there is a cross-reference to the English title used in the text.

That is all I have to say by way of introduction. *Levez le rideau!*

§

FRENCH OPERETTA

THE ESTABLISHMENT OF A TRADITION

THE ancestry of French operetta need be traced back no further than 1715, when the newly inaugurated 'Théâtre de l'Opéra-Comique' undertook managerial responsibility for the musical booths which had long been a popular attraction at the Paris fair-grounds of Saint-Germain and Saint-Laurent. The entertainment which it provided bore little resemblance to what we now understand by *opéra comique*, for it consisted merely of short sketches introducing topical songs and parodies of opera. They were put together by miscellaneous hacks and fell into two categories : the *vaudeville*, often bawdy, and the *comédie à ariettes*, equally trivial but comparatively decorous. No one attempted to strike a balance between these crude fabrications and the grandiloquent productions of the Académie de la Musique — *i.e.* the 'Opéra' — where Rameau reigned as uncrowned king. All in all, stage music in the French capital was going through a period of malaise.

The turning-point came with the visit of an Italian company of players in 1752. The *intermezzi* (see page 163) which comprised their repertory were basically no more ambitious than the *comédies à ariettes*, but each was the work of a single composer (often an accomplished one) and the artistic standard of presentation was vastly superior. Their unparalleled success was the immediate cause of the so-called *guerre des bouffons* ; many of the protagonists, among them distinguished musicians and philosophers, clouded the issue with weighty and irrelevant expositions of their pet theories, but in essence the dispute lay between the invading forces and the fairground proprietors. The outcome of the struggle was determined by Jean Monnet, a far-sighted impresario who fought the Italians with their own weapons by striving to develop a native product that would be capable of rivalling any importation. His first shot misfired, because the 'book' of *Les Trocqueurs* (1753, music by Antoine Dauvergne, *chef d'orchestre* at the Opéra) was imbued with the ribald traditions of *vaudeville*, but in 1757 he hit the target with *Le Caprice amoureux* (which some historians prefer to call by its sub-title *Ninette à la cour*) and *Le Peintre amoureux de son modèle*. Curiously enough their composer, Egidio Duni, was Italian by birth, but for once the dominating partner was the librettist, Charles Favart. (Among other composers with whom he collaborated were Gluck and Mozart.) He was not only an author but also an experienced man-of-the-theatre, and a year later he succeeded Monnet as manager of the Théâtre de l'Opéra-Comique. It was under his auspices that in 1759 François Philidor made his mark with *Blaise le savetier* and Pierre Monsigny with *Les Aveux indiscrets*. Such unassuming affairs were still described conventionally as *comédies à ariettes* or more loosely as *divertissements*, and for the time being they were still played — *faute de mieux* — at one or other of the fairgrounds. But by 1762, when Favart became lessee of the Salle de l'hôtel de Bourgogne in the rue Mauconseil, the French evolution of the *intermezzo* was recognised as a distinctive and reputable genre, fully deserving the appellation *opéra comique*.

For many years Favart relied largely on Duni, Philidor and Monsigny ; he might have done worse. Duni, though a second-rank composer, was an adaptable cosmopolitan whose skill in imparting a French flavour to a typically Italian art-form undoubtedly helped to smooth the road ahead for his younger contemporaries and their successors. Philidor was a professional chess-player, which goes far to explain how it was that he packed his music with ingenious *fugati*, canons and rounds, as well as providing the earliest known examples of straightforward 'tune-combination' ; unfortunately his chess-board mentality seems to have precluded a natural blossoming-forth of inspiration. Monsigny, by contrast, had a pleasing gift of melody but was unable to exploit it to the full because of sad deficiencies in technique. In consequence their combined achievements did not vie with those of the prolific and more versatile André Grétry (Belgian by birth, Parisian by adoption), who wrote some fifty little operas of which *Les Deux avares* (1770), *Zémire et Azor* (1771), *L'Épreuve villageoise* and *Richard Cœur de Lion* (both 1784) long enjoyed popularity in France and abroad. His technique was almost as weak as Monsigny's, but at his best he coupled Gallic grace with Mozartian delicacy. His proudest moment came in 1783 when he was invited to compose *Thalie au nouveau théâtre* for the ceremonial opening of the fittingly named Salle Favart in the boulevard des Italiens, which was henceforth to be the permanent home of *opéra comique*.[1]

During the first fifteen years or so of the Salle Favart's existence Grétry's good work was consolidated by Nicolas Dalayrac; elsewhere Gluck had cut away much of the dead wood surrounding *opéra* and, though *vaudeville* continued to flourish in the music-halls which were gradually replacing the fairground theatres, French stage music as a whole was beginning to wear a much healthier complexion. Audiences at the Salle Favart were left in no doubt as to the direction in which they were being led, for such works as Méhul's *Euphrosine et Coradin* (1790) and Boïeldieu's *Calife de Bagdad* (1800) made it clear that *opéra comique* had thrown aside its questionable associations and was now worthy to rank as the denizen of an opera house.

By the turn of the century, therefore, French opera (we can now justifiably use the term in its wider sense) was flowing in two adjacent and well-regulated channels. The dyke which separated them had a fundamental substructure, but during the next fifty years its walls were artificially buttressed. From the premise of incompatibility between Drama and Comedy it was argued that *ethos* of subject-matter rather than sincerity of expression should be the main criterion in differentiating *opéra* from *opéra comique*. Philip Hope-Wallace in *A Key to Opera* (1939) hit the nail on the head : '*Opéra* is heroic. *Opéra comique* is unheroic.' As we have seen, the distinction had a historical basis, but its arbitrary application was illogical. Though it may have been reasonable to assume that the spoken word was inadmissible in a 'heroic' opera, it was muddle-headed to enforce the groundless corollary that an *opéra comique* must willy-nilly include passages of dialogue or *recitativo*

---

[1] In Britain today Grétry might be almost forgotten but for the proselytising zeal of Sir Thomas Beecham; the charming 'pantomime' from *Zémire et Azor,* for instance, was one of his favourite 'lollipops'.

secco. Furthermore each of the recognised genres had — and still has — its own separate organisation and headquarters, pursuing a policy of mutual exclusion which has been an unconscionable time a-dying ; *Carmen* (which in France incorporates dialogue) had to wait until November 1959 before being played at the Opéra. (The Académie de la Musique was a peripatetic institution until the present Opera House was completed in 1875 ; the Théâtre de l'Opéra-Comique still occupies the site of the original Salle Favart — though there have been breaks in continuity. I shall not attempt to elucidate the apparent anomaly that spectacular ballets, often with a frankly sensual or frivolous appeal, have usually been staged at the Opéra rather than the Opéra-Comique, for such a diversion would involve a comprehensive investigation of the sociological aspect which would here be out of place.)

This obligation to conform with convention unquestionably imposed a brake on the initiative of serious composers for the theatre ; they could not hope to emulate Weber or Donizetti so long as the French corner of the operatic field was subjected to officious husbandry which effectively impeded the flowering of a native *Freischütz* or *Don Pasquale*. In case such a generalisation, covering half a century, be adjudged sweeping or superficial, let me particularise by focusing attention on the Opéra-Comique at the exact mid-point, New Year's Eve 1825.

. . . The fifty-year-old François Boïeldieu, doyen of authentic *opéra comique*, has just launched the classic *Dame blanche* ; he and four others — Ferdinando Paer (fifty-four), D. F. E. Auber (forty-three), Michele Carafa (thirty-eight) and Ferdinand Hérold (thirty-four) — have secured a virtual monopoly of new productions. Paer normally adheres to the traditions of Italy (where he was born), but is preferred for his rather uncharacteristic *Maître de chapelle*, which has held its place in the repertory since 1821. Carafa (another Italian) and Hérold are the youngsters of the group ; two years ago the former established himself with *Le Valet de chambre* and the latter with *Le Muletier*. Auber has a more assured, at times almost Mozartian approach, but he too has yet to reach the summit of his powers (not till 1828 will *Fra Diavolo* be completed) ; he has already done enough to raise hopes that he may presently outshine

even Boïeldieu as a master of *opéra comique*. Before the vision fades
we may catch a glimpse of Meyerbeer and Rossini standing in the
wings ; both have just settled in Paris at the age of thirty-three but
up to date their impact has hardly made itself felt. J. F. Halévy
(twenty-six) is still out in the cold, vainly seeking admittance at
the stage-door but dreaming, possibly, of a moment ten years hence
when the simultaneous presentation of his best *opéra* (*La Juive*) and
his best *opéra comique* (*L'Éclair*) will bring him fame and fortune. . . .

Now these eight composers, four Frenchmen and four immigrants, abided without question by the immutable lines of de-
marcation, and their operas fitted neatly into one or other of the
two acceptable categories. (Of all the works they wrote between
them for the Paris stage how many were to stand the test of time ?
Half a dozen perhaps.) Presently, however, some of the rising generation began to find the circumscriptions irksome, and the importance
of ADOLPHE ADAM (1803–1856) derives from his praiseworthy
attempts to breach the barriers, thus facilitating the subsequent
passage of Berlioz, Bizet and Massenet in one direction and of
Offenbach, Lecocq and Messager in another. His methods were far
from being revolutionary, but he did at least assess a libretto on its
merits, and he was quite capable of setting it to music without
regard for formal precedent. Consequently a few of his *soi-disant*
opéras comiques hovered on the verge of *opéra*, but it is of greater
moment that many others introduced *vaudeville* characteristics,
whereby they were either enlivened or debased according to the
point of view. From this union of two elements which had been
irreconcilable since the *guerre des bouffons* sprang the hybrid of
opéra bouffe, a term which for practical purposes may be considered
synonymous with *opérette*. (Strictly speaking, an *opéra bouffe* was
essentially 'burlesque', an *opérette* comparatively 'straight' ; but the
distinction was often blurred and in retrospect has only academic
significance.) Adam may thus be credited with the initiation of a
new art-form ; therein rests his chief claim to remembrance, for
though the ballet *Giselle* has achieved classic status his music rarely
rises above the level of a comfortable mediocrity.

Adam's father, perhaps because himself a musician, discouraged
young Adolphe's determination to adopt the same profession, but

eventually — with reluctant parental consent — he was enrolled at the Paris Conservatoire. Although he had lessons from Boïeldieu, whom he greatly admired, he was an awkward student and never looked likely to gain academic honours. He spent his evenings assisting in the 'kitchen' department of a music-hall orchestra, where his virtuosity on triangle and side-drum earned him an early opportunity to show his paces as a composer — albeit in the same undignified milieu. During this period he wrote about two dozen *vaudevilles* ; though as unsubstantial as tissue-paper they no doubt served their purpose, and for Adam the experience was useful. But it was only when Boïeldieu enlisted his aid in orchestrating the overture to *La Dame blanche* that his name was brought to the notice of the Opéra-Comique, where his curtain-raiser, *Pierre et Catherine*, was produced in 1829. This was followed a year later by his first large-scale work, the rather pretentious *Danilowa*, and in 1831 by the lighter-handed *Grand Prix*. Meanwhile he had secured the interest of his brother-in-law, François Laporte, who was in charge at Covent Garden ; *The First Campaign* and *The Dark Diamond* were staged there in 1832, but all we know about their content lies in Adam's own recorded words : 'J'ai remplacé la musique de ces deux ouvrages dans plusieurs opéras réprésentés à Paris.'

Thus far he had shown little inclination to defy convention, and back at the Opéra-Comique *Le Proscrit* (1833) followed in the train of *Danilowa*. However, *Le Châlet* (1834, libretto by Eugène Scribe and H. J. Mélesville) marked a noteworthy divergence ; Adam's instinct must have warned him that the time was not yet ripe for a fifty-fifty mixture of *opéra comique* and *vaudeville*, but he incorporated enough frivolity to enable this one-act piece to stake its claim as the first French operetta.[1] Moreover, it must rank as a good specimen, for in the main Adam here adopted an attractive and melodious style which perhaps owed too much to the lighter side of Rossini but pleased both singers and audience ; elsewhere the whiff of the music-hall was unmistakable, though discreet.

---

[1] Admittedly *Le Diable à Séville* by José Gomis, a refugee from Spain, had been given three years previously. But it sprang from *tonadilla* (see page 168), and the composer's death in 1836 cut short any influence he might otherwise have exerted on the future development of the French variant.

Le Postillon de Longjumeau (1836), despite an excellent first-act finale, somehow lacked spontaneity ; nevertheless it is an important land-mark in our story, for this time *vaudeville* intruded not on a curtain-raiser but on a full-length *opéra comique* which was otherwise more or less in the Boïeldieu manner. The incursions were multiplied in *Le Fidèle berger* (1838), but for *Le Brasseur de Preston* (also 1838) Adam chose a libretto which obliged him to adhere more closely to tradition. And so the vacillation went on. Of major works between 1839 and 1844 *La Reine d'un jour* was virtually an operetta (not a very good one), *Le Roi d'Yvetot* was a genuine *opéra comique*, *Cagliostro* drew near the frontiers of *opéra* and *Richard en Palestine* crossed over them.

By 1847 Adam had acquired such personal prestige and financial stability that he was able to realise a project he had long had in mind. He bought the lease of a disused theatre and equipped it for the presentation not only of his own operas, operettas and ballets, but also those of younger and lesser-known composers who could not gain entry to the Opéra-Comique. For the opening of this 'Opéra-National', Auber, Carafa, Halévy and Adam himself col-laborated in *Les Premiers pas*, and the inauguration was auspicious. But though the venture was sound in conception it was not proof against a political whirlwind ; it was brought to an untimely and regretted end by the revolution of 1848. Adam was left to count his losses which monetarily speaking were heavy, for his life's savings were involved, but he carried on his creative work with undiminished enthusiasm. The one-act *Toréador* — which had been hurriedly finished in eight days for the Opéra-National just before the cataclysm — was in 1849 revised and expanded to two acts for the Opéra-Comique ; with the possible exception of *Le Châlet* it was his most satisfying work to date. By this time the legitimacy of the new genre was recognised, and most of Adam's subsequent productions can be classed without apology as operettas. The full-length *Giralda* (1850, libretto again by Scribe) and *Si j'étais roi* (1852) were both very successful, but curtain-raisers continued to find him in even sunnier mood : *La Poupée de Nuremberg*, *Le Farfadet* (both also 1852) and *A Clichy* (1854) showed him at his best. Just before his death in 1856 he made his first and only contribution to Offenbach's Bouffes-Parisiens (see pages 21 and 55) ; this was *Les Pantins de Violette*.

Perhaps because of his close association with the Opéra-Comique the intrinsic worth of Adam's music was long overrated by responsible French critics, and his unorthodox approach troubled them less than one might have expected. Even Félix Clément, the leading musicologist of the mid-century and a regular old die-hard at that, accorded a few gracious words of praise to *Le Châlet*, *Giralda* and other equally light-hearted effusions, though whenever he detected any suggestion of impropriety in either words or action he pounced as heavily on the composer as he did on the author and director. (This tendency to confuse art with morals coloured many of his judgments on the music of other operettas, as we shall see in later chapters.) Clément's colleague Arthur Pougin waxed particularly fulsome over *Le Toréador*, which he acclaimed as a distinguished piece of elegant comedy, the work of a clever musician with a cheerful and friendly personality.[1] It was left to the German-born Francis Hueffer to put the case for the opposition in the first edition of Grove's *Dictionary of Music and Musicians*.

> His melodies are often trivial to absolute vulgarity : the structure of his concerted pieces is of the flimsiest kind : all this, no less than the choice of *hasardé* subjects, seems to indicate the gradual decline from the serene heights of Boïeldieu's humour to the miry slough which has swamped the sweetest growth of French national art, the comic opera [*i.e. opéra comique*], and the murky surface of which reflects the features of Beethoven's countryman, Jacques Offenbach.

All subsequent editors of *Grove* have retained the bulk of Hueffer's article — which was factual and informative — but have rightly expunged this peroration, where one of the most honoured names in music was dragged into the argument for the sake of a cheap jibe. To strike a balance between Pougin and Hueffer I shall para-

---

[1] 'Cette partition n'est pas seulement distinguée, elle est d'une élégance extrême ; elle n'est pas seulement gaie, elle est d'un comique achevé, qui ne tombe jamais dans la trivialité et ne fait aucune concession au mauvais goût ; elle n'est pas seulement l'œuvre d'un musicien habile, expérimenté, heureux et inspiré, mais encore celle d'un homme d'esprit, de goût, de sens et de bonne compagnie.'

phrase the comment of a great composer who was Adam's compatriot and almost exact contemporary.

His music is admirably suited to the requirements of the Opéra-Comique, for it is stylish, fluent, undistinguished, full of catchy little tunes which one can whistle on the way home.

In those few words Berlioz told us all we really need to know about Adam's quality as a composer.

For readers who are interested in technicalities, it can be recorded that he was addicted to drone basses, elementary 'tum-tum' and abrupt shifts of tonality (usually down a major third) ; such devices are tolerable in a short curtain-raiser where there is hardly time for them to outstay their welcome, but they become irritating when spread impartially over a full-length work, and in order to represent him in as favourable a light as possible I have chosen for quotation four passages where he accorded more positive support to his flow of melody. Thus Ex. 1 from *Le Châlet* shows some initiative in its harmonic progressions ; in Ex. 2 the orchestral accompaniment to the second verse of a song from *Le Farfadet* introduces a pleasing line of figuration for violas ; in Ex. 3 from *À Clichy* the phrases fall into unequal bar-lengths (5–5–4–4), and Ex. 4, a *pas-de-deux* from *Les Pantins de Violette*, demonstrates economic facility in tune-combination *à la* Philidor. But it will be noticed that in two cases out of four there is a subsequent lapse into the commonplace.

Ex. 1 Moderato

Ras-su-rez vous, soy-ez sans crain-te, Pen-dant un mois, c'est fort heur-eux, vous au-rez des sol-

dats ai-ma-bles et joy-eux, Car tout le ré-gi-ment doit pas-ser en ces lieux.

Ex. 2 Andantino quasi allegretto

ben staccato

Voi-là que Ni-na, la blon-de, ar-rive a-vec son pa-pa, *etc.*

Ex. 3 Andantino

Je sais bien que la pauv-re-té Est le des-tin du vrai po - è - te; Fuy-ant l'é-

clat et l'é-ti-quette, Elle a, par-fois, elle a, par-fois, son

rall.

bon cô-té, Et son de-vise est tra-vail et gaie-té!

Ex. 4 Allegro

ALPHONSE THYS (1807–1879) followed Adam's trail from the music-hall to the Opéra-Comique ; his early *vaudevilles* led to half a dozen one-act operettas of which *Aïda* (1835) was the first, *Le Roi Margot* (1844) the best, and *Les Échos de Rosine* (1854) the last. He specialised in burlesque of Italian opera in general and Rossini in particular. Other contemporaries in the same field were NARCISSE

GIRARD (1797–1860) and ALEXANDRE MONTFORT (1803–1856, exactly the same dates as Adam). Girard, principal conductor at the Opéra-Comique, was obviously impressed by the success of Adam's experiments and hoped to profit from it. Nothing would be easier, he thought, than to write an operetta or two ; that they would be produced at the Opéra-Comique was a foregone conclusion. But *Les Deux voleurs* (1841) and *Le Conseil de dix* (1842) were ingenuous to the point of fatuity ; Girard wisely discarded his pen forthwith and picked up the baton once more. Montfort's first two attempts, *Polichinelle* (1839) and *La Jeunesse de Charles-Quint* (1841), were also elementary, though the vocal writing had a professional touch. *L'Ombre d'Argentine* (1853) showed him to better advantage ; much of it was Italian pastiche, but here and there an inborn talent seemed to be struggling to express itself.

LOUIS CLAPISSON (1808–1866) was a more considerable figure; though trained as a violinist he soon took to composition and he espoused Adam's cause as early as 1838 with the very pretty *Figurante*, a work of some finesse for which his name deserves to be remembered. During the rest of his life he turned out on an average about one operetta a year, but he was often hampered by poor libretti, which he treated perfunctorily. Though he could write effectively for both voices and orchestra — witness the delicate opening ensemble 'Venez, venez' from *Le Coffret de Saint Domingue* (1854) — he never again caught his first fine careless rapture. Apart from the tuneful and popular *Gibby la Cornemuse* (1846), only *Frère et mari* (1841), *Les Bergers trumeaux* (in frankly eighteenth-century style, 1843), *Dans les vignes* (also 1843) — all in one act — and *La Fanchonnette* (1856) realised something of his early promise. (In *La Fanchonnette* he had for once the benefit of a good libretto ; the authors were J. H. Vernoy de Saint-Georges and A. de Leuven.) Clapisson's latent charm can best be illustrated by a few bars of intermission from *La Figurante*.

Ex. 5 Andante

It was the versatile Adam, better known for his ballet-music, who was the originator of this new genre ; the specialist Clapisson, despite his shortcomings, played a large part in helping to establish it. But twenty-three years after *Le Chalet* first saw the light Adam was in his grave and Clapisson had shot his bolt. The situation was critical ; French operetta, despite its promising beginnings, needed a composer of forceful character and outstanding ability to save it from lapsing into desuetude. It found him in Jacques Offenbach.

III

OFFENBACH — THE GREAT DAYS

JUDA EBERST was a Jewish singing-teacher from the Hessian town of Offenbach, now a suburb of Frankfort ; on becoming Cantor at a Cologne synagogue he took to himself the name of his birthplace. His son JAKOB OFFENBACH was born on 20th June 1819 and as a child showed such proficiency on the cello that the family raised sufficient funds to send him to the Conservatoire at Paris. After little more than a year's study he secured a position in the orchestra of the Opéra-Comique, a remarkable achievement for a boy of sixteen. This gave him invaluable experience ; besides becoming familiar with the standard repertory he must have contributed his modest share to successful new productions like Adam's *Postillon de Longjumeau* and Clapisson's *Figurante* of which he could hardly fail to realise the significance. The appointment also brought in its train some useful contacts, notably an introduction to another emigrant from Germany, Friedrich von Flotow (see page 62), who was a good friend to his young compatriot and engaged him to orchestrate parts of the opera *Le Naufrage de la Méduse* (a composite affair to which several composers contributed).

Presently Offenbach diplomatically changed his first name to JACQUES and became a naturalised Frenchman. He augmented his meagre salary at the theatre by playing at dances and soirées ; later at fashionable concerts. Before long his prowess on the cello was recognised both in France and abroad ; in 1844, for instance, he appeared in London, sharing the bill with an infant prodigy of the violin, Master Joseph Joachim, and being accompanied, the programme tells us, 'by Doctor F. Mendelssohn-Bartholdy'.[1]

---

[1] 'He is on the violoncello what Paganini was on the violin.' — *Dramatic and Musical Review*, 15th May 1844. (Later the same year Offenbach married the seventeen-year-old Herminie d'Alcain ; thereafter she rarely left his side.)

By this time, too, occasional engagements as conductor were beginning to come his way ; now and again he was handed the baton at the Opéra-Comique itself. But his great ambition was to be acclaimed within those august portals not as cellist or even as conductor, but as composer. His early activity in that sphere was largely restricted to 'salon music' — songs, waltzes, quadrilles and the like — though he wrote a few pieces exploiting the potentialities of his own instrument, including a recently discovered concerto and a fantasia for seven cellos based on the melodies of Meyerbeer's *Robert le Diable*. All this he regarded only as a preliminary canter ; he hankered to win his spurs in the *operatic* world. But the management of the Opéra-Comique had not been impressed by his immature musical farce *Pascal et Chambord* — given at the Palais-Royal in 1839 — and refused to consider *L'Alcôve* (1847). It was played with success, however, at an obscure music-hall.

During the revolution of 1848 Offenbach did not add to his personal stature. He found convenient 'family reasons' for visiting his native Cologne, where he temporarily reassumed the name Jakob and indulged in some fence-sitting antics that were hardly edifying. Jewish by race, German by birth and French by adoption, he would have liked to enjoy the privileges of all three while escaping from the responsibilities involved. When he returned to Paris — now once more *Jacques* Offenbach — he again importuned the Opéra-Comique. His contract as cellist and occasional conductor was renewed, but as composer he was still ignored. With characteristic persistence he refused to give up the struggle and went on writing short musical plays which were produced at small concert-halls or suburban theatres, sometimes even in private houses. *Le Trésor à Mathurin* (1851) later achieved recognition in more dignified surroundings as *Le Mariage aux lanternes*, but the only one of these pieces that demands more than a passing word is *Pepito* (1853), for this was a prototype of the one-act trifles with which he was later to flood the market.

Admittedly Offenbach never repeated the experiment of raising the curtain to the strains of a duet between flute and top-register cello (one likes to think that he stepped down from the conductor's desk to play the cello part himself), but thereafter several precedents were established : the burlesque of Italian opera ; the sentimental ballad in 3/8 or 6/8 time ; the 'ensemble de perplexité'; the 'chanson à boire'. These *Pepito* precursors were indeed less perfunctory than many specimens which followed them over the years. The take-off of 'Largo al factotum' was really funny, Manuelita's ballad had the added interest of a flute *obbligato*, and the representative features of the 'ensemble de perplexité' and the 'chanson à boire' were cleverly combined : while the young people sang of love the third character (a boozing old hotel-keeper) drank himself into a coma.

Ex. 6

Other stock ingredients were to be added to his later operettas — the 'tyrolienne' (*i.e. Ländler*), the dreamy waltz, the polka, the can-can, the military ensemble with a 'ra-ta-plan' refrain[1] — but the convention of building on a stereotype (so different from Adam's practice) was established with *Pepito*.

As the Opéra-Comique remained stubborn, Offenbach presently formed a syndicate to buy the lease of a derelict building in the Champs-Élysées, had it completely re-furbished, and opened it on 5th July 1855 as the 'Théâtre des Bouffes-Parisiens'. In taking this ambitious step he could probably afford to disregard the disastrous precedent of Adam's 'Opéra-National', and he was certainly put on his mettle by the success of the 'Folies-Nouvelles' inaugurated two years previously by his rival Hervé (see page 70). By the terms of the licence not more than four persons were allowed to appear on the stage in singing parts (though in practice five or six occasionally

---

[1] 'Ra-ta-plan', first popularised by Donizetti, soon became ubiquitous ; it even found its way into Verdi's (tragic) *Forza del destino*. And see the Sullivan quotation, Ex. 126 (page 189).

C

did so) and accordingly Offenbach for the time being limited himself to one-act pieces. His rapidity in composition may be gauged from the fact that during the next two and a half years he produced twenty of them, besides finding time to write four ballets, one of which, *Le Papillon*, was given at the Opéra. Although other composers — whom we shall meet later — contributed to the success of the 'Bouffes', its founder had the lion's share of both work and credit. Early in 1858 the licensing restrictions were relaxed and soon afterwards they were withdrawn altogether; Offenbach was then able to embark on that series of full-length operettas with which his name has ever since been associated in the public mind, though to the end of his life he continued to throw off a curtain-raiser or two every year as well.

During the period of which we are now speaking most of the libretti were written jointly by Henri Meilhac and Ludovic Halévy (a nephew of the composer). Although often shallow and occasionally vulgar, they were at least well put together. Offenbach, for all his own hasty methods, would tolerate no skimping on the part of his collaborators. Indeed he refused to start work until the whole libretto was completed to his satisfaction, and this forethought certainly helped to ensure dramatic unity.[1] So far as the one-act pieces are concerned individual comment would be wearisome, for their basic constructional pattern — of which the standard components have already been noted — remained virtually unchanged. A modicum of stylistic contrast was achieved, however, by variations in character and *locale*; most of these little buffooneries fell thereby into several readily distinguishable categories, *e.g.* the sentimental (*La Chanson de Fortunio*, 1861), the farcical (*Croquefer*, 1857), the satirical (*Les Deux aveugles*, 1855), the provincial or countrified (*La Rose de Saint-Flour*, 1856) and the naughtily-Parisian (*Un Mari à la porte*, 1859).

The musical content of these one-act pieces will not be left out of account when Offenbach's technique is discussed in Chapter V; though they were absolutely characteristic in their fertile melodic invention and rhythmic verve, it must be admitted that the sophisti-

---

[1] Meilhac and Halévy later served Bizet well with a workmanlike adaptation of Prosper Mérimée's *Carmen*, their only excursion outside the realm of triviality.

cated elegance which graced the best numbers from his more ambitious operettas was as a rule conspicuous by its absence. Space must be found, however, to quote a preamble from *Le 66* (1856) to which Bizet might not have been ashamed to put his name.[1]

The taste of the audience was catholic and the disarming simplicity of peasant-boy-meets-peasant-girl in *Lischen et Fritzchen* (1863, Ex. 8) was applauded just as vociferously as the boulevardier's jaunty invitation in *Le Brésilien* (also 1863, Ex. 9).

Although Offenbach rarely misjudged his public, his instinct was at fault in *Les Trois baisers du diable* (1857), a grim, *Freischütz*-like affair set in the Pyrenees. It failed completely at the Bouffes-Parisiens but deserves a mention because here and there it foreshadowed the Dappertutto scenes from *The Tales of Hoffmann*.

Offenbach's first two-act operetta, *Orphée aux enfers* (1858), was singled out by Edward Dannreuther in *The Oxford History of Music* (Vol. VI, 1905) as showing him at his best. It is not clear whether the author was referring to the 1858 original or to the greatly

---

[1] *Le 66* is the authentic title, though *Grove* lists the work as *Les 66!*, which suggests a secret society of brigands or anarchists ; in fact the plot hinges solely on the number of a lottery ticket.

expanded 1874 version (see page 38). In either event the judgment was a rational one : most of us would place *Orphée* on a short list, although ultimately we might not award it the palm. Here Offenbach certainly had a subject which enabled him to indulge to best advantage his talent for uninhibited tunefulness. The galop is one of the healthiest and most invigorating pieces of dance music ever written, and the burlesque which related the stock figures of classical mythology to contemporary Second-Empire 'types', if occasionally rather crude, could have left a bad taste only on a hyper-sensitive palate. What contemporary criticism could not overlook was the use of a famous melody from Gluck's *Orfeo ed Euridice* as a frivolous *Leitmotiv* ; the hero (who appeared as a violinist, not a lutenist) played it on the slightest provocation, sometimes in situations that might cause its well-loved strains to be held up to ridicule. One may now be permitted to question whether 'Ché faro' is really such a magnificent tune as one has been brought up to believe, but a hundred years ago it was sacrosanct, and one can well understand how its continual reproduction in an unsuitable context — from today's standpoint merely boring — was then regarded as the next thing to blasphemy. Of course *Orphée* was by no means the only one of Offenbach's operettas which lampooned the popular classics, but many French musicians smiled inwardly at the burlesque of Wagner in *Le Carnaval des revues* (1864) and were inclined to forgive the skits on Italian operatic convention that recurred constantly and were the sole *raison d'être* of *Monsieur Choufleuri* (1861) ; it was when he guyed Gluck in *Orphée*, Grétry in *Le Savetier et le financier* (1856) and Meyerbeer in *Mesdames de la Halle* (1858) that he placed himself beyond the pale. And there he remained ; unrepentant to the very end, he parodied Méhul in *La Fille du tambour-major* twenty years later. That the works of Grétry, Méhul and even Meyerbeer are today half-forgotten, while many of Offenbach's still survive, should not blind one to the fact that in the mid-nineteenth century these composers were revered ; to mock them was an intolerable affront.[1]

---

[1] On the other hand, the direct quotations from Gounod's *Faust* in *Bagatelle* (1874) and from Mozart's *Don Giovanni* in *The Tales of Hoffmann* were dramatically justified and in consequence gave no offence.

Orphée aux enfers (which caricatured mythological characters) was a huge success with the general public. That could not be said of *Geneviève de Brabant* (which treated a historical subject with the same disrespectful levity), though the music was cast in the same mould and technically showed an advance. Offenbach thought highly of *Geneviève* (originally 1859) and revised it twice (in 1867 and in 1875), but the first version remains the most satisfying. It included, for instance, an admirable 'ensemble de perplexité' which on revision became a mere solo, based on a melody which had been an acceptable contribution to a trio but was rather a poor affair when left on its own. For the one-act *Daphnis et Chloé* (1860) — which by reason of its subject stands rather apart from his other curtain-raisers — Offenbach returned to mythology, but a new pair of librettists, L. F. Nicolaie and E. de Vaulabelle, saw the characters through a less distorted mirror than Meilhac and Halévy would have done. The restraint that this imposed on musical jibing may not have suited the taste of the regular audience in the Champs-Élysées, but it evidently made a favourable impression on ambassadors from the boulevard des Italiens, for Offenbach was at last invited to compose a piece for the Opéra-Comique. *Barkouf* (also 1860) was the result.

As he had spent so many years trying to force an entry it is surprising that when the opportunity came he did not provide something at least as well composed as *Geneviève* or as straightforward as *Daphnis*. Instead he chose a libretto in which the principal character was — a dog! Having thus loaded the scales against himself he overturned them completely by writing music of extreme triviality.[1] One number alone calls for mention as a curiosity : a waltz in E major on a *basso ostinato* of two notes — C♮, B♮. *Barkouf* had seven performances ; it was to be seven *years* before the directors of the Opéra-Comique gave another chance to a composer who was evidently still unworthy of their serious regard.

At this time Offenbach's fortunes were at a slightly low ebb. Not only had *Barkouf* been a fiasco ; all was not well behind the

[1] The critic of *La Presse* thought it time that Offenbach packed up, but : 'Ce n'est pas le chant du cygne, c'est le chant de l'oie'.

scenes at the Bouffes-Parisiens, and following a succession of dis-
agreements he resigned from the managerial board. His connection
with the house was not completely severed, and his works continued
to receive occasional hospitality, but most of his subsequent triumphs
were secured at the Théâtre des Variétés, the Gaîté, the Palais-Royal,
the Renaissance or the Folies-Dramatiques. A few pieces had their
premières at Bad-Ems in the Palatinate, a favourite summer resort for
Parisians of the Second Empire ; [1] among them were *Lischen et
Fritzchen* (see page 23) and *Les Bavards* (1862), a poor affair in which
the only noteworthy number was an excellent patter-song lasting
for eighty breathless bars. Meanwhile Offenbach had paid two
successful visits to Vienna, where his operettas were received with
acclamation ; while there he wrote a 'romantic German opera'
Die Rheinnixen (1864), of which nothing has survived except the
'Goblins' Song', a haunting waltz-tune. The composer could not
bear to let it slip into oblivion with the rest, and seventeen years
later in *The Tales of Hoffmann* it established itself as one of the
'top pops' of all time — not as a waltz, but as 'the' barcarolle.
Offenbach's impact on Vienna was tremendous (see Chapter XIII),
but the traffic was not all one-way. He himself had learnt much
by the time he returned to Paris that autumn and was reunited with
Meilhac and Halévy. Though *Les Géorgiennes* amounted to little,
the deserved success of *La Belle Hélène* promised that his popularity
at the Théâtre des Variétés would be as great as it had been at the
Bouffes-Parisiens. Here the composer was once more in impertinent
mood — though there were no quotations from Gluck this time.
La Belle Hélène was not only charming and vivacious but held a
touch of refinement that was somehow lacking in *Orphée aux enfers*.
Moreover it was full of good tunes ; one should reflect that its
glorious waltz might never have been written had not the composer recently been to Vienna.

Just before his next production — *Les Bergers* (1865) — Offenbach wrote a long letter to J. H. de Villemessant, editor of *Le Figaro*,

---

[1] It was here that the King of Prussia met the French Ambassador on 13th July
1870 ; the discreditable episode of the 'Ems telegram', which reported their conversation to Bismarck, precipitated 'an unnecessary, insensate war'. (The phrase
is H. A. L. Fisher's.)

who rather surprisingly published it in full. In the first paragraph Offenbach explained that this time Meilhac and Halévy had provided a 'beautiful three-act poem' with a pastoral background, adding that they in turn had assured *him* that the musical score was a 'threefold masterpiece'. This modest announcement was followed by a synopsis : the first act was a serious setting of the 'charming episode of Pyramus and Thisbe',[1] the second an eighteenth-century pastiche evoking the spirit of Watteau, the third a musical realisation of Courbet. This last was evidently intended to be the tit-bit, but unfortunately there was a snag.

> Nous avons choisi, autant que possible, les tableaux où les femmes sont habillées. Vous apprécierez notre réserve.

After stressing that never before had he devoted so much loving care to the preparation of an operetta, Offenbach ended a remarkable epistle by inviting theatre-goers to listen carefully to the first act, to laugh a lot at the second, and to split their sides ('se tordre') during the third. Alas for his expectations! The first act of *Les Bergers* (which opened with a chorus that was both original and impressive) was on the whole well-received, the second raised an occasional titter, but the third was listened to in stony silence — possibly a protest against the short supply of *femmes déshabillées*. Stony silence so far as the music is concerned, that is to say ; a speech making fun of the Constitution of 1789 was loudly booed, and in the ensuing uproar the police had to intervene.

Undeterred by this set-back Offenbach and his librettists again ventured on dangerous ground with *Barbe-bleue* (1866), in which some of the satire could be taken as applying to the existing régime, but by now the Emperor Napoleon III regarded Offenbach much as a sixteenth-century monarch might have regarded his court jester ; impertinence could be tolerated so long as entertainment was provided. Anyway, politics played little part in *La Vie parisienne* (also 1866), a topical travesty of life in the great city set to music as amusing and sparkling as that of *La Belle Hélène*. Taken by and large it was probably Offenbach's best operetta ; the subject certainly

---

[1] 'Je me suis cru obliger d'emboucher mes pipeaux sur un mode plus élevé.'

enabled him to demonstrate that his humour was completely in tune with the spirit of the age.[1]

What is one to say of *The Grand Duchess of Gerolstein*? It was not the worst of the hundred or so operettas that Offenbach wrote, but it was undoubtedly the worst of the round dozen for which his name is best remembered. Most of the music was either pretentious or downright commonplace, and its *succès fou* in 1867, at the time of the Great Exhibition, was almost entirely due to a skilful publicity build-up of the artiste who appeared in the title rôle — Hortense Schneider, 'la Grande Duchesse de Gérolstein, du théâtre, et du demi-monde'. That year was more significant in Offenbach's musical development for his second Opéra-Comique production, *Robinson Crusoé*. (Defoe might have been surprised to find his hero accompanied throughout by a 'jolie cousine', but such a piquant garnish was well suited to the taste of a Parisian audience.) Offenbach had learnt something from the failure of *Barkouf* and went to a great deal of trouble to redeem his reputation in high circles : *Robinson Crusoé* included an 'entr'acte symphonique' and several of the elaborate ensembles were admirably constructed.

---

[1] *La Vie parisienne* as played in 1929 at the Lyric Theatre, Hammersmith — with words by A. P. Herbert and music arranged by A. Davies Adams — was not so much a revised version of this particular work as a clever pasticcio to suit contemporary Playfair requirements. It was very 'artistically' done, but Offenbach lost something in the process, and one regrets that no place was found for the servants'-hall chorus from the original (Ex. 10), where the infectious rhythmic gaiety is so typical of the composer. (The item was included, of course, in the more traditional Sadler's Wells revial of 1961.)

The following year saw *Le Château de Toto* (of which a little was very good but much was repetitive) and, far better known, *La Périchole*. This had great success and has been widely praised (even by distinguished critics), perhaps beyond its deserts. The famous 'letter song' shows Offenbach at his weakest — it was the sort of thing that two young Englishmen, Frederic Clay and Arthur Sullivan, were churning out by the jugful (in their off-moments) on the other side of the Channel. Then in 1869 Offenbach committed another indiscretion at the Opéra-Comique : though *Vertvert* showed him on his best behaviour in the charming barcarolle —

Ex. 11 Andantino

Le ba-teau march-ait len-te-ment, Pous-sé par le vent et la ra - me.
Un é-poux, peut-être un a-mant, Cou-sait près du-ne jeu-ne fem - me.

— the dead parrot which figured largely in the plot found no more favour than had the live dog of *Barkouf*. Nor did the buffooneries of the year inflate the composer's reputation. *La Diva* was at least original in conception, being supposedly based on the life-story of Hortense Schneider (who needless to say impersonated herself with *empressement*), but *La Princesse de Trébizonde* was unremarkable.

In *Les Brigands* (1870) Meilhac, Halévy and Offenbach for the last time aimed pointed shafts at the régime which had nurtured them and was so soon to crumble into dust. The chorus of carabiniers — not sung, but spoken in 'tramp-tramp' rhythm — was a biting satire :

> Nous sommes les carabiniers,
> La sécurité des foyers,
>   Mais par un malheureux hasard
> Au secours des particuliers
>   Nous arrivons toujours trop tard.[1]

[1] *Les Brigands* was translated by W. S. Gilbert, who later incorporated several of Meilhac and Halévy's jokes in *The Pirates of Penzance*. His rendering of 'Nous sommes les carabiniers' lacked pungency :

> 'We are mighty carbineers,
> All with glorious careers,
>   But it is most unfortunate
> That though we have no kind of fears
>   Somehow we are always too late!'

It was not long before the 'tramp-tramp' that had been such a joke became a sinister reality, and Parisians had more serious things to think about than glamorous divas or comic brigands. Once again Offenbach's record in a national emergency did him little credit. He retreated at once to his country house at Étretat in Normandy and later (when the Germans broke through at Sedan) to Bordeaux. Soon he found it prudent to move still further afield, and while the city of his adoption was first besieged and afterwards humiliated he was dividing his time between San Sebastian, Milan and Vienna. It was a changed Paris to which he returned in October 1871.

IV

OFFENBACH — UPS AND DOWNS

It will be convenient to take advantage of this break in Offenbach's active career to analyse and attempt to explain the harsh criticism from serious musicians which his operettas had to counter during his lifetime, and to compare it with the fulsome adulation granted him after his death in circles that could not possibly be described as irresponsible or frivolous.

At first glance the contemporary attitude looks to have been both prejudiced and ill-natured. Reputable commentators stressed his vulgarity, his bad taste in parodying Gluck or Meyerbeer; they accorded but grudging praise to his melodic fertility and rhythmic sparkle; they ignored his constructive skill and extremely competent orchestration. This may be forgiven when one realises that his name must inevitably have been associated in their minds with the environment in which the majority of his pieces were played. It could plausibly be argued that when the coffers overflowed at the Bouffes-Parisiens and the Théâtre des Variétés artistic merit had little to do with it, for these resorts were fulfilling much the same purpose as an exclusive *maison tolérée*; it was common knowledge that many a stall-holder attended solely in the expectation of a later and more intimate rendezvous with one of the charming creatures on the other side of the footlights. This in turn led to an uprush of splenetic jealousy between the established actresses and the established courtesans, for many versatile young ladies regarded temporary success in either profession as the stepping-stone to a more lucrative and permanent engagement in the other. They were often disappointed. Lise Tautin, for instance, who displayed her good features, trim figure and pretty coloratura voice in countless operettas, never distinguished herself in the *demi-monde*, while contrariwise there was a complete fiasco when Cora Pearl once took the stage — the fabulous Cora, whose exploits elsewhere were a revelation to all who shared them and a legendary by-word with those who had not to date enjoyed such a privilege. That amazing woman Hortense Schneider, however, was an exception. *On the stage she was a fine singer and a superb actress ; off it*

> Ambassadors cropped up like hay,
> Prime Ministers and such as they,
> Grew like asparagus in May

and the rulers of more than one European country were proud to number themselves among her conquests. When in *The Grand Duchess of Gerolstein*, for instance, this gorgeous Juno flashed her eyes in open invitation to the *jeunesse dorée* —

Ex. 12 Andantino

Di-tes lui qu'on l'a ré-mar-qué dis-tin-gué, di-tes lui qu'on le trouve ai - ma - ble; Di-tes lui que s'il le vou - lait on ne sait de qui l'on ne se - rait ca - pa - ble.

— the atmosphere was so charged with electric cross-currents that any attempt at detachment was quickly short-circuited.[1]

No wonder that many of Félix Clément's comments were fretful; after recording the good reception given to half a dozen numbers from *Orphée aux enfers* he had to add :

> These melodies might be adjudged charming and original, were they not associated in one's recollection with stage situations that were grotesque or even licentious.

Nor was this attitude confined to France — J. Schluter in *Die allgemeine Geschichte der Musik* (1863) described the same operetta as 'typical brothel-music' — but after the German army had goose-stepped through Paris to the strains of an Offenbach march (while the composer rested in Vienna) objective criticism, already difficult for musicians who were moralists, became impossible for those who

---

[1] The world of Second-Empire operetta was riddled with social and political intrigue ; for an *exposé*, see S. Kracauer's *Offenbach und sein Jahrhundert* (1926), available in an English translation as *Offenbach and the Paris of his time.* Hortense Schneider herself afterwards married and settled down ; she died in 1920 at the ripe age of eighty-four.

were patriotic Frenchmen. Saint-Saëns, for instance, had been a regular and appreciative visitor to the 'Bouffes' before the war, but his youthful enthusiasm for Offenbach now cooled perceptibly, and responsible opinion in the early seventies was well crystallised by Gustave Chouquet in his *Histoire de la musique dramatique en France* (1873).

The crowds thronging the theatres had no more knowledge or love of music than the man who threw a sou to the barrel-organist's monkey ; rather than listen to Mozart or Rossini they preferred to have their senses titillated by the buffooneries of Jacques Offenbach. Here was a clever man : one hesitates to call him a charlatan because he knew enough about music to parody its established conventions. He and his librettists made a point of jeering at our middle class and owed their pecuniary success to the continuance of a régime under which rewards were distributed not to those who practised the art of music but to those who ridiculed it. In such an atmosphere it was easy for the operetta to lampoon the opera. No one minds a joke, but in Offenbach's burlesques the jokes were utterly extravagant: often a melody of real charm would be caricatured in a refrain of extreme vulgarity. As for the dialogue — so long as it was sufficiently filthy it was judged to be marvellously original! For too many years honours were showered on the perpetrators of these monstrosities, which could not have been tolerated by the community had not the greater part of it been indifferent to anything but money and the ephemeral pleasures which money can buy. This moral infection was a threat to our cultural existence, and after the disasters of 1870 and the humiliations of 1871 our unfortunate country will plunge into ruin if she does not quickly recover her good sense and her good taste by throwing out once and for all these impudent corroders of the theatre who seem to take such a malicious delight in undermining our national heritage, never realising, perhaps, that they are thereby hastening our ultimate doom.[1]

Now Chouquet was a broad-minded critic ; his later and more temperate assessment of Offenbach's contribution to music has remained the basis of relevant entries in *Grove* up to and including

---

[1] This is a free rendering rather than a literal translation of Chouquet's diatribe, and I have omitted his graphic description of Offenbach as a 'pillaging Uhlan'.

the fifth edition. In his *Histoire*, however, one feels that he was a little arbitrary — and perhaps unkind — to single out a composer of operettas as the symbol of his country's decadence.

The harsh but well-informed criticism of Chouquet is easier to tolerate than the absurd comparisons of Nietzsche in *Der Wille zur Macht* (1888), where his possibly sincere admiration for Offenbach provided the author with a grand excuse to indulge in some windy rhetoric.

> *Offenbach* : French music imbued with Voltaire's intellect, free, with a slight sardonic grin, but clear and intellectual almost to the point of banality (Offenbach never titivates), and free from the mignardise of morbid or blond-Viennese sensuality.
>
> If by artistic genius we understand the most consummate freedom within the law, divine ease, and facility in overcoming the greatest difficulties, then Offenbach has even more right to the title of genius than Wagner has : Wagner is heavy and clumsy ; nothing is more foreign to him than the moments of wanton perfection which this clown Offenbach achieves as many as five times, six times, in nearly every one of his buffooneries. But by genius we ought perhaps to understand something else.

For most of us the first paragraph is meaningless nonsense except for the three words in parenthesis which constitute a definite but very questionable statement. The second paragraph (despite one felicitous phrase) looks like *dangerous* nonsense until the last sentence cancels everything, and we realise that Offenbach has been dragged into the argument merely to give another sip of honey to one of the busiest bees that ever buzzed in a philosopher's bonnet.

The only full-length study of Offenbach published before the close of the nineteenth century was André Martinet's *Offenbach, sa vie et son œuvre* (1887) ; this was scholarly and well-documented but almost entirely factual. No comprehensive *appraisal* of his work appeared until 1909, when Paul Bekker contributed a pen-portrait to the series *Musik*, edited by Richard Strauss. It included a thoughtful analysis of 'Offenbach the musician', but some of the judgments had little sure foundation : the generalisation that Offenbach's melodies 'rarely exceed the span of an octave' will be disproved by a quick glance at the brief quotations in the present book, and the few indirect references to such ancillary but important features as counterpoint and orchestration were perfunctory and occasionally misleading.

In his scores there are few trimmings, either of the penny-plain variety or tuppence-coloured ; there are no trivial superfluities, no dazzling decorations. On the contrary, every note of every instrument is an essential part of the pattern.

Bekker evidently concurred with Nietzsche's terse 'he never titivates', but what would he have called those delightful little instrumental interpolations of which Ex. 13 (from *La Belle Hélène*) is typical ? They may not be 'dazzling' but they are certainly 'decorations'.

Ex.13 Allegretto

Au_ Mont I - da trois dé - ess - es Se que-rel-laient dans un bois.

A few years later Offenbach's reputation was subjected to the strain of undiscriminating eulogy from another quarter. After the 1914–1918 war it became the fashion with certain intellectual cliques in Paris (and elsewhere) to affect nostalgic admiration for a type of frivolity usually associated with the Second Empire ; Offenbach's music provided a convenient jumping-off board. In 1923 Louis Schneider (who also wrote biographies of Monteverdi and Schumann) went so far as to describe him as the Mozart of his day.[1] Now Offenbach adored Mozart, and it may be true that up to a point he 'practised the cult' (Schneider's phrase) ; a mid-nineteenth-century composer of operettas who knew his *Così fan tutte* and *Figaro* backwards was bound to do so from time to time. And surely enough, on perhaps one page out of fifty we may light on a short passage (usually in an ensemble) where the manner at least reminds us of the Master. When Schneider, however, cites three numbers — one each from *Le Mariage aux lanternes*, *La Chanson de Fortunio* and *La Périchole* — 'qui sont tombées du ciel comme certains *andante* et certaines ariettes de Mozart', he could hardly

---

[1] 'Les deux compositeurs, sur le terrain mélodique, sont frères.'

have chosen worse examples to reinforce his point; they had
popular success because they were fluent and sentimental, but not
one of them showed a trace of that Mozartian elegance which
Offenbach at his best did occasionally achieve.[1] In this country,
too, he had a vogue with the *avant-garde*, and in 1937 the distinguished
poet and essayist Sacheverell Sitwell published a panegyric in praise
of *La Vie parisienne* which as literature was a joy to read but as
musical criticism left one puzzled. Was the biographer of Domenico
Scarlatti and Mozart really sincere in his glorification of Offenbach?

These Schneider/Sitwell tendencies showed themselves mainly
where there was a natural reaction against any form of Teutonic
hegemony. (Ironically, the reaction appeared to favour the German-
born Offenbach rather than Gounod, Lalo, Massenet or Chabrier.)
On the other side of the Rhine objectivity still held sway. Anton
Henseler's *Jakob Offenbach* (1930) was a monument of erudition
on the composer's upbringing, career and private life, while also
covering many aspects of his creative art. But though Offenbach
was an outstanding figure in the history of operetta and deserves a
niche in the history of music as a whole, Henseler's conscientious
elaboration of detail strikes one as being slightly out of proportion.
The devotion and industry that produced these 500 closely printed
pages (about 200,000 words) compel one's admiration, but the
treatment was perhaps unnecessarily exhaustive.

Commentators during the early eighteen-seventies (of whom
Chouquet has been taken as representative so far as France is concerned) could write only of Offenbach's pre-war achievements,
but it is significant that later critics too — apart from paying lip-
service to *The Tales of Hoffmann* — have largely concentrated their
attention on the period that began with the opening of the Bouffes-
Parisiens in 1855 and ended when that establishment temporarily
closed its doors in 1870. Superficially at least this was right and
proper, for the Second Empire was Offenbach's heyday; thereafter his personality for a time became shadowy and unreal —

---

[1] In two of the same three songs the Hungarian philosopher Max Nordau —
whose *Degeneration* (1892) outdid *Nietzsche contra Wagner* in vindictiveness — heard
'the sound of every church bell in the holy city [Cologne] and the voices of the
Loreley at eventide' (article on Offenbach in *Pester Lloyd*, 28th January 1912);
as with Schneider, the association must have been subjective.

it was as though a ghost were striving to participate anew in the earthly pleasures now denied him.

When he returned to Paris after his voluntary exile Offenbach picked up two unfurnished scores which had been laid aside eighteen long months before. One of them he completed in a few days by using over again some of the music from *Barkouf* ; this was appropriate enough, for in *La Boule de neige* (December 1871) the dog of *Barkouf* reappeared as a bear — the 'gardien terrible' of Ex. 33 (page 49). The other was the outcome of collaboration with Victorien Sardou, a serious-minded playwright whose lurid drama *La Tosca* later inspired music very different from any that Offenbach ever wrote. They were hardly tactful to choose the year 1872 in which to present *Le Roi Carotte*, which was partly a satire on French incompetence in the face of Prussian efficiency. Sardou on his own might have been forgiven, but his association with Offenbach — already *persona non grata* — was ill-timed, and the vials of wrath that were poured on both author and composer obliterated any attempt to form an impartial judgment on the merits of the piece, which were considerable (in particular there was a comic 'railway song'.) In *Fantasio* (libretto by Paul de Musset, after his brother Alfred), which was given at the Opéra-Comique the same year, Offenbach struggled hard to please highbrow critics and avoid the commonplace ; in consequence the musical texture often hovered between the complex and the tenuous. Henseler draws attention to a passage in the overture which was clearly anticipatory of the trio 'Chère enfant' from Act III of *The Tales of Hoffmann*, and much of the music was in the same unexceptionable vein. But impertinence and healthy vulgarity had often been concomitant with Offenbach's tunefulness ; in *Fantasio* all three qualities were lacking. The same search after 'refinement' at the expense of melodic spontaneity was only slightly less pronounced in his next three Parisian operettas — *Les Braconniers*, *La Jolie parfumeuse* (both 1873) and *Madame l'Archiduc* (1874). There was a tendency to rely on contrapuntal technique that was not always adequate for the occasion, and the burlesque when it came was no longer *musical* burlesque. In *Les Braconniers* poverty of invention could not hide behind the 'superfluities' whose very existence was denied by Paul Bekker and of

D

the would-be amusing 'duetto bouffe anglais' from *Madame l'Archiduc*
only the words deserve (exact) reproduction.

> COMTE.   Oh! yes splendid' l'Italie
>   London y préfer
> COMTESSE. Oh! yes moi comme vous y préfer
>   Birmingham and manchester.
> COMTE.   Oh! Venise elle est jolie
>   Very beautiful
> COMTESSE. Y préfer Dublin oh! Liverpool!
>   Very Nice Liverpool.

Nevertheless these operettas, along with the one-act *Pomme d'api*
(1873) and *Bagatelle* (which were more or less in the old Bouffes-
Parisiens tradition) served to provide Offenbach once again with a
regular public. But the mood had changed — there was now an
overwhelming desire to escape from realities — and he did not truly
catch it until 1874 when he produced a sumptuous new version of
Orphée aux enfers. It was expanded to nearly twice its original
length by half a dozen spectacular 'tableaux' which required not
only 50 soloists but '16 Coryphées et 60 Dames du Ballet ; 100
Choristes, Hommes, Dames et Enfants'. Here was escapism with a
vengeance. Moreover much of the new material showed Offenbach
at last coupling his new methods with his old manner. One number
at least, the elaborately scored 'ballet des mouches', was a *tour de
force* ; it may well have been a source of inspiration for Tchaikovsky,
who frankly acknowledged his indebtedness to Parisian influences.

Meanwhile Offenbach had been travelling abroad again. In
Vienna, an audience which had just heard Johann Strauss's first
operetta *Indigo* (see page 124) failed to appreciate the supposedly

humorous antics of a bungling amateur orchestra which were featured largely in *Der schwarze Korsär* (1872), a work which is only remembered because some of the music lived again in *Der Gold-schmidt von Toledo*, a pasticcio fabricated by Alfred Zamara (page 135), which was played in Germany and Britain between the two world wars. In London *Whittington* [1] made even less impact — the title and the production date (26th December 1874) alike indicate its character — but in few pantomimes before or since can the principal girl's conventional ballad have been graced with such a polished little preamble.

During the next three years (1875–1877), despite the preoccupa-tion of a long visit to the United States where he conducted some of the old favourites, Offenbach found time to complete six more full-length operettas — *La Boulangerie a des écus*, *La Créole*, *Le Voyage dans la lune*, *La Boîte au lait*, *Le Docteur Ox* and *La Foire Saint-Laurent* ; they all showed the same introversive tendencies which we have already noted. Meilhac and Halévy having by now virtually received their *congé*, the libretti were less amusing and less well constructed than heretofore — two were based on Jules Verne — but there was certainly an advance in technical assurance ; for instance, the principal character in *Le Docteur Ox* was satisfactorily identified throughout with a *Leitmotiv*. Indeed, from a musician's standpoint, these later operettas would be more pleasing than the earlier ones, did not the actual tunes so often lack a divine spark. In *La Boîte au lait* there was a soprano solo ('Il ne veut pas garçon traîner sa triste vie') which Sullivan may have had at the back of his mind when ten years later he wrote 'The Sun whose rays' in the same key ; there were basic similarities in the rhythm of the 'verse' and the melody of the refrain, but as *inspirations* there was

---

[1] So published ; in London it was inevitably billed as *Dick Whittington and his Cat*, but Paris heard it later as *Le Chat du diable*.

no comparison. If Sullivan on this occasion owed something to Offenbach it was merely a *quid pro quo*, for two numbers from *Maître Péronilla* (1878) bore an astonishing initial resemblance to 'My name is John Wellington Wells' from *The Sorcerer* (1877).

By this time Offenbach was not only re-established in popular favour ; even the élite were inclined to be indulgent to an *enfant prodigue* showing signs of repentance. His old enemy Clément found *Maître Péronilla* 'agréable' and *Madame Favart* (which followed it) 'une de ses meilleurs'. Actually *Madame Favart* (libretto by H. C. Chivot and A. Duru), in spite of some attractive music, was little more than an extended eighteenth-century pastiche on the lines of the second act of *Les Bergers* ; in Paris it enjoyed only a *succès d'estime*, though it ran for over a year in London.[1] It would have been more fitting if Clément had reserved his award for *La Fille du tambour-major* (1879) : a satisfying reconciliation between refinement and carefree gaiety eluded Offenbach to the end, but here he came nearer to achieving it than anywhere else. (This was Donizetti's *Daughter of the Regiment* viewed through an inverted telescope and provided with a more topically acceptable set-up of political loyalties.) It was the last operetta which he lived to complete, for he died on 5th October 1880 ; the posthumous *Belle Lurette* and *Moucheron* were rounded off by Delibes. (Curiously enough, the most attractive item in *La Belle Lurette* was written by a foreigner ; it was an unashamed presentation — not a parody as has sometimes been stated — of the *Blue Danube* waltz).

Offenbach looms so large on our canvas that his portrait would be thrown out of perspective if at this juncture one were to ignore *The Tales of Hoffmann* merely because it does not belong to the genre of operetta. After all, to be recognised as the composer of a successful *opera* had been his greatest ambition ever since the moment when he first set foot in Paris as a practically penniless student, and death alone prevented its realisation. Though he had spent many years of intermittent toil on the preparation of a piano score

[1] This was due to the enterprise of H. B. Farnie, who, like Favart himself a century earlier, combined the functions of librettist and impresario. In his London production of *Madame Favart* Florence St. John reached the zenith of her career and Herbert Beerbohm Tree had his first important part.

he never quite finished it; the last touches were added and the whole was orchestrated by Ernest Guiraud. The first performance eventually took place on 10th February 1881. These are the cold facts, but they embody a tinge of romance which provides sufficient justification for the sentimental imp that lurks in any but the most inhuman heart to urge the fitting corollary — that *Hoffmann* must be Offenbach's masterpiece. Nevertheless the realist will still maintain that *Orphée aux enfers*, *La Belle Hélène* and *La Vie parisienne* form his chief claim to immortality, for unquestionably they hold his quintessence. That is not to say that *The Tales of Hoffmann* was freakish or even uncharacteristic. On the contrary : so far from being a flash in the pan it marked the culmination of Offenbach's nine-year struggle to rescue his name from irrevocable association with trivialities. The libretto (by Jules Barbier and Michel Carré) gave very little opportunity for indulgence in frivolity or extravagant burlesque, so that he was able to ride over vulgarity ; and there were not many lapses into the commonplace. Judging the opera as a whole, its merits were in the main of this somewhat negative order, partly because it was virtually impossible for a composer of modest calibre to endow three independent and contrasted 'tales' with a sense of musical and dramatic unity. But since his melodic inspiration was flowing more freely than in some of the concurrent operettas there is no difficulty in locating a few of Nietzsche's 'moments of wanton perfection' ; one need only wait for the middle section of the 'Legend of Kleinzach', for 'Ah! vivre deux', for 'Elle a fui', and finally for that pathetic vignette of tender feeling, 'C'est une chanson d'amour'. This was not, strictly speaking, poor little Antonia's swan-song, but it would be appropriate to regard it as Offenbach's.

V

OFFENBACH — SOME TECHNICAL ASPECTS

To most Anglo-Saxons the prosodic conventions of French verse
will probably always appear somewhat artificial. It is hard to
reconcile its shadowy outlines with the workaday language which
one learnt at school and hears spoken when travelling abroad or
listening to Radio-Paris. The first discrepancy is quickly noticed :
the final 'e' (in 'vite' for example), that remains obstinately mute in
conversation, is just perceptible in an official pronouncement ; in a
poem it becomes an essential part of the scansion ; in music it
may even acquire sufficient importance to be associated with a
'down beat'. This is a comparatively trifling instance of the
apparent anomaly that in French song (before Debussy's day, at
any rate) there is little suggestion of normal spoken accentuation.
Look at Adam's treatment of the line 'Voilà que Nina, la blonde,
arrive avec son papa', quoted in Ex. 2 on page 16. Consider, too,
the opening phrase of a well-known song from *Louise*, which *looks*
like '*Depuis le* jour'. No British composer would dream of setting
the words 'When first we loved' *à la* Charpentier '*When* first *we*
loved', but to a Frenchman the word 'accentuation' in such a
context is meaningless, for the approach of both versifier and
composer is guided solely by those indefinable nuances (so elusive
to a foreigner) which for centuries have characterised French poetry
— and on a less exalted plane French operatic libretti.[1]

---

[1] The difficulty has been recognised in France itself. Over two hundred years
ago Voltaire wrote : 'Hitherto French music — or at least French vocal music —
has not satisfied the taste of any other nation. It could hardly do so, because French
prosody differs from that of all other European languages ; we always stress the
last syllable, whereas everybody else leans on the penultimate or, like the Italians,
on the syllable before. Our tongue is the only one that ends words with mute
'e's, which are not pronounced in ordinary utterance but must be sounded in singing
with complete uniformity — *gloir-uh, victoir-uh, barbari-uh, furi-uh.* That is enough
to make our airs and recitatives unbearable to anyone not accustomed to them.'

Offenbach, whose roots lay elsewhere, overestimated this flexibility, and when hurrying over his work often ignored even the *sense* of the words ; in Ex. 9 on page 23, for instance, 'voulez-vous' is given two different accentuations in consecutive bars. He eventually became equally careless in setting German, sometimes with disastrous results ; his native language, so much less elastic than French, can rarely have been stretched on so painful a rack as in *Fleurette* (a one-act piece written for the Viennese in 1872).

Ex.16

On the other hand, when he took a little trouble, he could give added point to a verbal quip by the simplest of means, such as urging forward the rhythm. Here is the reprobate old maestro who gives his name to *Il Signor Fagotto* (Bad-Ems, 1863).

Ex.17

The cadence of a duet from *La Jolie parfumeuse* is even more dexterous ; here the rhythm is held back, and the momentary unison of the two voices imparts just the right emphasis to the essential line.

Ex.18

More often, words are but an excuse for the musical illustration of some amusing situation. The endless repetition of short and sometimes pointless verbal phrases becomes a tiresome mannerism, yet on occasion it serves to draw attention to Offenbach's extraordinary facility for making a tasty omelette out of one small egg. Nothing could be more economical, nor in its trifling way more effective, than the trio in *Ba-ta-clan* (1855) from which Ex. 19 (page 44) is taken.

Offenbach's orchestration was always skilful, often delicate and occasionally subtle. Pluton's song from *Orphée aux enfers* became a duet for Vénus and Pluton in the 1874 revision, but in both versions the number opens with three bars for solo clarinet and solo bassoon in octaves ; the same phrase is then repeated by solo flute and solo oboe an octave higher. When the voice enters (here we are following the 1874 edition) the accompaniment is what Nietzsche presumably meant by 'intellectual almost to the point of banality', but how could he have missed the 'titivation' of clarinet and flute ?

Ex.20 Allegretto

The composer made a point, too, of including grateful solos for his instrumentalists in the unpretentious overtures ; in *L'Ile de Tulipatan* (1867), for instance, a clarinet cadenza leads to this presentation of the main theme.

Ex.21

During his characteristic Second-Empire period Offenbach rarely escaped from the despotism of the four-bar phrase.[1] The three-bar phrases of a minuet from *Orphée aux enfers* were exceptional, and in any case the item was probably intended as pastiche, if not parody. He seems to have felt the need for variety, however, and though unable to achieve it instinctively, he occasionally did his best by sustaining the last note of the melody for an extra bar or so. 'Dans Venise la belle' from *Le Pont des soupirs* (1861) was a four-bar notion artificially extended to five bars ; so was a less well-known song from the same work.

Un jour la vil - le de Ve - ni - se en - ten-dit la bri - - - - se. ___

Another makeshift, not so obvious, was the insertion of a one-bar phrase for a different character, for the chorus, or for the orchestra, as in the next three quotations. The first is from *La Belle Hélène*, the other two are both from *Les Brigands*.

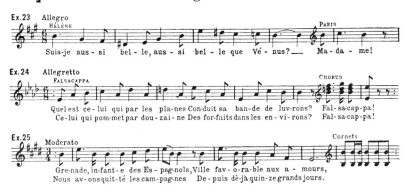

Sometimes four bars were filled out in the same way to six (*e.g.* in the duet 'Partout on chercherait en vain' from *Les Bavards*) or even seven (see Ex. 11 on page 29), but it was not until Offenbach's closing years, when he was conscientiously trying to bring his technique into line with his other accomplishments, that he succeeded in making this trick sound convincing. In *La Créole* $3 + 2 = 5$ quite acceptably—

[1] Some of his less talented imitators were thereby rendered aesthetically bankrupt.

Eh, bien! non, vrai je suis trop lâ - che, A la fin des fins fin - is - sez.

— and in the one-act *Pierrette et Jacquot* (1876) there is an interesting little duet where 7 is the sum not of 'natural' 4 + 'redundant' 3 but of natural 4 + natural 2 + redundant 1.

Al - lons les gars et les fil - les, Pre - nez vos bâ - tons. Pre - nez vos bâ - tons.

The vigorous three-bar rhythm of the chorus 'En route!' from *Le Voyage dans la lune* brings one up with quite a jerk because the four-bar phrase is still something of a fixation, but one notes with appreciation that here and there in these later operettas Offenbach tempers the rigidity by interpolating an odd half-bar. In *La Belle Lurette* there is a suggestion of undecimal time.

At - ta - quez le gou - ver - ne - ment, le roi, sa femme et la jus - ti - ce.
At - ta - quez mêm' le par - le - ment, la fav - o - rite et la po - li - ce.

Though one cannot say definitely that Delibes left this passage in its original form or even be sure that he did not write it himself, Offenbach was by that time quite capable of it — witness the extraordinary evolution of a straightforward waltz-tune in the overture to *La Fille du tambour-major*.

(An earlier curiosity was a short 5/4 item in *Il Signor Fagotto* ; Henseler assessed it as a burlesque of Berlioz' 'strivings after the antique'.)

If Offenbach's melodies rarely broke free from the strophic restrictions imposed by the elementary conformation of the lyrics, they suffered still more — in the opening stanzas at least — from subjection to the tyranny of tonic/dominant/sub-dominant. A rare song from *Un Mari à la porte* showed that when he did throw off these shackles, not only harmonic but melodic and rhythmic balance alike shared the benefit.[1]

On the other hand, he had a flair for effective character-contrast within the confines of a single number. In *Mesdames de la Halle*, for instance, the rhythmic sprightliness of —

— is closely followed by a suave *legato*.

Considered separately, neither extract promises a particularly good tune, but the juxtaposition almost persuades us of its realisation. It was in cadences, however, that Offenbach was most consistently

[1] Another exceptional case (from *Robinson Crusoé*) is cited on page 49.

successful ; many a commonplace ditty was redeemed by its conclusion (*e.g.* 'Ah! le sommeil va me surprendre' from *Les
Géorgiennes*) and he sometimes showed individuality by indulging
a talent for simple chromaticism, thereby producing effects both
charming and original. Ex. 32 is taken from *Le 66*, Ex. 33 from
La Boule de neige.

In the long run his technical resource was not sufficient to make him
a master of modulation, although when he was on the top of his
form he could give us an occasional surprise, as in 'Oh, la femme
blanche bien belle' from *Robinson Crusoé* (where by the fourth
bar he was in the flat sub-mediant major). In an item from *Monsieur
et Madame Denis* (1862), the development of orchestral figures was
quite accomplished (Ex. 34, page 50), and the A♮ in the final chord
of the quotation imparted an almost Schubertian touch.

Ex. 34

Now and again Offenbach's harmonic waywardness led him off the beaten track. There are so many obvious misprints in the published vocal scores that one is always on guard, but I am inclined to give him credit for this passage from *Le Roi Carotte*, even if I have to echo Fridolin's cry, 'Est-ce possible ?'.

Ex. 35

One can find a double meaning, however, in Chouquet's accusation that Offenbach 'se moquait de l'orthographie et de la syntaxe musicales' (*op. cit.* page 33). A professor of harmony would quickly explain away these clashes in *Le Vent du soir* (1857) —

Ex. 36

— but what could he say or do about the barcarolle from *The Tales of Hoffmann* (Ex. 37) ?

Finally, after perhaps too much space has been devoted to criticism of Offenbach's shortcomings and too little to praise of his undoubted talents, it is a pleasure to be able to commend without reserve one tiny but significant feature of his harmonic style — the effective use which he often makes of a simple contrast between major and minor. Nowhere is it better exemplified than in a naïve melody from *Pepito*.[1]

There was another alluring instance in the 'Ronde normande' from *Le Château de Toto* with its haunting refrain, and although the same urge drove Offenbach to over-exploitation of the 'Neapolitan sixth', this wayward hovering between the major, the

---

[1] According to Henseler this number was an independent composition dating from a few years earlier. But its separate publication in Cologne — with words adapted from an old German folk-song 'Cathrein, was willst du mehr' and a dedication to Fräulein Catherine Weyden (daughter of an old family friend) — roughly coincided with the production of *Pepito*, where it is so admirably in place that one prefers to think it was part of the original conception.

minor and the 'more minor' was such an agreeable feature of
his normally unexciting harmony that it may be fitting to bring
this brief review of his technical resource to a full close on a *tierce
de Picardie* from the posthumous *Moucheron*.

JACQUES OFFENBACH (1819–1880)

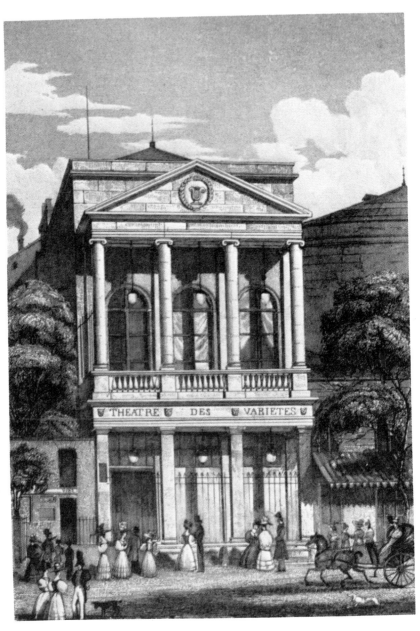

Théâtre des Variétés, Paris, in the 1860's

VI

ILLUSTRIOUS CONTRIBUTORS

THE gods loved GEORGES BIZET (1838–1875) even as they had loved Franz Schubert ; they snatched him in full flower before his genius was recognised in the mortal world. Schubert's great C major symphony was rescued from oblivion comparatively soon, but he had been in his last resting-place for forty years before the 'Unfinished' was performed or *Rosamunde* recovered intact. Down to this day patient and fruitful research is carried on by some of his devoted admirers — and what musician would wish to be excluded from that category ? As with Schubert, so with Bizet. Some of his best music achieved neither success nor publication during his lifetime ; the youthful Symphony in C, for instance, which is now in the repertory of every symphony orchestra, had to wait eighty years before being played in public. It is true that he lived to hear *Carmen*, but its cold reception caused acute mental depression which weakened his powers of resistance to chronic physical ailments. Two months after the first performance of his masterpiece Bizet was dead, and it would not be far from the truth to say that he died of a broken heart.

Bizet's music as a whole, however, is not our present concern — only the fact that as a young man he fancied himself as a composer of operettas. The immature *Maison du docteur* (1854) never saw the light of day, but *Le Docteur Miracle* (1856) tied for first place in a competition organised by Offenbach and so was played once at the Bouffes-Parisiens.[1] After gaining the Prix de Rome with a cantata, *Clovis et Clothilde*, Bizet tried to repeat his triumph in 1859 with a

---

[1] *Le Docteur Miracle* was revived at the Bath Festival, 1959. In spite of two or three attractive items it is, I feel, inferior to Lecocq's version which shared the prize (see page 74).

full-length operetta, *Don Procopio*. Appropriately enough he chose an Italian libretto, and much of the music adhered to the conventions of Rossini and Donizetti, though here and there his individuality broke through. There were several instances of a harmonic device which later became almost a mannerism (sidestepping from the established key and then immediately returning to it), parts of the long trio 'Se lei di parola' remind one of the first movement of the symphony (written four years previously), while another number — a little march — was unashamedly based on a theme from its finale. In relation to *Djamileh, L'Arlésienne* and *Carmen, Don Procopio* is negligible, yet for all its inconsistencies of style it stands comparison with any but the best of Offenbach's operettas, let alone those of his less talented contemporaries. The Prix-de-Rome adjudicators, however, would have no truck with such a trifle ; Bizet was furious, but nevertheless soon decided for himself that his true *métier* lay elsewhere. (He was not deterred from using one or two of the tunes over again in *The Pearl Fishers* and *The Fair Maid of Perth*.)

Meanwhile, a composer of almost equal calibre and much greater experience also tried his hand at a musical farce, but *Le Médecin malgré lui* (1858, after Molière) by CHARLES GOUNOD (1818–1893) fell between two stools. Though melodious, cultured and technically impeccable (the serenade 'Est-on sage' was Mozart brought up to date), Gounod's treatment was lacking in humour and failed to reconcile operatic methods with the manner of operetta. The stupendous success of *Faust* the following year inevitably directed his attention to regions where he was more at home, though he again dallied with comedy in *Philémon et Baucis* (1860). Some of the sentimental numbers had considerable charm — notably 'Ah! si je redevenais belle' — but elsewhere the music lapsed into vulgarity, as so often happened when Gounod strove to achieve a light touch that did not come naturally to him.[1]

---

[1] But *audi alteram partem*. 'Le *Médecin malgré lui* is witty, light-handed and perfectly adapted to Molière. Here and in *Philémon et Baucis* Gounod is at his best.' So wrote Martin Cooper in his admirable book *French Music* (1951) ; I am distressed to find myself at variance with this acknowledged expert.

When Offenbach opened his little theatre in the Champs-Élysées he combined the functions of managing director and resident composer ; he hoped — confident fast worker that he was — to be able to supply nearly all demands himself. But he overrated his capabilities and endurance, considerable though they were. Adam would no doubt have been welcomed on equal terms, but he died before he could provide a successor for *Les Pantins de Violette*, and the necessity for keeping the doors open obliged Offenbach to give frequent opportunities to less experienced composers. Prone to regard the establishment as his special preserve, he often disparaged the abilities of local boys who made good — it may be significant that after *Le Docteur Miracle* there were no more competitions — and for his understudies the position can have been no sinecure. But to start with, at any rate, he turned an unusually lenient — or was it discriminating ? — eye on LÉO DELIBES (1836–1891), who had already secured a production of his *Deux sous de charbon* (1855) at Hervé's Folies-Nouvelles and now came forward with *Les Deux vieilles gardes* — afterwards given in London as *The Patient* — and *Six demoiselles à marier* (both 1856). Always better behaved than Offenbach from the view-point of the élite, Delibes actually beat his sponsor in the race for the Opéra-Comique's rival theatre, the Lyrique, with his one-act *Monsieur Griffade* (1857). From that moment there was a cooling-off in the personal relationship, though the Bouffes-Parisiens still welcomed the younger man from time to time. Altogether Delibes wrote about fifteen operettas during this period ; most of them were in one act and about half were played at the 'Bouffes'. Presently he turned his attention to ballet and achieved fame with *Coppélia* (1870) and *Sylvia* (1876). But old associations were tugging, and in due course he wrote three ambitious works for the Opéra-Comique — *Le Roi l'a dit* (1873), *Jean de Nivelle* (1880) and *Lakmé* (1883). The last two are outside our present scope and here it need only be recorded that they were both successful, though the posthumous *Kassya* (completed by Massenet, 1893) was a failure. *Le Roi l'a dit*, however, belongs to the operetta category, for the atmosphere is frivolous and the music is an apotheosis of the composer's earlier style. It is a charming work which — apart from an occasional overdose of saccharine — shows Delibes at his best. The overture is still played occasionally, and anyone who has had the good fortune to hear it will recall the fetching little tune (Ex. 40) that seems to foreshadow the 'pizzicato' from *Sylvia*.

Ex.40 Moderato

In the second-act finale this is cleverly developed as an eleven-part ensemble, for the chorus is a mere formality that accords with eighteenth-century tradition — it is excluded altogether from the last act — and a surfeit of soloists has to make good the deficiency.

Although Delibes' youthful *jeux d'esprit* bore a superficial resemblance to the buffooneries of Offenbach with which they often shared the bill, there were profound differences in the approach. Offenbach indulged far more than did Delibes in flagrant burlesque. (Here was an unusually clear demonstration of the distinction between *opéra bouffe* and *opérette*.) Offenbach — even after he became established — had only one object in view, namely to please the public; Delibes, though by no means indifferent to money or renown, wrote mainly to please himself. Offenbach scribbled down the first thing that came into his head; Delibes, whose melodic invention was less fertile, relied on a surer instinct to distinguish the genuine from the meretricious : in the 'sérénade' from *La Cour du roi Pétaud* (1869), quoted in Ex. 41, the tune was more original and the accompaniment far more polished than in the much-praised 'letter song' from *La Périchole*. Moreover, such numbers as the long and varied duet 'Entrez, beau naufragé' from *Monsieur de Bonne-Étoile* (1860) captured a Gounod-like serenity which was beyond Offenbach's grasp.

Delibes' technical equipment, too, was superior; the five-bar rhythm and 'moving bass' of a march from *L'Omelette à la Follembûche* (1859) were not at all out of character, and effective instrumentation often added interest to the conventional portrayal of amusing situations, as in *L'Écossais de Chatou* (1868) — see Ex. 42. In *Le Roi l'a dit* his contrapuntal resource encouraged him to exploit fugal stretto (Ex. 43), but it must be admitted that he lacked that

Ex. 41 Allegretto

Si j'a - vais cent cœurs, Ils ne se - raient rem-plis que d'elle, —

Si j'a - vais cent cœurs, Au - cun d'eux n'aim-e - rait ail - leurs.

Ex. 42 Allegro non troppo SOPRANO Ad - mi - rab - le can - deur. BARITONE

TENOR Ad - mi - rab - le can - deur. _____ Ser - vez en -

SOPRANO
TENOR

-fin, j'ai soif! j'ai faim! Il croit qu'il va sou - per, Ah, je ris de bon cœur.

Picc.
Fl.

Ex. 43 Moderato maestoso

(continued over)

unfailing store of rhythmic sparkle and that impertinent sense of
humour which were Offenbach's priceless assets.

The name of JULES MASSENET (1842–1912) is not normally
associated with operetta, but of his first half-dozen works for the
stage two at least accorded with the terms of the definition we have
agreed to accept, and two more were border-line cases. The one-act
Grand' Tante (1867) achieved only seventeen performances, but it
was nevertheless prophetic, for in the duet 'L'amour que je rêvais si
doux' the lovers used the same accents as Manon and Des Grieux
seventeen years later ; throughout the touch was light, and triviality
was successfully avoided. The more ambitious *Don César de Bazan*
(1872), on the other hand, was almost entirely trivial without being
noticeably light-handed ; fortunately for Massenet's reputation it
was quite uncharacteristic. In 1874 came *L'Adorable Bel-Boul*, which
he designated as an operetta and afterwards regarded as an indiscretion ; it was eventually withdrawn from circulation. (Camille Le
Senne, in the *Encyclopédie de la musique*, accorded it a more explicit
title — *L'Adorable belle-poule*.) The charming *Cendrillon* (1879),
though perhaps really an *opéra comique*, must pass under review if
only to counteract the bad impression made by *Don César*. Here the
music recaptured the mood of *La Grand' Tante* ; admittedly the
well-known waltz (so beloved of Sir Thomas Beecham) was too
sugary and too prolonged to carry a universal appeal, but the
ingenious quartet 'Félicitez-moi', with a persistent running figuration, showed equal delicacy and greater artistic sensibility. At the
end of his life Massenet turned to comedy once more in the experimental 'haulte farce musicale' *Panurge* (produced posthumously in
1913) ; it was skilfully contrived in an unexpectedly modern
idiom, but was too pretentious to rank as a true operetta.

One might have expected that the man-of-the-world brilliance
of CAMILLE SAINT-SAËNS (1835–1921) would from time to time
have found expression in this typically Parisian form of entertain-

ment which he himself much enjoyed. But his only essay was a failure and the reason is not far to seek. Whereas Gounod had tried to set farcical comedy in an operatic manner, Saint-Saëns reversed the process by choosing a dream-like allegory as the excuse for a display of accomplished trivialities. Nevertheless the score of *La Princesse jaune* (Opéra-Comique, 1872) is worth dipping into ; this tantalising composer has as usual hidden a grain or two of wheat under the chaff. The overture is in sonata form and shines with the wonted classical polish, but the best number is the finale, built on a catchy tune which adheres to the Bouffes-Parisiens tradition.

No two compatriot contemporaries could provide a greater contrast than the slick professional Saint-Saëns and the frustrated amateur EMMANUEL CHABRIER (1841–1894). This is not the place to attempt comparative assessment of their stature, but the latter is certainly the more important figure so far as operettas are concerned. Although only two have been published and his biographers René Martineau and Georges Servières each credit him with only four — not the same four — he did in fact write seven all told : *Vaucochard et Fils premier* (1863), *Fish-ton-kan* (1865), *Le Sabbat* (1876), *L'Étoile* (1877), *Cocodette et Cocorico* (1878), *Monsieur et Madame Orchestre* (also 1878) and *Une Éducation manquée* (1879). It is believed that parts of *Vaucochard* were incorporated in Chabrier's last piano piece, *La Ronde champêtre* ; apart from that we have only the scores of *L'Étoile* and *Une Éducation manquée* on which to form a judgment. Here are eight bars from the former which typify its charm, delicacy and humour.[1]

Ex. 44
Andante

Pour vous re-met - tre un homme en son as - siet - te Non rien ne

pp très léger

(continued over)

[1] When in 1899 Ivan Caryll set to music an English version of the same libretto in *The Lucky Star* (see page 217), he paid Chabrier the compliment of using the excellent first-act finale of *L'Étoile* — eighteen pages of vocal score — almost intact.

Une *Éducation manquée* (one act) surpassed even *L'Étoile*. Offenbach's likeable predilection for contrasting tonic minor with tonic major has already been recorded ; how much more subtle was Chabrier's treatment (Ex. 45) of the same key-relationship! (*Cf.* the 'Mauresque' from *Dix pièces pittoresques* and the song *Pastorale des cochons roses.*) Note the effect of the recurring D♯ in bars 7, 8, 9, 10 and 13.

pe-tit vau-rien Que je n'ai rien, rien, rien, rien à t'ap-prend - - - re.

And there was a waltz-duet — 'J'en prends un, j'en prends deux' — which testified that when Chabrier chose to write in that rhythm he had no need to fear comparison with Offenbach, Johann Strauss, Waldteufel, Tchaikovsky or anyone else ; a few years later *España* was to drive the point home. Yet during Chabrier's lifetime *Une Éducation manquée* received only a few semi-private performances with piano accompaniment and, like *L'Étoile*, has only survived at all through the perseverance of enthusiasts who have arranged an occasional revival.

It would be pleasant to draw a veil over the rest of Chabrier's stage music, and I should be justified in doing so — for he wrote no more operettas — were it not that *Le Roi malgré lui* (1887) has often been mistakenly referred to as a 'comic opera'. The misapprehension may have a double origin : for one thing the title reminds one of both *Le Roi l'a dit* and *Le Médecin malgré lui* ; for another the work is officially classed as an *opéra comique*. But the designation is merely technical, due to the inclusion of spoken dialogue and a happy ending ; *Le Roi malgré lui* is in fact no more comic than *Fidelio* or *Der Freischütz*, both of which, by the same criteria, are *opéras comiques*. Stylistically it is a hotch-potch ; the harmonies at times foreshadow Debussy, while the dramatic treatment is for the most part in the 'grand' manner which Chabrier had first espoused in *Gwendoline* (1886) and which he maintained to an ever-increasing extent as his admiration for Wagner developed into the obsession which hastened his tragic mental collapse. Most musicians prefer to remember him for *España*, for the *Joyeuse Marche*, for a handful of unassuming songs and piano pieces ; *L'Étoile* and *Une Éducation manquée* deserve to be added to this short list of compositions on which his immortality depends.

VII

LESSER LIGHTS (1)

THE opening paragraph of this chapter must be accorded to that peripatetic cosmopolitan FRIEDRICH VON FLOTOW (1812–1883). Although he was born within sight of the Baltic and the only work by which he is now remembered was first produced in Vienna, most of his early life was spent in Paris, where his talent for expressive if rather superficial melody earned him popularity several years before *Martha* (1847) spread his fame round the world. Member of a noble and wealthy Prussian family, he possessed a kind heart as well as a coronet, and we have already seen how he gave practical encouragement to Offenbach when it was most needed. The cordiality of their relationship was unimpaired by the latter's subsequent success, and in 1895 Flotow wrote an operetta, *La Veuve Grapin*, for the Bouffes-Parisiens — a characteristic gesture of good will. As regards example and precept his influence on French music did not amount to much, but many of his associates who were less well endowed with worldly goods had reason to be grateful for the opportunities which his friendship and interest afforded them.

One such was ALBERT GRISAR (1808–1869), who on a chronological basis should perhaps rank with Clapisson as a predecessor of Offenbach rather than as a contemporary. But though he first took the stage in 1833 — with *Le Mariage impossible* — and was firmly established as a composer while Offenbach was still struggling to achieve recognition, his few operettas (as distinct from his *opéras comiques*) all belong to the last eighteen years of his life, a period which roughly coincided with the great days of the Bouffes-Parisiens ; one of them — *Douze innocentes* (1865) — was actually produced there. Grisar was born in Antwerp ; as a young man he was apprenticed to a business firm in Liverpool, but neither commerce nor Merseyside appealed to him, and at twenty-two we find him studying music in Paris, where — apart from occasional visits to Belgium and Italy — he remained for the rest of his life. Success came in 1838 with *Lady Melvill*, in which he was aided and abetted by Flotow ; in 1864 Grisar rewrote it (without assistance this time) and re-christened it *Le Joaillier de Saint-James'*. During the intervening years he produced a dozen or so *opéras comiques*. Most of them showed eclectic tendencies : one notices the influence of Flotow again in the one-act *Gilles Ravisseur* (1848), of Rossini in *Les Porcherons* (1850) and of Weber in *Le Carillonneur de Bruges* (1852). His operettas, which were *all* in one act, displayed sound if rather parsimonious workmanship and a welcome facility in rhythmic devices, but they lacked character, and poverty of invention was all too evident. Nevertheless there were some attractive items, especially in the first two — *Bonsoir Monsieur Pantalon* (1851) and *Le Chien du jardinier* (1853) — where he owed much to his librettist, J. P. Lockroy.

Another Belgian, FRANÇOIS GEVAERT (1828–1908), though remembered mainly for his standard treatise on orchestration, distinguished himself in several branches of composition. His first opera (*Hugues de Somerghem*) and a one-act operetta *La Comédie à la ville* — in which the only sign of immaturity was the squareness of the choral writing — were both played at Ghent before he was twenty-one. In Paris he made a mark with the gay but uneven *Georgette* (1853) and the more consistent *Billet de Marguerite* (1854), but of his subsequent works for the stage only *Le Diable au moulin* (1859), *Le Château Trompette* (1860), *Les Deux amours* (1861) and possibly *Le Capitaine Henriot* (1864) were sufficiently unassuming to rank as operettas. He took great care over his scores. The overtures were particularly well-constructed and many of the light songs and ensembles combined perkiness with a refreshing rhythmic freedom ; elsewhere — as in the duet 'Rassurez-vous, ne craignez rien' from *Le Capitaine Henriot* — there was a tendency to imitate the Verdi of the *Rigoletto* period without much success. After 1864 he devoted most of his time to teaching and musicology ; it would be interesting to read the comments of Gevaert, the staid pedagogue, on the blatant 'consecutives' perpetrated by Gevaert, the dashing young composer of *Le Château Trompette* (Ex. 46).

Ex. 46   Andante misterioso

AIMÉ MAILLART (1817–1881), JEAN GAUTIER (1822–1878),
THÉOPHILE SEMET (1824–1888) and JULES DUPRATO (1827–
1892) resembled Grisar and Gevaert in that they wrote with their
eyes fixed firmly on the Opéra-Comique while not disdaining
an occasional operetta.   Maillart made only one contribution to
the genre — the somewhat rustic *Moulin des tilleuls* (1849).   His
opéras comiques — of which *Les Dragons de Villars* (1856) long held
the stage — came later ;   though they showed him in a more
favourable light they were overpraised by his contemporaries.
(Arthur Pougin ranked Maillart above Verdi, a judgment he
delivered *after* having heard *Aida*.)   Jean Gautier was quickly off
the mark with *L'Anneau de Mariette* (1845), which was a happy-go-
lucky affair.   But he soon settled down :   *Le Mariage extravagant*
(1857) had great success, and *Le Docteur Mirobolan* (1860) deserves
honourable mention if only for an ingenious fugato put forth
by two bassoons during the overture and recurring later.   Of
Semet's works perhaps *La Petite Fadette* (1869) alone was a true
operetta.   This was a revised and largely redeemed version of a
vaudeville written way back in 1850 ;   the tunes were good, and a
romance in 5/4 time — part of the accretion — exposed a nice vein
of originality.   Jules Duprato's *opéras comiques* were written in a
fluent but rather conventional style (reminiscent of Flotow) which
was well maintained in three agreeable one-act operettas — *M'sieu
Landry* (1856), *Une Promenade de Marie-Thérèse* (1863) and *Le
Bonhomme Hiver* (1882).

To a certain extent the career of VICTOR MASSÉ (1822–1884)
ran parallel with Offenbach's.   Junior by less than three years he
followed him to the Paris Conservatoire, achieved a stage production
at twenty-one (as against twenty), first tasted real success at twenty-
seven (twenty-seven) and died when he was sixty-two (sixty-one) ;
furthermore Massé, like Offenbach, left his most ambitious work

barely completed and did not live to hear it. Aesthetically, however, the two composers had little in common. Félix Marie Massé — as he was christened — came from Brittany. He was sincere and high-minded ; a cantata (*Le Rénégat de Tanger*, 1845) and a 'Messe Solenelle' showed the trend of his youthful aspirations. But the theatre soon beckoned him, and after misfiring once or twice he hit the target with the one-act operetta *La Chambre gothique* (Folies-Dramatiques, 1849), which showed him to much better advantage. The charming *Chanteuse voilée* (1850) earned him entry to the Opéra-Comique (which remained his spiritual home) but as early as *Galathée* (1852) he inclined to adopt a lofty 'dramatic' style which he could not live up to. *La Reine Topaze* (Théâtre-Lyrique, 1856), *Le Cousin de Marivaux* (Baden-Baden, 1857) and *La Mule de Pedro* (Opéra, 1863) evinced the same unfortunate tendency to an even greater degree. Their musical content was basically unsubstantial, but he strove so hard to disguise the fact by overloading the detail with pretentious artificiality that one is bound to assess them at his own valuation as *opéras* or *opéras comiques*, and if one were to adopt a proper standard of criticism the judgment would be a harsh one. Only two works from this period — *Les Noces de Jeannette* (1853) and *Mariette la promise* (1862) — belong undisputably to the category of operetta. (In some reference books *La favorita e la schiava* is dated 1855, but that was merely when Venice first heard this Italianised version of an unnamed French operetta which had been written about the same time as *La Chambre gothique*.) *Les Noces de Jeannette* remains Massé's *chef d'œuvre* ; for once the graceful tunes were allowed to develop naturally and the orchestral accompaniments held little trace of his wonted turgidity.[1]

In 1866 Massé was appointed professor of composition at the Conservatoire. This was a set-back to his operatic projects, for the duties left little time for creative work, but after the Franco-Prussian war he amused himself by writing a few 'opérettes de famille', evidently intended for private performance. They were mere trifles, bubbles light as air, but they gave a glimpse of what might have been, for deft workmanship endowed their unassuming numbers

---

[1] Between 1860 and 1864 *Les Noces de Jeannette* was occasionally staged at Covent Garden, a most unusual honour for a French operetta.

with a touch of distinction. In *Une Loi somptuaire* (1874), for instance, there was an 'air de rouet' which was quite a little gem ; its *rondeau* form permitted the interpolation of two episodes, one in the dominant and the other in the mediant (first minor, then major), and the contrasted returns to the tonic were admirably contrived. Unfortunately this form of musical relaxation did not satisfy Massé's inner urge, and in the mid-seventies he turned his hand to 'grand' opera, a medium for which his talents were conspicuously ill-fitted. From an armchair in 1961 one cannot question the motives which prompted the decision, but one has to place on record that in *Paul et Virginie* (1876) and the posthumous *Nuit de Cléopâtre* (1885) few of his virtues were apparent and all his weaknesses were laid bare. Had he been content to explore more thoroughly the vein which he had uncovered in *Les Noces de Jeannette* and the 'opérettes de famille' it might have been difficult to set a limit to Massé's achievements, for his flow of melody, though less glib than Offenbach's, was nevertheless considerable and rarely lapsed into the commonplace. It is a matter for regret that this resource was so often misapplied.

XAVIER BOISSELOT (1811–1893), ERNEST BOULANGER (1815–1900) and FRANÇOIS BAZIN (1816–1878) entered the field about the same time as Massé. Boisselot made only a brief appearance, for when the promise of *Ne touchez pas à la reine* (1847) was negatived in the vulgar and heavy-handed *Mosquita la sorcière* (1851) he gave up composition and took to the manufacture of pianofortes. The case of Boulanger — a professor at the Conservatoire — was a curious one. By the time he was thirty he had written three miniature operas, all quite effective, in the manner of Adolphe Adam ; they were *Le Diable à l'école* (1842), *Deux bergères* (1843) and *Une Voix* (1845). His subsequent output, however, suffered from an extraordinary irresolution of approach, with results that were often artistically disastrous. For instance, *La Cachette* (1847) was pretentious melodrama, *Les Sabots de la marquise* (1854, a great success, it must be admitted) was a mixture of attractive pastiche and crude burlesque, in *Le Docteur Magnus* (1864) a fantastic theme was treated with irresponsible levity, and finally *Don Mucarade* (1875) was merely a clumsy imitation of Offenbach. François Bazin's first attempt at operetta — the well-constructed *Trompette de Monsieur le Prince* (1846) — also raised hopes that were never realised, except perhaps in the comparatively serious *Madelon* (1852), which introduced a touch of genuine sentiment to an essentially frivolous art-form. A perusal of the vocal scores of *Maître Pathelin* (1856) and *Le Voyage en Chine* (1865) fails to elucidate why they were translated into German and Danish and welcomed abroad, for the music plumbs the depths of triviality.

FERDINAND POISE (1828–1892) demands rather more attention. His *Bonsoir voisin* (1853) ran for over a hundred performances at the Théâtre Lyrique, and a warm reception was accorded to *Le Thé de Polichinelle* at the Bouffes-Parisiens in 1856. Though most of his later pieces were given at the Opéra-Comique, for which their refinement and 'musicality' made them eligible, they belonged definitely to the genus operetta. The best of them were *Les Absents* (1864), *La Surprise de l'amour* (1877) — in which the heat and burden of three acts was borne by four characters only — and *L'Amour médecin* (1880). (A clever librettist, C. P. Monselet, collaborated in the two last-named works, which were based on comedies by Marivaux and Molière respectively.) Unlike Massé, Poise never allowed his ambition to outrun his ability, but he had not the same gift of spontaneous melody and his music was at times disfigured by irritating mannerisms, *e.g.* an over-fondness for drone basses and for a certain little rhythmic figure. On the credit side must be placed not only his skilful handling of dramatic situations — the trio 'Lui vivant devant moi' from *Don Pedre* (1858) is suggestive of Verdi — but also his adroit orchestral figuration and his dissension from the prevalent four-bar jog-trot.

ÉMILE JONAS (1827–1905) was less accomplished than Poise but far more prolific. As a Jew he was welcomed at the Bouffes-Parisiens by its founder, and as a competent hack he must have been a great stand-by ; when an *apéritif* was called for at short notice he was always ready to mix an acceptable tumblerful of weak Offenbach-and-water. Jonas's early operettas may be acquitted of vulgarity, for such a charge would presuppose the existence of an animate impulse which is here barely perceptible. In the whole array I can find only two numbers that manifest any positive attribute : one is a duet ('Joli rosier') from *Le Roi boit* (1857) which introduces a welcome touch of syncopation to the melody, and the other is an ensemble (see Ex. 47) from *Le Canard aux trois becs* (1867) which quite prettily exploits a specialised form of polyphony originated by Philidor and later brought to a fine art by Sullivan.

Ex.47 Moderato

As time went on Jonas managed to infuse a small measure of vitality into his music, and presently he earned recognition in London with *Cinderella the younger* (1871) — afterwards played in Paris as *Javotte* — and in Brussels with *Le Chignon d'or* (1874). In the eighties he tried his hand at *opéra comique* : *La Bonne aventure* (1882) — especially in the concerted sections — displayed a modicum of technical resource which must have been recently acquired, but *Le Premier baiser* (1883), so far from betokening the consummation of an intimate *liaison*, marked the conclusion of a fleeting acquaintance.

The obscure and unassuming LOUIS PIERRE DEFFÈS (1819–1900) had a surer touch ; *La Clef des champs* (1857), *Le Café du roi* (1861) and *Lanterne magique!!!* (1862) were almost worthy of Offenbach himself, and several other pieces secured production at the Théâtre-Lyrique, at the Bouffes-Parisiens or in Bad-Ems, but his output was small and apparently he worked only spasmodically. In later life his two *opéras comiques* — *Les Noces de Fernande* (1880) and *Jessica* (1898, based on *The Merchant of Venice*) — were both well received.

The other contributors to the repertory of the Bouffes-Parisiens while Offenbach remained in charge were a very mixed lot. They included the conductor ALPHONSE VARNEY (1811–1879) who lived again in his son Louis (see page 87) ; LÉON GASTINEL (1812–1883), composer of forgotten oratorios ; the singing-teacher GIULIO ALARY (1814–1891) ; the piano-builder HENRI CASPERS

ANDRE MESSAGER (1853-1929)

HERVÉ (1825–1892)

(1825–1906 [1]) ; the novelist ERNEST L'ÉPINE (1826–1893) ; and the organist RENAUD DE VILBAC (1829–1884). In fairness it must be recorded that Gastinel's *Opéra aux fenêtres* (1857, given in London as *An eligible Villa*), L'épine's *Croquenille XXXVI* (1860) and perhaps Alary's *Orgue de Barbarie* (1857) were musically superior to most of Jonas's paltry gewgaws. (Alary had been born in Milan of French parents, and during this period he was writing unashamedly in the Italian manner ; in 1866 his *Locanda grantis*, despite its title, captured more of the Parisian spirit.[2]) Caspers' *Dans la rue* (1858) and *Baronne de San Francisco* (1861) were very commonplace, but he appeared to much better advantage away from the 'Bouffes'. *Ma Tante dort* (Théâtre-Lyrique, 1860), which was an amusing little affair in the classical manner and included a charming *rondeau* ('Chez les valets'), was later successful at the Opéra-Comique and abroad ; it even survived the turn of the century, being given a single performance at the Vienna Opera House in 1914.

This does not quite complete the list, for two young lady composers made their début at the 'Bouffes'. *La Pomme de Turquie* (1857) was by PAULINE THYS (1836– ?), daughter of Alphonse Thys whom we met on page 16 ; *Le Son de Lise* (1859) by a protégée of Flotow who was christened Marie de Reiset, later became the Vicomtesse de Grandval, and wrote music under the successive pseudonyms of 'Caroline Blangy' and CLÉMENCE VALGRAN (1830–1906). Their subsequent operettas were performed elsewhere, as were their *opéras comiques*, of which they wrote one apiece : Valgran's *Piccolino* (1869), a tribute to her patron, was less assured in execution than Thys's *Mariage de Tabarin* (1876), which was translated into Italian and given at Naples in 1881 as *La congiura di Chevreuse*. Pauline's gifts, modest though they were, surpassed those of her father ; she modelled her style on Offenbach or Gounod according to circumstances and had quite a flair for expressive melody which gave singers scope for effective vocalisation. It is interesting to note that she anticipated Dame Ethel Smyth in so far as she wrote

---

[1] Alfred Loewenberg (*Annals of Opera*, 1946), whose accuracy was as a rule impeccable, killed Caspers off prematurely in 1861, the year of his *father's* death.

[2] It is worth noting that Alary, like Grisar, Massé, Bazin and Deffès, composed some of his overtures in sonata form.

F

all her own libretti. Either she shared the same prejudices or else professionals like Meilhac and Halévy were disinclined to have their names associated with such a disturbing manifestation of feminine efficiency. At all events, by taking the reins into her own hands she managed to avoid the animadversions of the puritanical Félix Clément. Not so the collaborators of her colleague the Vicomtesse : 'the libretto of *Piccolino* offends both morality and good taste'.

The Bouffes-Parisiens was not the only theatre in Paris wholly consecrated to frivolous operettas, for in 1853 HERVÉ (1825–1892) had opened the 'Folies-Nouvelles' in the boulevard du Temple. 'Hervé' was the third of three pseudonyms adopted by an enterprising and versatile youth from the Pas-de-Calais whose real name was Florimond Ronger. (The others, quickly abandoned, were 'Jules Brément' and 'Louis Heffer'.)   At seventeen he presented *L'Ours et le pacha* at the Bicêtre *hospice d'aliénés* — with a cast and orchestra comprising not only attendants but also some of the more reliable inmates.[1]   *Don Quichotte et Sancho Pança* (1848) was thrown in as a makeweight at Adam's ill-fated 'Opéra-National', and presently there followed an engagement as conductor at the Palais-Royal. But Hervé did not hit the headlines until he started on his own at the Folies-Nouvelles with a quadruple bill and a fivefold personal flourish.

(1) *Prologue d'ouverture*, in one act, words by Charles Bridault, music by Hervé.

(2) *Fausse Douairière*, pantomime in two acts, words by Charles Bridault and Paul Legrand, music by Hervé.

(3) *Pierrot amoureux*, in one act, words by Paul Legrand and Charles Delaquis, music by Hervé.

(4) *La Perle d'Alsace*, 'pastorale strasbourgeoise' in one act, words by Hervé, music by Hervé.

His breakneck energy exceeded even Offenbach's, for in the course of forty-four years (he virtually abandoned composition in 1886) he perpetrated some hundred and twenty operettas, at least half of

---

[1] About thirty-five years later another young man performed much the same functions at the lunatic asylum at Powick near Worcester. Unlike Hervé, he was not driven by the experience to adopt a succession of pen-names ; he rested content with his own — Edward Elgar.

which were in two or more acts. Furthermore he wrote many of the libretti, and appeared so frequently as conductor or leading baritone that one is almost constrained to believe that he must sometimes have undertaken both rôles simultaneously. Although he did not completely monopolise the Folies-Nouvelles — we have already noted how young Delibes was there given his first chance — it is none the less significant that Offenbach was never admitted ; nor did Hervé's name appear on the Bouffes-Parisiens prospectus until after Offenbach had resigned from the managerial board. Mutual suspicion and jealousy long kept them at daggers drawn, but years later they became friends ; in 1878 Hervé actually consented to play the part of Pluton in a revival of *Orphée aux enfers*.

His best-known operettas — *L'Œil crevé* (1866), *Chilpéric* (1868), *Le Petit Faust* (1869) — came towards the end of his most prolific period. The outbreak of war sent him, along with Jonas, to London, where he wrote *Aladdin the Second* in English and *Le Trône d'Écosse* in French.[1] On his return to Paris he contented himself for the rest of the decade with about one operetta annually, and this self-discipline helped to ensure that *La Belle poule* (1873) and *Panurge* (1879) were less perfunctory than the vast majority of his previous outpourings. From 1881 onwards, however, he concentrated on *vaudevilles* for the Théâtre des Variétés (thus renewing an association which had been inaugurated with his *Joueur de flûte* in 1864) ; hereabouts his only substantial work was *La Nuit aux soufflets* (Opéra-Comique, 1884). In 1886 he settled permanently in London on being appointed musical director of the Empire Music-hall in Leicester Square, and his last piece of any consequence, *Frivoli*, was produced that autumn at the Theatre Royal, Drury Lane.[2]

Lacking Offenbach's musical background, professional training and operatic experience, Hervé relied partly on a remarkable gift

[1] *Le Trône* introduced twelve pretty 'gardes de la reine', all named in the programme. One imagines that the stage-door johnnies turned down Sarah-For-Ever and Diana Kiss-Me-Not as being unapproachable, Mary Bad and Katy Yes as too-easy game, and that it was Eva Thank-You and Jenny Hyde-Park whom they hopefully asked out to supper.

[2] One of the small parts was played by Marie Tempest, then aged twenty, who shortly afterwards came to the fore in Messager's *Béarnaise* (page 93) and Cellier's *Dorothy* (page 184).

for facile melody (which was not of itself a passport to anything more than transient success) and partly on the skill of his regular librettists, H. Crémieux and A. Jaime. His technical equipment was woefully inadequate ; only here and there does one find any indication of *savoir-faire*. A two-part chorus from *La Belle poule* stands out a mile —

— but generally speaking he appears at his modest best in the dainty little waltzes to which he was so much addicted : there was a particularly charming one in *La Marquise des rues* (1879). His harmonic resource remained negligible to the end, and many of his orchestral accompaniments were not only ungrammatical but fatuous. It is almost incredible that a composer with nearly a hundred operettas behind him could do no better than Ex. 49 for the leading lady of *La Veuve de Malabar* (1873), and indeed there was a pitiful amount of this kind of thing. Nor did Hervé share Offenbach's aptitude for musical burlesque. A song from *Chilpéric* was alleged to be a skit on the love duet from Act III of *Lohengrin*, but it was really nothing more than a feeble imitation of one of Gounod's graceful garden-scene melodies, and though that composer was also parodied in *Le Petit Faust* such exhibitions of bad taste were comparatively rare. Possibly this restraint helped to inflate Hervé's reputation in circles where Offenbach's operettas were tabooed, but it is still puzzling that musicians or the world at large should ever have thought him capable of challenging his contemporary's supremacy. Viewed in retrospect a far more dangerous rival was Charles Lecocq, whose considerable achievements demand a chapter to themselves.

L'u - sa - ge veut qu'à do-mi-ci - le On fé - li - cite au Ma-la-bar Les jeun - es

gens au cœur fa - ci - le Qui tom - bent dans le grand traqu'-nard!

VIII

LECOCQ

ALEXANDRE CHARLES LECOCQ (1832–1918), like his close contemporaries César Cui, Saint-Saëns and Max Bruch, linked a bygone
age with the present. (All four were born during the lifetime of
Cherubini — which overlapped that of Rameau who was older
than J. S. Bach — yet not one of them closed his eyes until well after
Carlo Menotti and Benjamin Britten had opened theirs.) By temperament Lecocq was introspective and self-critical ; he was fully
aware of his limitations, and in his diary he made some naïve and
extraordinarily frank comments on his own compositions. It is
therefore not surprising that he rarely attempted anything ambitious,
and that during a long career his total output of operettas — forty-
odd — was less than half Offenbach's and only about one-third of
Hervé's. But he was an incomparably better musician than the
latter, and — leaving aside a few lapses during the eighteen-eighties
when he temporarily lost his grip — his work attained a higher
standard of consistent merit than Offenbach's without ever quite
reaching such summit-points as *La Belle Hélène* or *La Vie parisienne*.

Five years' study at the Paris Conservatoire gave him an admirable grounding, and during his student days he aspired to 'serious'
composition. Nevertheless in 1857 he entered for Offenbach's
Docteur Miracle competition, and his setting tied with Bizet's for first
prize. It was a clever little affair which showed a refreshing inde-
pendence of outlook (the amusing 'omelette quartet' was quite a
tour de force). But evidently this sort of thing was not wanted at the
Bouffes-Parisiens and no further invitations eventuated. Unlike
Offenbach and Hervé, Lecocq had only one strong string to his bow;
moreover he lacked their self-assurance and too easily became
despondent. For seven frustrating years he made a meagre living
as an organist, and in 1864 seized avidly on the chance of writing

74

another buffoonery, this time for Hervé's Folies-Nouvelles : *Le Baiser à la porte* was the turning-point, for it led to similar productions elsewhere. He soon stabilised a connection with the Théâtre de l'Athénée, where in 1868 he presented three full-length operettas — *L'Amour et son carquois*, *Fleur de thé* and *Les Jumeaux de Bergame*. (*Fleur de thé* was originally called *Le Mikado* ; the title was changed at the request of the Japanese Ambassador in Paris. Although Gilbert and Sullivan got away with it in London sixteen years later, *The Mikado* itself ran into political trouble in 1908, when the Lord Chamberlain banned a revival on the grounds that it might offend Japanese sensibilities.) In 1869 Lecocq at last returned to the Bouffes-Parisiens with *Gandolfo* and *Le Rajah de Mysore*, but three of his best operettas had their *premières* in Brussels — *Les Cent vierges*, *La Fille de Madame Angot* (both 1872) and *Giroflé-Girofla* (1874). They did not reach Paris until a year or two later ; thereafter they swept the world.

The Second Empire had been a perfect background for Offenbach ; during the first few years of the Third Republic Lecocq was the more dominating figure of the two, for while Offenbach was under a cloud Lecocq consolidated his position. Although he never quite repeated the triumph of *Madame Angot* his next nine or ten operettas were all nearly as good. (Most of them were produced at the Théâtre de la Renaissance.) Some of the ensembles — of which 'Bon appetit, belle cousine' from *Giroflé* and 'Ne faisons pas de bruit' from *La Petite mademoiselle* (1879) may be cited as examples — were very skilfully contrived, and if one adopts a standard of criticism appropriate to the genre it would be difficult to praise too highly such charming numbers as 'Aimons-nous tous bas' from *La Petite mariée* (1875), the 'duo des adieux' from *La Marjolaine* (1877) and 'C'est pourtant bien doux' from *Le Petit duc* (1878). By the end of the decade, however, Lecocq began to show signs of having over-written himself ; he had allowed the composition of operettas to become a mechanical habit. Though by that time he was so well established that almost anything went down with the public, the success of *Le Jour et la nuit* (1881), *Le Cœur et la main* (1882) and *La Princesse des Canaries* (1883) proved ephemeral because much of their content was repetitive or perfunctory. Lecocq

himself realised this, and when in 1886 he was invited to compose a
piece for the Opéra-Comique he pulled himself together. The
result was *Plutus*, where perhaps valour outran discretion. *Les
Grenadiers de Mont-Cornette* and *Alibaba* (both 1887) marked a
return to his more acceptable manner, but they did not find the
success they deserved, and his tendency to self-criticism quickly
reasserted itself after the complete failure of *La Volière* in 1888. For
a time he gave up composition altogether, and his later operettas
came to little, though *La Belle au bois dormant* (1900) deserves mention
for the sake of the romance 'Mon âme était toute joyeuse', which
was worthy of Chabrier. Lecocq's last work, *La Trahison de Pan*
(Aix-les-Bains, 1911), was an interesting little experiment in *durchkomponiert* form ; though perhaps not very spontaneous, it proved,
as had Verdi's *Falstaff*, that a composer of seventy-nine could still
be young in spirit.

Many of Lecocq's operettas enjoyed popularity in England, where
Le Cœur et la main, as *Incognita*, was not the only one to bear a new
and inscrutable title. *La Petite mariée* appeared first as *The Elopement*
(which was fair enough) and afterwards as *The Scarlet Feather* ; by a
master-stroke of Victorian metamorphosis *Les Cent vierges* became
The Island of Bachelors. His most helpful librettist was L. F. Nicolaie
(who wrote under the name of 'Clairville'), but A. Vanloo and
E. Leterrier played their part in helping to ensure the success of
Giroflé-Girofla and *La Petite mariée*.

So far as technique is concerned, Lecocq was Offenbach's superior
and Delibes' equal. He had learnt the job thoroughly in a hard
school, and though his operettas inevitably contained many pages
of triviality, almost every bar, even in the simplest passages, showed
a quality of accomplished workmanship which is difficult to analyse
but is easily recognisable by a musician. Cecil Forsyth in his
Orchestration (1914), apropos of a passage from *The Yeomen of the
Guard*, advised students to consider 'not only the notes which
Sullivan has written but the many other notes which he might have
written and didn't' ; one might apply the same comment to
Lecocq's orchestral accompaniments, where the right balance was
achieved with the utmost economy of means. Another characteristic which he shared with his British contemporary was adroitness

in bringing new life to well-worn conventions; here are a few
bars from *Kosiki* (1876).

As early as *Ondines au champagne* (1866, anglicé *The Sea-Nymphs*)
Lecocq showed his fancy for a 'moving bass' —

— and though he rarely indulged in elaborate counterpoint he was
much addicted to simple canons. For instance, *La Vie mondaine*
(1885) opens with an amusing chorus for schoolboys; presently a
girls' school passes by, marching *en crocodil* and singing the same
words, *mutatis mutandis*, to the same tune. The cheeky boys cannot
bear to be left out of the fun, so they join in again — one bar behind!
Lecocq was adept, too, at raising expectancy with a touch of the grand
manner, as at the lead-in to a song from *Le Pompon* (1875). As

for that rigid adherence to four-bar phrases, which was such an irritating feature of Offenbach's early operettas and almost sterilised those of Jonas, with Lecocq the defect was somehow translated into a virtue, for it ensured a symmetry that accorded well with the character of the music. Harmonic initiative was a more tangible asset, amenable to progressive analysis; although in *Docteur Miracle* days the search after originality was somewhat capricious, it led to a complete reconciliation between spontaneity and subtlety thirty years later in *Alibaba*.

Unfortunately the admirable qualities which Lecocq acquired through study and developed through long experience were all but balanced by a serious weakness that was inherent ; just at the very moments when one might have expected the tide of inspiration to be at the flood it was apt to ebb sluggishly away, leaving the composer high and dry on a sandbank, from which his technical resource, considerable though it was, could not always rescue him. In such a predicament he was often driven to disguise poverty of invention with note-repetitions, arabesques and other such well-worn devices. A four-bar snatch from *Le Testament de Monsieur de Crac* (1871) — Ex. 54 — is a typical instance of this revealing mannerism ; another occurs in the well-known 'Chœur des merveilleurs' from *La Fille de Madame Angot* (Ex. 55).

It is only fair to quote, by way of contrast, the vital, surging waltz-
tune 'Tournez, tournez' — also from *Madame Angot*.

Ex.56   Tempo di Valse

Because of his independent approach and disinclination to follow
formal precedents, it was Lecocq rather than Offenbach who may
be accounted the direct descendant of Adolphe Adam.   Had he
been born with that impelling gift of melody which the conscientious
Massé hoarded so thriftily and the thoughtless Hervé squandered so
improvidently, French operetta might have found in him its supreme
exponent.

IX

LESSER LIGHTS (2)

IN France the decade of the eighteen-thirties brought forth quite a bevy of youngsters who were later to practise the art of operetta or at any rate try their hand at it. We have already met, putting them in order of age, Valgran, Lecocq, Saint-Saëns, Delibes, Pauline Thys and Bizet. The names of Lacome and Pfeiffer must now be added to the list. PAUL LACOME (1838–1920, real name Paul Lacome-d'Estelenx) was an honest imitator of Lecocq, though curiously enough he sometimes extended the same flattery to Mendelssohn. He has gone the way of most imitators, but his best music was by no means negligible, for it was adequately tuneful and the careful workmanship displayed a professional touch. Between 1870 and the close of the century he turned out on an average one operetta every eighteen months ; the most successful were *Jean, Jeannette et Jeanneton* (1876) and *Ma mie Rosette* (1890), but *Pâques fleuries* (1879), *Le Beau Nicolas* (1880) and *Myrthille* (1885) showed him in an equally favourable light.[1] GEORGES PFEIFFER (1835–1908) was a versatile musician who did good work in several branches of composition. His three operettas — *Capitaine Roche* (1862), *L'Enclume* (1884) and *Le Légataire universel* (1901) — were widely spaced chronologically ; *L'Enclume* was the best of them, and the effective 'air et chanson de l'enclume' (the 'production number' as it would nowadays be called) was its outstanding feature.

[1] Paul Lacome is sometimes confused with the symphonic composer Paul Lacombe (1837–1927), an obscure recluse who studied music by correspondence and spent nearly all the ninety years of his life in his native Carcassonne. Their names and dates are so similar that misapprehension is pardonable, though one is surprised to find it perpetuated in Schmidl's *Dizionario universale dei musicisti* (the article on Victor Roger). Sterling Mackinlay in his *Origin and Development of Light Opera* (1927) — see page 257 — went further astray when he attributed Lacome's *Ma mie Rosette* to *Louis* Lacombe, a distinguished pianist from Bourges who turned to composition and wrote several operas, but never descended to operetta.

The eighteen-forties saw the birth of Chabrier and Massenet but they produced no habitual practitioner of Lecocq's calibre ; Audran and Planquette — as will soon be made evident — were clear leaders in an undistinguished field. The most promising of the 'also ran' was PAUL VASSEUR (1844–1917), who rescued the Bouffes-Parisiens from imminent post-war ruination with *La Timbale d'argent* (1872). That this piece should have had a great vogue enraged Félix Clément; a special invitation to the 150th performance found him in belligerent mood.

> The libretto is absolutely immoral. . . . I had imagined that the success of this piece must be due to some redeeming feature in the music — but it has none ; the tunes are monotonous, the orchestration is noisy, and there is hardly an original idea from start to finish.

From this wholesale condemnation he might at least have had the courtesy to exclude the introduction to the second act, which may be unoriginal but has no time to become monotonous and is certainly not noisy.

Ex.57 Tempo di menuetto

Unfortunately Vasseur's courtship of popularity progressed so rapidly in its initial stages that he became superbly complacent. The forward path was strewn with fewer primroses than he expected, for he had failed to take into account the possibility that he might not be blessed with the fertile inventiveness of an Offenbach or a Hervé. He even let go his grip on the sound principles of musician-ship to which he had held fast in much of *La Timbale* and *La Petite*

reine (1873) ; his subsequent operettas, besides being often un-
melodious, were almost unbelievably slipshod, and their sole interest
lay in the occasional emergence — especially in *Le Billet de logement*
(1879) — of an unexpected flair for tender sentimental expression.
HENRI MARÉCHAL (1842–1924) had more steadiness of artistic
purpose. His compositions included eight or nine works for the
stage, but not many of them fell into the category of operetta : he
was a favourite pupil of Victor Massé, and as time went on developed
his preceptor's tendency to apply inappropriate 'operatic' methods
to situations which demanded a lighter touch. But his first two
attempts — *Les Amoureux de Catherine* (1876) and *La Taverne des
Trabans* (1881) — deserve commendation, for here he introduced
rhythmic and harmonic originality without sacrificing vocal or
orchestral delicacy. A tenor aria and a brilliant scena for coloratura
soprano from *La Taverne* were particularly effective.

R OBERT PLANQUETTE (1848–1903) was less prolific than most
contemporaries in the same field ; apart from a few ballads and
comic songs his output consisted entirely of operettas, and he only
wrote about twenty. His capabilities and achievements fell short
of Lecocq's, but within his limits he was a conscientious craftsman
who never grudged attention to detail ; once or twice, when revivals
were in prospect, he went so far as to revise works that had already
been well received in their original form. In one respect —
rhythmic *élan* — Planquette more nearly emulated Offenbach than
any other composer who has so far been mentioned in these pages.
That in itself is worthy of note, and when this instinctive urge was
combined with an acquired contrapuntal technique — as in the
first-act finale of *Les Cloches de Corneville* (1877) — the effect was
unequivocal.

It is for *Les Cloches* (where he had the assistance of Lecocq's regular librettist 'Clairville') that Planquette's name is remembered by Anglo-Saxons, and not for twenty years did he write anything better. Thanks to the driving enthusiasm of H. B. Farnie (see page 40 footnote) it brought him fame in Britain and America surpassing any that he achieved at home, and two of the pieces that followed during the next ten years — *Rip van Winkle* (1882) and *Nell Gwynne* (1884) — were written to English libretti and first played in London. *Les Voltigeurs de la 32ᵉ* (1880) and *Surcouf* (1887) were also riotously welcomed on our side of the channel as *The Old Guard* and *Paul Jones.* But when all is said, many of Planquette's tunes lacked spontaneity, and he was prone to use the same basic ideas — melodic or rhythmic — over and over again. The opening phrase of *Le Chevalier Gaston* (1879), for instance, besides being itself momentarily reminiscent of Dvořák's *Carnival* overture, was echoed in *Les Voltigeurs* and again in *Rip van Winkle.* Although this tendency to repeat himself became tiresome in *Captain Thérèse* (1890) and *Le Talisman* (1893), *Mam'zelle Quat'sous* (1897) showed the composer in a new light. Not only the sparkling overture but at least one of the entr'actes and much of the dance music (especially the delightful 'kissing polka') had a touch of originality and refinement worthy of Delibes. On the evidence of *Mam'zelle Quat'sous* one is constrained to feel that Planquette's invention had hitherto been stifled by the necessity of setting trivial doggerel in a like manner, and that his true métier might have been the ballet; he died too soon for the validity of this conjecture to be proved or disproved. It is pleasant to record, however, that in the posthumous *Paradis de Mahomed* (completed by Louis Ganne in 1906, see page 101) the more mature approach was well maintained; in particular there was a stirring ensemble based on a tune of exceptional strength and vigour.

Ex.59

Ho-la! ho - la! ___ le sol-eil bril- le, ___ Il fait grand jour, jeu-nes é-poux Re-veil-lez vous! ___

Son of a wealthy Breton industrialist, GASTON SERPETTE (1846–1904) gave up legal studies to learn composition with Ambroise

Thomas at the Paris Conservatoire, and when his promising cantata
Jeanne d'Arc won him the Prix de Rome in 1871 he thought the
world was at his feet. But the world was older than the self-
confident young composer, who to justify his choice of career was
soon driven to court the Bouffes-Parisiens and other like establish-
ments with trivial buffooneries. In this milieu he settled down,
but — perhaps because he never had an instantaneous success comparable with that of *La Fille de Madame Angot* or *Les Cloches de
Corneville* — his achievements aroused no widespread interest and
authorities are at variance even as to the extent of his output. *Grove*,
in what apparently purports to be a complete list, tabulates only
sixteen operettas, without divulging that one of them — *La Dot de
Brigitte* (1892) — was partly the work of Victor Roger (page 100),
and Thompson's *International Cyclopaedia of Music and Musicians* is
quite definite with seventeen. On the other hand, Riemann's *Musik-
Lexikon* says thirty-one ; this must be nearer the mark, for my own
researches have unearthed twenty-seven, not counting revisions and
collaborations. One is pleased to note that a perspicacious contributor to Schmidl's *Dizionario universale dei musicisti* correctly
credits Serpette with a share in *Rothomago* (Alhambra, London,
1880), which has elsewhere been attributed complete to George
Jacobi (page 204).

In his first few attempts all Serpette could do was to imitate
Offenbach, and although he did so with more panache than Jonas, it
is not surprising that in 1880 Arthur Pougin felt called upon to issue
a picturesque reproof to a promising young composer who was
evidently prostituting his talent by purveying commonplace trivialities.[1] Possibly Serpette took his remarks to heart, for he revised
La Nuit de Saint-Germain (Brussels, 1880) before presenting it in
Paris as *Fanfreluche* three years later ; this was his most consistent
piece of work, except perhaps for the tiny *Princesse* (Théâtre des
Variétés, 1882), which comprised only an overture and four numbers.

---

[1] 'Il est fâcheux de voir un jeune artiste pourvu d'une bonne instruction, ayant
fait d'excellentes études qui lui ont valu l'honneur d'obtenir le grand prix de Rome,
et qui n'a pas pour lui l'excuse de besoin, se lancer dans la voix de la musique
burlesque et manquer véritablement de respect pour son art, alors que tant d'autres
lui donnent de meilleurs exemples et conservent, même dans les situations difficiles,
le souci de leur avenir et de leur bonne renommée.'

La Princesse, being hardly more than a refined *vaudeville*, earned no mention in the reference books, but in such a miniature Serpette's frail talent could do itself justice ; on a larger canvas his limitations were all too obvious.   Good-natured parody was his most engaging characteristic :   a burlesque of conventional drinking songs ('La chanson de l'eau claire') in *La Branche cassée* (1874) ;   an eighteenth-century minuet in *Le Moulin du vert galant* (1876) ;   a habanera in *La Petite muette* (1877) ;   an outrageous skit on the 'Jewel song' from Gounod's *Faust* in *Le Petit chaperon rouge* (1885) which was too ingenuous to give offence ;   these were all quite amusing.   As time went on Serpette tried to add interest to his operettas by introducing fantastic, exotic or extravagantly ridiculous elements which were often reflected in the titles — *Tige de lotus* (1883), *Le Singe d'une nuit d'été* (1884), *Me-ne-ka* (1892), *Le Carnet du diable* (1895) — but the appropriate flavour was imparted in a slapdash manner which did not improve the taste.   This striving after originality at any cost also led to the unusual experiment of an operetta in the form of a monologue — *Insomnie* (1884) ;   the disturbed night was a very short one.   Several of Serpette's pieces were played abroad ; one of them — *Cuvée réservée 1810* — was given in London in 1904 as *Amorelle* without, it seems, having ever achieved a production in its original form or in its native country.

FIRMIN BERNICAT (1843–1883) specialised in one-act pieces which he called operettas but which in reality were *vaudevilles*. Starting with *Deux à deux* in 1872 he wrote fourteen more — all extremely vapid — during the next seven years.   *Le Triomphe d'Arlequin* (1879) was slightly less feeble than the others, but *Les Deux Omar* (1876), *La Jeunesse de Béranger* (1877) and *La Cornette* (1879) also caught the public fancy.   Most of them were given at music-halls — the Alcazar or the Eldorado.   A three-act operetta, *Les Beignets du roi* (Brussels, 1882), was rather more accomplished and included at least one or two attractive examples of pastiche.[1] Bernicat's sudden death interrupted a second full-length work — *François-les-bas-bleus* ; it was completed by his younger contemporary André Messager (see page 92).

FRANCIS CHASSAIGNE (1843– ?) also graduated at the Eldorado

---

[1] *Les Beignets du roi* reached Paris six years later as *Les Premières armes de Louis XV.*

G

Music-hall, where the first of several *vaudevilles* (*Deux mauvaises bonnes*) was played in 1876. Later, like Bernicat, he embarked on two full-length operettas ; unlike him he lived to finish them both. They were *Le Droit d'aînesse* (1883) and *Les Noces improvisées* (1886), which suited the taste of audiences at the Théâtre des Nouveautés and soon afterwards enjoyed fair success in London as *Falka* and *Nadgy*. Chassaigne must surely have had a military background, for his normal style, in which march-rhythms and brass-band effects predominated, was more suited to a barrack square than to a music-hall, let alone an opera house. Exceptionally, the soprano solo 'Quand, le matin, tu partais pour la chasse' from *Actéon* (1878) and the 'chanson bohémienne' from *Le Droit d'aînesse* were gracefully conceived and sufficiently naïve to disarm criticism.

ÉMILE PESSARD (1843–1917) belonged to a different world. He was the son of a flautist and showed a nice sense of proportion in deciding to take up the double-bass ; he went on to win the Prix de Rome and later held important posts as professor of harmony at the Paris Conservatoire and inspector of music for municipal schools. As a composer for the stage he made his début with the operetta *La Cruche cassée* (Opéra-Comique, 1870) ; though there was perhaps an overstress on sentiment, the approach was cultured, and the ensembles — notably the duet 'Je me souviens que dès l'aurore' — were both attractive and refined. *Don Quichotte*, which followed in 1874, was carelessly written and in retrospect negligible, but an *opéra comique* — *Le Capitaine Fracasse* (1878) — and another operetta — *Le Char* (also 1878) — displayed more resolution. These two works, together with an *opéra* — *Tabarin* (1885) — were products of Pessard's transition period ; he was struggling to widen his outlook, but so far the only outward sign was a plethora of diminished sevenths, chromatic scales and elaborate violin figuration. Several years elapsed before his conscientious application was rewarded and his talent found full expression in two more operettas — *Les Folies amoureuses* (1891) and *Mam'zelle Carabin* (1893) ; though the quality was uneven their best numbers showed a high degree of initiative. For instance the overture to *Les Folies amoureuses* had a rare rhythmic freedom recalling the precedent of Offenbach's *Fille du tambour-major*, and in the song 'C'est en plein décembre' from *Mam'zelle Carabin* the harmonic progressions were at once spontaneous and original.

In 1887 the Théâtre des Nouveautés gave hospitality to an operetta called *L'Amour mouillé*. The curtain rose on a group of pretty girls basking on the sun-drenched coast of the Mediterranean, and their two-part chorus 'Ah! sommeillons!' caught the languorous atmosphere to perfection. (The little six-note figure in the last bar of Ex. 60 later darts from key to key like a dragon-fly at summer noon.)

Ex.60 Allegro moderato

Who was the composer of this enchanting evocation ? If asked to name him off-hand one might hesitate between Bizet and Massenet ; it was in fact LOUIS VARNEY (1844–1908). Second-rate artists now and again startle one with a flash of inspiration akin to genius ; that Varney should have done so here — and perhaps in the ballet-music from *La Fée aux chèvres* (1890) — is surprising though not without parallel. But he poses some more delicate questions. Why did he write no music until he was thirty-six and then suddenly start churning out operettas at the rate of about one every six months, continuing to do so for the next twenty years although the small measure of success which they enjoyed could have given him little incentive ? Why did his first and best work, *Les Mousqetaires au couvent* (1880), conform with conventions that were a generation out of date ? (The facile melodic style, the persistent drone basses, the characteristic harmonic shifts and the occasional touches of pomposity inevitably remind one of Adam ; in the waltz numbers

alone is there any sign of a later impact — Offenbach, say, or
Delibes.) Why did the mixture remain the same as before in
Fanfan la Tulipe and *Coquelicot* (both 1882) but then grow pro-
gressively weaker as time went on, so that *Le Pompier de service*
(1897), *Les Demoiselles des Saint-Cyriens* (1898) and *Le Fiancé de
Thylda* (1900) belonged not so much to the world of Adolphe Adam
as to that of his inexpert imitator Narcisse Girard ? The only tenable
solution I can find involves a charge of filial peculation.

We have already met Varney *père* (on page 68) ; like Girard,
he was an operatic conductor who must often have interpreted the
music of Adam, Montfort and Clapisson. As a composer, he is
remembered for his *Chant des Girondins* ('Mourir pour la patrie')
which swept France in 1848, but during the next ten years or so he
wrote many more songs and several operettas. *Le Moulin joli*
(Gaîté, 1849) was an innocuous little affair in contemporary style ;
that *Le Polka des sabots* (1859) and a few others secured production
at the Bouffes-Parisiens must have been due to his prestige as a
conductor. From about 1860 onwards his activities in that field
occupied all his time, but it seems reasonable to suppose that he
may have left behind him a quantity of unpublished and unper-
formed music dating from the forties and fifties. Was this store-
cupboard raided after his death by his son Louis, who had been his
close associate for many years ? I must make it clear that I am not
accusing Varney *fils* of appropriating forgotten compositions *in toto*
and passing them off as his own, but I do suggest that he may have
selected individual items, revised them to suit his purpose, and so
have been able to present one by one a series of operettas each of
which, to some extent at least, was a parental pasticcio. Of course
large-scale alterations and additions would have been necessary, and
a few exceptional numbers like 'Ah! sommeillons!' *must* have been
Louis Varney's own work, but I can find no other satisfying explanation for his sudden emergence as a composer little more than
a year after his father's death ; for his subsequent prolificity ; for
the apparently out-of-date approach ; for the eventual deterioration
in quality (which would be consequent upon the gradual dwindling
of the pile of old manuscripts). There the matter must rest, for the
Varney family have already taken up more space than their achieve-

ments, separately or in conjunction, could justify. If my deductions
are false, as they well may be, I gladly apologise to Louis Varney's
memory. In any case, the opening chorus of *L'Amour mouillé* will
remain in mine.

EDMOND AUDRAN (1840–1901) was born at Lyons, studied
with Duprato at the École Niedermeyer in Paris and then settled in
Marseilles, where all his early works were written and some produced ; only one of his first few operettas — *Le Grand Mogol* (1877)
— ever reached Paris. In 1879, however, he secured admission to
the Bouffes-Parisiens with the plausible buffoonery *Les Noces
d'Olivette*, which was followed by four more in as many years.
Frankly, they were poor affairs ; that *La Mascotte* (1880) caught the
public fancy as nothing had done since *La Fille de Madame Angot*
can only have been because Audran had a knack of endowing the
most paltry tune and the most elementary tonic/dominant bass with
an infectious rhythmic vigour. However, he did not allow success
to spoil him, as had Vasseur ; on the contrary it spurred him to take
more trouble over his work. In *Les Pommes d'or* (1883) one finds
considerable melodic enterprise, and there were further signs of
initiative in *La Cigale et la fourmi* (1886), *Le Serment d'amour* (also
1886, quoted in Ex. 61), and *La Fiancée des verts poteaux* (1887).

Presently, too, Audran began to explore a pleasant vein of
eighteenth-century pastiche ; the gavotte 'Le maître qui en haut'

from *Miss Hellyet* (1890) and the minuet 'Ah! qu'ils sont bien' from *L'Oncle Célestin* (1891) were good examples of this trend. *L'Article de Paris* (1892), though a comparative failure, was musically his best work to date ; the 'chœur des tapisseurs' and a song in 5/4 time entitled 'Fin de siècle' were both admirable. *Madame Suzette* (1893) — apart from a second-act finale on operatic lines — and *L'Enlèvement de la Toledad* (1894) marked a return to his earlier and more perfunctory manner, but perhaps it was a case of *reculer pour mieux sauter*, for they led to his *chef d'œuvre* — *La Poupée* (1896). This time success was fully deserved ; the composer had been provided with an exceptionally good libretto by Maurice Ordonneau and he applied his full resource in setting it to music. A lead-in from verse to refrain shows how far he had travelled since the 'tum-tum' days of *La Mascotte*.

Ex.62 Andante

Monsieur Lohengrin had its *première* less than six weeks after *La Poupée*. On internal evidence it might have been composed during the interim, but as compensation for many hurriedly written pages and a pointless parody of Wagner's wedding-march there was one charming 'duettino' — 'Elle a tort celle qui pense'.

We have now reached another turning-point in the story of French operetta. Conceived by Adam in the eighteen-thirties, its teething troubles of the forties had been resolved by Offenbach, who guided its adolescence through the fifties and brought it to manhood during the sixties. In the eighteen-seventies Lecocq had been its foremost exponent and Audran's regeneration perhaps came just in time for him to be awarded the same accolade for the eighties, although in the absence of any stronger challengers a good case might also be made out for Planquette. But before the nineties were under way — and indeed before Audran himself had reached his zenith — the firmament saw the rise of a new star, bright enough to outshine them both.

X

MESSAGER

ANDRÉ MESSAGER wrote only seventeen operettas (as against Hervé's hundred and twenty), but he occupies an eminent position among French campaigners, for he combined a flow of spontaneous melody worthy of Offenbach with a flair for economic workmanship at least the equal of Lecocq's ; moreover, to much of his music (though not all) he brought a measure of Massenet's fluent grace, Saint-Saëns's aristocratic elegance, even Fauré's refined subtlety. Of the other regular exponents Delibes alone had comparable potentialities, and in his case they were never fully realised ; after *Le Roi l'a dit* — written at the age of thirty-six — he was content to rest on his laurels so far as operettas were concerned. By contrast Messager never wrote one until he was over thirty, and then carried on the good work to the end of his life.

Born on 30th December 1853 at Montluçon (almost exactly in the centre of France), he was apparently an unruly child, and when he was seven his parents sent him to live with some in-laws. It was from them that he learnt the rudiments of music, soon acquiring some proficiency on both piano and violin. The family had independent means, but during the Franco-Prussian war their investments slumped to such an extent that it became necessary for young Charles Prosper (as he had been christened) to adopt a profession. To the dismay of his father — a civil servant — he chose the unlucrative one of organist and entered the École Niedermeyer in Paris, an institution primarily devoted to the training of church musicians. His progress was so rapid that before he was twenty-one he was appointed organist at the Saint-Sulpice. Nor was his general musical training neglected (one of his mentors was Gabriel Fauré). Messager soon secured the production of a few small ballets at the Bouffes-Parisiens, but he was not altogether satisfied with them ;

perhaps he was shrewd enough to realise that the occasional felicitous
Fauré touch —

Ex.63 Allegretto moderato

— threw the surrounding trivialities into unwelcome relief.[1]   At all
events, in 1881 he gave up his post at the Saint-Sulpice for a less
exacting one at the Jesuit church of Saint-Paul-et-Saint-Louis, eked
out his income by conducting at the Folies-Bergère, and embarked
on an intensive course of lessons in composition with Saint-Saëns.
Presently he seized an opportunity of visiting Bayreuth, where he
absorbed all that he needed of the Wagnerian cult.   In the same year,
1883, he was engaged by a publishing firm (Enoch) to complete
François-les-bas-bleus, left unfinished by Bernicat.   On the title-page
Bernicat gets most of the credit — only small type is accorded to
the modest addendum 'terminée par A. Messager' — but according
to internal evidence Messager took over half-way through.   There
are at least two numbers in the second act which Bernicat could
hardly have written and, though he may have sketched out the
third, the hand that filled in the detail had far more assurance.   For
Messager his share in *François* established a profitable connection
with the Théâtre de Folies-Dramatiques, where his *Fauvette du
temple* (written during 1884) was presented on 17th November
1885.   Though his style was still inconsistent (indeed it always
remained so) Saint-Saëns' precepts had borne fruit.   Two duets, the
expressive 'Et tous deux bien amoureux' and the more elaborate
'Dans un mois je mets ma rob' blanche', were particularly good.
There were waltzes and polkas with an Offenbach lilt, a mild burlesque of Adolphe Adam was thrown in for good measure, and a
few passages (such as Ex. 64) were endowed with genuine poetic
feeling.

[1] The quotation is from *Les Vins de France* (1880).   The ballets of his maturity,
notably *Les Deux pigeons* (1886) and *Scaramouche* (1893), were much more homo-
geneous.

Ex.64

Lento

Que vo-tre cœur roux Cède à ma pri-è - re, Si vous saurez Pier - re, oui, je suis à vous.

Neither *La Béarnaise* (produced at the Bouffes-Parisiens only three weeks after the *première* of *La Fauvette* at the rival institution) nor *Le Bourgeois de Calais* (Folies-Dramatiques, 1887) were quite so satisfying, but nevertheless both pieces contained some charming music and they certainly showed up well beside the current operettas of Messager's elder contemporaries like Planquette, Serpette and even Lecocq, who by then was past his best. *Isoline* (Théâtre de la Renaissance, 1888), the setting of a romantic fairy tale by Catulle Mendès, was outside the ordinary run and cannot rank as an operetta, but *Le Mari de la reine* (Bouffes-Parisiens, 1889) followed the authentic tradition. The quartet 'Nous vous disons ce qu'il faut faire' was a *tour de force* — a brilliant vocal scherzo taken at breakneck speed and alternating back and forth between 2/4 time and 6/8. *La Basoche* (Opéra-Comique, 1890) has claims to be considered Messager's masterpiece, for his varied attributes were never displayed to better advantage. No light soprano could wish for a more grateful solo than 'Il était un' fois un' bergère'; the villanelle 'Quand tu connais Colette' had remarkable rhythmic freedom; the long ensemble 'Midi! Midi!' was most skilfully contrived for both voices and orchestra; best of all, perhaps, was the little song for the Duke, 'Eh! que ne parliez-vous?', a miniature in impeccable taste. Furthermore, by this time Messager had learnt to incorporate idiomatic excursions without disturbing stylistic balance.

Ex.65   Assai vivo

This gradual absorption in his music of contemporary harmonic trends, though significant, was only one facet of his individualism. He strove, like Victor Massé before him, to raise the artistic standards of operetta to the level expected from an *opéra comique* without sacrificing the characteristic buoyancy of the genre. Being blessed not only with sincerity of purpose but also with a recognition of his own limitations, he succeeded where Massé had failed.

Hélène (Théâtre Vaudeville, 1891), spoken drama with a background of almost continuous music, calls for no comment here, but in Messager's next *operetta* the libretto of G. Hartmann and A. Alexandre (after Loti) was exactly suited to his talents and temperament. The figure of a Japanese geisha-girl who is wooed, won, and then deserted by a naval officer seems to have an irresistible attraction for composers. Messager treated the subject more seriously than Sidney Jones (three years later) and with greater delicacy than Puccini (ten years later), so that *Madame Chrysanthème* (Renaissance, 1893) occupies a position midway between *The Geisha* (see page 213) with its inoffensive flippancy and *Madam Butterfly* with its combination of sentimentality and *verismo*. It was a remarkable achievement, for while the touch had operetta-lightness throughout no susceptibilities were ruffled when the placid surface was disturbed by an undercurrent of pathos. Yet Messager, who had a healthy tendency to self-criticism, soon came to feel that in *Madame Chrysanthème* he had mistakenly been endeavouring to reconcile two irreconcilables, that his operettas were slowly but surely developing into something very like *opéras comiques*.[1] Whereupon his approach to the problem underwent a *volte-face*. 'Henceforth', he seems to have said to himself, 'it will be better if I make no more experiments with fairy tales, lyric dramas, exotic evocations and what-not. I may perpetrate a genuine *opéra comique* from time to time if I feel in the mood, but my operettas will be light-hearted and frankly frivolous.' The inauguration of the new policy was by no means auspicious, for *Miss Dollar* (Théâtre Nouveau, 1893) was almost entirely trivial except for the soprano song 'Ces mots si doux.'

---

[1] Some of them had already been so designated, though not, one feels, with much conviction.

Disappointed by its reception, Messager decided to try his luck across the channel.

His work was already well known in London, where all his operettas had been played and several had enjoyed great popularity. *La Basoche* had followed Sullivan's *Ivanhoe* as the second — and last — production at D'Oyly Carte's ill-starred Royal English Opera House (now the Palace Theatre), and presently Carte again called on Messager to fill a gap, this time at the Savoy. *Mirette* was given there in 1894, but after some forty performances it was withdrawn for revision ; on revival two months later it did little better. The libretto (an English one) was admittedly very poor, but the composer must bear some part of the blame ; only the second-act finale — which closed with an extraordinarily effective off-stage chorus — found him in his best form.[1] Back in Paris *La Fiancée en loterie* (Folies-Dramatiques, 1896) showed that Messager, like so many other French composers before and since, was at home with Spanish as well as native dance-rhythms. It was slightly less perfunctory than either *Miss Dollar* or *Mirette* but was deservedly put in the shade by Audran's *Poupée*. As a counter-blast Messager came forward with his first true *opéra comique*, the five-act *Chevalier d'Harmental*, based on Dumas. The somewhat pretentious style was so strikingly different from that of *La Fiancée* that it emphasised his determination to regard himself as a dual-purpose composer, but because neither *La Fiancée* nor *Le Chevalier* met with any success he quickly realised that after all art was not divisible. For a time he was so despondent that he contemplated giving up composition altogether, but in the event he decided to embark on two more operettas. To them he devoted as much care as he had to his abortive *opéra comique*, while giving free rein to his inborn melodic impulse and still to a large extent refraining from the harmonic subtleties which he now sincerely felt to be out of place in light music. It seems that these might have added greatly to the charm of *La Basoche* and *Madame Chrysanthème*, but Messager no doubt had good reasons for his restraint.

---

[1] Writing in the French periodical *Musica* fourteen years later, Messager disclosed that his wife, the Irish-born song-writer Hope Temple, had helped in the preparation of *Mirette* ; whether this was an excuse for its failure or merely a tactful expression of marital appreciation was not made clear.

Having made this reservation one can wholeheartedly praise *Les P'tites Michu* and *Véronique* (Bouffes-Parisiens, 1897 and 1898). The tunes, though inevitably not all of equal merit, were consistently suave and graceful ; the ensembles were superbly well constructed ; the orchestration was masterly. (*Véronique* had a good libretto, too ; it was by A. Vanloo and G. Duval.) For some reason neither of these operettas reached London until after a lapse of six years, but in 1904 *Véronique* captured all hearts. That in this country it is better remembered than *Les P'tites Michu* may partly be due to the fact that two of its weaker numbers — the sentimental 'letter song' and the catchy 'swing song' — were exactly suited to Edwardian taste ; indeed they had a certain affinity with the ballads and waltzes of Edward German which were then all the rage. In France enthusiasm was more controlled ; responsible opinion insisted (rightly) that Messager had slipped from his pedestal with *Miss Dollar*, and it was not yet ready to concede that he had earned redemption, though his old friend Fauré, for one, was quick to appreciate the merits of his two latest productions.[1]

Véronique marked the climax of Messager's career as a composer ; thereafter he concentrated his energies mainly on conducting and administration. Universally respected and admired as a cultured musician (whatever the shortcomings of his recent operettas), he became in 1899 director and principal conductor at the Opéra-Comique, with which he had long been associated, and he endowed the theatre with a fresh lease of life by sponsoring new works and encouraging the younger generation : it was under his auspices and baton that Debussy's *Pelléas et Mélisande* received its first performance in 1902. Shortly afterwards he accepted the post of artistic director at Covent Garden, where he remained for five years ; from 1907 until the outbreak of war he discharged the same functions at the Paris Opéra. These duties left him little time for composition, but while in London he wrote for the Paris Opéra-Comique the

[1] 'Ne pensez pas que dans *Les P'tites Michu* ou *Véronique* . . . sa plume ait eu moins de distinction que dans les ouvrages de premier place comme *Les Deux pigeons* ou *La Basoche*. Sa veine mélodique est également généreuse dans ces diverses productions ; elle va d'un rythme alerte, aisé renouvelé de formes, de lignes très pures et toujours distinguées, sans ambiguité comme sans banalité, et sans cesse une écriture fine, mais simple, la réhausse de ses plus délicats ornements.'

operetta *Les Dragons de l'impératrice* (1905) — which was nearly as good as *Les P'tites Michu* — and an *opéra comique* (*Fortunio*, 1907) — which was better than *Le Chevalier d'Harmental*. On taking over direction of the Paris Opéra he never abused his opportunities to push forward his own works ; indeed the only composition dating from this period was his third and best *opéra comique* (*Béatrice*, 1914), which was given at Monte Carlo. During the war Messager spent much time in London, where he had many friends, and completed his second English operetta ; it must regretfully be recorded that, as before, an attempt to cater for the British market involved a lowering of sights. *Monsieur Beaucaire* (Birmingham, 1919, afterwards Princes Theatre, London) certainly came like a breath of fresh air to audiences bemused by current vulgarities, for it was tuneful and refined, and the score included some delightful examples of eighteenth-century pastiche ; but much of the music was again curiously reminiscent of *Merrie England* and *Tom Jones*. Only here and there — *e.g.* in the duet 'Lightly, lightly' with its delicate chromatic figuration — could one recognise without question the Messager of old.[1]

In 1919 he took the Paris Conservatoire Orchestra on a long tour of the United States ; on his return to France he agreed to help out the Opéra-Comique in an emergency by reassuming the directorship for a limited period. The arrangement lasted for little more than a year, and soon afterwards Messager found time to write three more operettas, described as *comédies musicales*. They were *La Petite fonctionnaire* (1921), *L'Amour masqué* (1923, libretto by Sacha Guitry) and *Passionnément* (1926, libretto by M. Hennequin and A. Willemetz). *L'Amour masqué* was the best of them, and was certainly more representative of the Messager we all know than *Monsieur Beaucaire* had been. There were some lapses into triviality, but the duet for the two servants 'Veuillez accepter quelques roses' was a little gem. In his last operetta of all — *Coup de roulis* (1928) — he again captured something of his pristine spontaneity, notably in two excellent ensembles — 'Appuyez-vous un peu sur nous' (sparkling in its humour) and 'Avez-vous vu ?' (which displayed unusual rhythmic freedom). By this time Messager was living in

---

[1] The *French* version of *Monsieur Beaucaire* was not staged until 1925.

semi-retirement and suffering from much ill-health ; after a long
illness he died in Paris on 24th February 1929.

We have already noted how after *Madame Chrysanthème* Messager used his flair for harmonic originality very sparingly, but he
did not allow it to fall into utter disuse.   One lights on an occasional
enchanting progression : here is a deceptively simple one (*a*) from
Les Dragons de l'impératrice.

Ex.66 Allegro vivo

Songe   à quels dan-gers tu l'ex - po - ses, Vois - tu bien, s'il te prend pour moi,

It is permissible to feel that his reluctance to use this attribute more
freely in his later operettas detracted from their interest — especially
as it could offset a lack of initiative in modulation — but he had
others which he employed with equal effect and greater consistency
of purpose.   For instance, he often established a basic form of 'till-
ready' accompaniment which had point and charm of its own, main-
taining it thereafter throughout the number.   This trick came to
light as early as *François-les-bas-bleus*, and two later examples —
one *à la* barcarolle from *Le Mari de la reine* and another of ineffable
grace from *Véronique* — are worth quoting.

Ex.67a Allegretto moderato

Ex.67b Moderato con moto

He was also addicted to light orchestral figuration (usually given to
the violins) and his constructive skill in concerted items was plain
to see even in his weakest operettas ; he was particularly fond of
introducing imitative or interlinked phrases into vocal duets.
Everybody knows *Véronique's* donkey trotting here and there, so I
prefer to illustrate this facility by a few bars from *Les P'tites Michu*
(Ex. 68).

Ex.68 Moderato quasi andante

Messager's only technical defect was one common to many composers of operetta — too close an adherence to repetitive rhythmic figures and four-bar rigidity ; yet such was his innate artistry that criticism on that score would be academic pedantry. The fault is apparent in this passage from *Véronique*, but who cares ? — it shows him at his best.

Ex.69 Andante grazioso

(It is interesting to note, however, that in his last few operettas, which were less characteristic than *Véronique*, Messager seems to have striven to subdue this weakness, if weakness it be. An instance from *Coup de roulis* has already been cited, and the 'couplets du charme' from *L'Amour masqué* were even more remarkable. Here slow 2/4 time and unexpected three-bar rhythm prevailed throughout each verse until rounded off with four bars — four bars only — in waltz-time.)

Messager, like Lecocq, spanned an era. Auber, Rossini and Meyerbeer were all still alive when he began his studies, yet he survived the first world war and witnessed the rise and decline of 'Les Six' (more than one of whom made tentative essays in operetta as we shall see in the next chapter). For forty years he carried aloft the torch kindled by Adolphe Adam in 1834 ; after his death it soon flickered out.

XI

SIXES AND SEVENS

NOT many of Messager's close contemporaries went in for operetta. Of those who did, Vincent d'Indy and the brothers Vidal scored only one apiece, Toulmouche three. Victor Roger, on the other hand, knocked up thirty off his own bat and also proved a useful partner for Lacome and Serpette.

Léon Vallas, biographer of the illustrious VINCENT D'INDY (1851–1931), stigmatised *Attendez-moi sous l'orme* (1882) as 'an undistinguished trifle'. A trifle it certainly was, but although much of the music was ordinary there were a few passages, notably in the introduction, where his future harmonic trends were foreshadowed. JOSEPH VIDAL (1859–1924) was primarily a musicologist and his brother PAUL VIDAL (1863–1931) a pedagogue. Joseph's *Mariage d'Yvette* (1896) did not enjoy the same success as had Paul's *Éros* (1892), which, considering his background, was commendably unpretentious; the 'sérénade à la lune', with an evocative orchestral accompaniment, was particularly attractive. FRÉDÉRIC TOULMOUCHE (1850–1909), who was for many years musical director at the Théâtre des Menus-Plaisirs, wrote several *opéras comiques* and operettas; one of the latter — *La Veillée des noces* (1888) — was later given in London, but *La Perle du Cantal* (1895) was more ingratiating. Toulmouche had not much enterprise and his output was small, but his music was stylish; here and there it caught a suavity akin to Messager's. VICTOR ROGER (1853–1903) was more prolific but very inconsistent. The librettists P. Ferrier and F. Carré helped him to establish a reputation with *Joséphine vendue par ses sœurs* (1886), but he allowed it to fade away during the next six years with some very mediocre productions, of which *Les Douze filles de Japhet* (1890) and *Le Coq* (1891) alone made much impression. Thus far his only positive characteristic was a flair for effective twists of rhythm.

With *Les Vingt-huit jours de Clairette* (1892) he got his second wind, and thereafter occasionally showed signs of greater initiative. For instance, the duet 'Avant que la loi prononce' from *Miss Nicol-Nick* (1895), besides being tuneful, was intriguingly poised between the keys of A♭ major and F major, and the dramatic aria 'C'est fatal, partout où je passe' from *Le Voyage de Courberon* (1896) was largely based on alternating four-bar and three-bar phrases. But the success, such as it was, of *Agence Crook et Cie* (1898) and *Le Jockey malgré lui* (1902) owed much to the librettist Maurice Ordonneau, who also collaborated from time to time with the proficient but uninspired EDMOND MISSA (1861–1910) — three of whose more serious works, by contrast, were based on Shakespeare, Goethe and Ouida respectively. His best operettas, *La Belle Sophie* (1888) and *La Doctoresse* (1890), were youthful ; *La D'moiselle de Tabarin*, written in 1909, was not played until after his death.

LOUIS GANNE (1862–1923), well known as a conductor, was a cultured musician with little aptitude for composition except in miniature. He exercised a wise restraint in *Rabelais* (1892) and *Les Colles des femmes* (1893), which lacked character but were unassuming and inoffensive. In its simple way the soprano ariette 'Si je vous gêne' from *Les Colles des femmes* was very charming indeed. Ganne was an accomplished craftsman ; when he was engaged to complete *Le Paradis de Mahomed* (see page 83) he made a good job of it, although he was incapable of matching Planquette's rhythmic verve. I can trace only five subsequent operettas from his pen ; two of them, *Hans, le joueur de flûte* (1906) and *Rhodope* (1910), were produced at the Monte Carlo Opera House, where at that time Ganne was resident musical director. (*Hans* was well-received in Paris four years after its *première* on the Côte d'Azur.) Up to a point the career of CLAUDE TERRASSE (1867–1923) resembled that of Messager, for he too was a provincial (from Grenoble), studied at the École Niedermeyer, and became an organist. He wrote two operettas in his early twenties — *Panthéon-Courcelles* (1889) and *L'Amour en bouteilles* (1890) — but, like Messager, he did not take seriously to composition until he was over thirty. There the similarity ends, for Terrasse's music had no pre-requisites of permanence. The first decade of the twentieth century, when he wrote about seventeen

H

operettas, was his period of greatest prolificity. *L'Heure du berger* (1900), *Les Travaux d'Hercule* (1901), *Le Sire de Vergy* (1903), *Monsieur de la Palisse* (1904) and *Paris, ou le bon juge* (1906) were the most successful, although they were not noticeably less trivial than the others. In his later works — e.g. *L'Ingenu libertin* (1907) and *Les Transatlantiques* (1911) — burlesque was the dominating feature. *Cartouche* (1912) was perhaps his best effort ; the second-act finale was well constructed, although his technical deficiences were laid bare in the choral sections. Terrasse wrote some catchy tunes, but they were inadequately supported by drone basses and elementary 'tum-tum' ; in ensembles the workmanship was negligible. It would be fair to say that he stood in the same relationship to Roger as Hervé did to Offenbach.

By now French operetta looked to be on its last legs, but it received a shot in the arm from an unexpected quarter. The year 1911 saw the Opéra-Comique production of *L'Heure espagnole* by MAURICE RAVEL (1875–1937), which was a highly successful attempt to bring the genre up to date. It bore little resemblance to the classic expositions of Messager and none at all to the effusions of Terrasse. Though it inevitably needs a different standard of appraisal it can nevertheless be reasonably accounted an operetta. (The libretto by Franc-Nohain was brilliant, witty — and indelicate.[1]) I shall not quote from *L'Heure espagnole*, since it needs to be seen and heard as a whole ; it must suffice to record that it is utterly captivating, and just as typical of Ravel as are *Daphnis et Chloé* and *La Valse*, besides showing a good sense of 'theatre'. His lead was followed by the generator of 'Les Six', ERIK SATIE (1866–1925), whose *Piège de Méduse* (1913, unpublished) was perhaps a dangerous precedent for those few of his disciples, whether or not they belonged to the same select group, who tried to emulate him by demonstrating their versatility in an occasional operetta : GEORGES MIGOT (1891–   ) in *Le Rossignol en amour* (1924), DARIUS MILHAUD (1892–   ) in *Esther de Carpentras* (1925) and ROLAND-MANUEL[2] (1891–   ) in *Isabelle et Pantalon* (1928). These talented composers were barking up the wrong tree, for though

---

[1] Ernest Newman's playful rendering of the title was 'The Immoral Hour'.
[2] Real name, Roland Lévy.

their productions accorded with the definition of operetta propounded in Chapter I and some of the separate items were brilliantly conceived — *e.g.* the amusing chorus of invalids ('Nous réclamons au chocolat') from *Isabelle et Pantalon* — the music of your true operetta should surely appeal to the 'ordinary' as well as the 'advanced' listener ; artless *bonhomie* is apt to find atonality an uncomfortable bedfellow. However, GEORGES AURIC (1899–   ) and MANUEL ROSENTHAL (1904–   ), comparative youngsters, did not stampede with the rest. Auric's jazz rhythms are not to everybody's taste, but one at least of the three operettas which he wrote before putting his mother-wit at the disposal of the film magnates — *Les Oiseaux* (1928, after Aristophanes) — held echoes of the authentic tradition.[1] So did Rosenthal's *Rayon des soieries* (1930) and *Poule noire* (1937) ; the latter ventured to poke gentle fun at Beethoven's *Fidelio*.

Of the more conventional exponents of French operetta between the wars, the most cultured was REYNALDO HAHN (1875–1947). He was born in Venezuela, brought to Paris when he was three, taken to the Bouffes-Parisiens when he was seven, sent to the Conservatoire when he was eleven, and at forty had made a name for himself with operas, song-cycles and 'incidental music'. His first operetta, *Ciboulette* (libretto by R. de Flers and F. de Croisset), which is also his best-known, did not come till 1923 ; he wrote a further half-dozen of which *Brummel* (1931), *Ô mon bel inconnu* (1933) and *Malvina* (1935) were musically the most interesting. Apart from *Le Temps d'aimer* (1926), which was a regrettable excursion into the field of pseudo-Viennese musical comedy, Hahn's operettas were carefully composed ; too carefully perhaps, for his scores are encumbered with a superfluity of notes and one longs for a few more 'rests'. (Where Auric provided a soufflé, Hahn offered a suet-pudding.) Though his harmonic style was eclectic and in places disfigured by affected chromaticism (he was obviously influenced by Franck and d'Indy as well as Ravel), he sometimes achieved a neo-classical diatonic purity — in the 'chœur des maraîchers' from *Ciboulette*, for instance. He was not an inspired melodist

---

[1] Among the films for which Auric has composed or arranged music is *Moulin Rouge*, based on the life of Toulouse-Lautrec.

but had a happy knack for getting the best out of a tune, especially in cadences. Ex. 70 is taken from *Ô mon bel inconnu.*

The next composer on our list was also an immigrant — JOSEPH SZULC (1875–1956), a native of Warsaw. His *Flup* (libretto by G. Dumestre) had been the rage of Brussels in 1913; he brought it with him to Paris in 1920. During the next twenty years he delighted the low-brows and satisfied the middle-brows with a series of typically 'French' operettas which were commonplace in conception but skilfully put together. They incorporated rag-time and jazz and were full of uninhibited rhythmic vigour. Very occasionally, as in the ensemble 'Pour trouver le chemin de mon cœur' from *Flossie* (1929), Szulc showed awareness of tradition (Lecocq, say), but audiences preferred his 'Shimmys' and 'Foxs', of which 'Pour qui cett' petit' bouche en cœur' from *Le Coffre-fort vivant* (1938) was a good example.

LOUIS BEYDTS (1895–1953) had his year of glory in 1931 with *Le Moineau, Le Club des canards mandarins* and the one-act *S.A.D.M.P.* (libretto by Sacha Guitry), but he quickly faded from the scene. Though his manner was essentially trivial, sound technique enabled him to add a superficial glitter to his music with chromatic progressions and occasional touches of parody; the soprano aria 'On vous dérange' from *Le Moineau* reached its climax with a reproduction of the tenor's 'E non ho amato mai tanto la vita' from 'E lucevan le stelle' in Puccini's *Tosca*. Less questionable were some skilful alternations between slow-waltz and 4/4 time in *La S.A.D.M.P.*

-er La po - é - sie Qui s'en dé - gage Et rendre hom - age A l'a - mu - san - te fan - tai - sie De leur lan - ga - ge.

MAURICE YVAIN (1891–), a cunning musician and adapter, made it his business to seek out forgotten tunes from the seventeenth and early eighteenth centuries and dress them in 'musical-comedy' garb. His operettas (of which he wrote about twenty) were thus a curious though not always incongruous mixture of pastiche and jazz, while a keen sense of humour prompted the interpolation of burlesque; in *Gosse de Riche* (1924), for instance, there was a comic ensemble ('Nous n'somm's pas des bourgeois') which effectively ridiculed the inordinate admiration for 'modern' art and music perennially prevalent in Montparnasse — and Chelsea. Yvain was far from being an outstanding composer of operetta; indeed his work belongs to the same category as Szulc's. But it was more polished, and the concerted writing — seen at its best in *Elle est à vous* (1929) — was always a pleasing feature. Having noticed (as my readers themselves will have done by now) the monotonous regularity with which the word 'amour' occurred in the titles of operettas, Yvain decided the time was ripe for a change; he therefore substituted 'bouche'. *Ta Bouche* (1921, his first success), *Pas sur la bouche* (1925) and *Bouche à bouche* (1926) justified the innovation. Ever since the spectacular *Au soleil de Mexique* set a seal on his popularity in 1935, however, he has written nothing save a little film-music and today lives in retirement at Saint-Cloud.

The story of French operetta has now been told, if not from A to Z, at least from A (for Adam) to Y (for Yvain). Its ending has been a sorry one. Leaving aside exceptional specimens like *L'Heure espagnole* which lie apart, Hahn's alone of the works that have come under notice in this chapter compare favourably in artistic merit with those of even minor practitioners of the previous generation like Gevaert, Massé, Poise and Lacome, let alone join Messager's *P'tites Michu* and *Véronique* as worthy successors to *La Belle Hélène* and *La Vie parisienne*. The name of *their* composer has frequently cropped up out of direct context, and another reminder of his pre-eminence may help to set the picture in perspective. Moreover, the significance of Jacques Offenbach's achievement will only become fully revealed as we review the gradual spread of operetta throughout Europe.[1]

[1] I am most grateful for the courteous hospitality of the director and staff of the Paris *Conservatoire de la musique*, in whose excellent library I was able to consult the scores of many operettas which I had sought in vain elsewhere.

§

ROUND THE CONTINENT

XII

GERMANY AND SCANDINAVIA

THE cult of opera, originating in Italy around 1600, was slow to take root in Teutonic countries. Heinrich Schütz can be credited with the lost *Dafne* (1627), but it was not until nearly a century later that a fellow Saxon, Reinhard Keiser, realised the potentialities. Keiser wrote over a hundred operas, all but a few of which were in German ; on the other hand his successors Johann Adolph Hasse (a Prussian) and Karl Graun (another Saxon), who flourished in the seventeen-fifties, had a decided preference for Italian. Johann Adam Hiller (a Silesian, and a specialist in comedy) struck a new note by using the translation of an English libretto by Charles Coffey for *Der Teufel ist los* (1766). His *Lottchen am Hofe* (1767) and *Die Jagd* (1770) were also cosmopolitan in character, for they bore stylistic resemblance to the *divertissements* of Duni and Monsigny (see page 8). Written in German and incorporating dialogue, Hiller's productions were the first representative *Singspiele* or 'song-plays', *i.e.* plays interspersed liberally with songs and sparsely with ensembles.[1]

In the assemblage of states collectively known as Germany, Hiller's methods were followed by Anton Schweitzer (from Bavaria), Johann André (Hessen), Johann Schulz (Lower Saxony, of whom more presently), Georg Vogler (Bavaria), Johann Friedrich Reichardt (Prussia), Peter Winter (Württemberg), Johann Christian Abeille (Bavaria) and Phillip Riotte (Palatinate). All had their moments of success, and Goethe himself was not above writing libretti for Schweitzer, André, Vogler and Reichardt. But the supreme exponent of *Singspiel*, Wolfgang Amadeus Mozart, was born in Austria. His essays ranged from *Bastien und Bastienne* (1768)

---

[1] The Italian operas which Haydn wrote during the seventeen-seventies were an interesting mixture of *opera seria* and *opera buffa* (see page 163) ; his *Abgebrannte Haus* (1776) was a *Singspiel* in Austrian dialect.

— written at the age of twelve — to *The Magic Flute* (1791). When setting Italian libretti he replaced dialogue with the conventional recitative of *opera buffa*, but *Così fan tutte* (1790), when played in German as *So machen's alle*, was no less a *Singspiel* than were *Die Entführung aus dem Serail* (1782, commonly known as *Seraglio*) and the one-act *Schauspieldirektor* (1786). In *The Magic Flute*, where the sublime and the ridiculous met on equal terms, genius established an unmatchable prototype for composers of operetta as yet unborn.

Among Mozart's Viennese contemporaries were Carl Dittersdorf, Johann Schenk and Joseph Weigl. They too wrote an occasional Italian opera but concentrated on German *Singspiele*. Dittersdorf's *Doktor und Apotheker* (1786), Schenk's *Dorfbarbier* (1796) and Weigl's *Schweizerfamilie* (1809) were admirable specimens. Adalbert Gyrowetz (a Bohemian by birth) and Wenzel Müller (a Moravian) were more prolific but less accomplished; they enjoyed only ephemeral success. Later Franz Schubert dashed down a few trifles in the same style, of which *Die Zwillingsbrüder* (1820) was played during his lifetime and several others have been resuscitated by enthusiasts; they did not show him at his wonderful best.

Meanwhile in Germany the operas of the mediocre Konradin Kreutzer, the great Carl Weber and the forgotten Peter Lindpaintner, though *Singspiele* in the strict sense of the term, were stressing 'romance' rather than the *buffo* element on which Hiller and Mozart had so largely relied. Surprisingly, the arch-romanticist Heinrich Marschner wrote one short opera in a light vein — *Der Holzdieb* (1825), which he actually described as an 'Operette' — but the only contemporary who consistently exploited the genre for purposes of comedy was ALBERT LORTZING (1801–1851). His mother and father were members of a wandering troup of players; he was born almost literally on the stage and his childhood was spent 'on tour'. In his twenties he conducted 'travelling opera' before taking up

resident posts first at Leipzig and afterwards at Vienna. He married
Rosalie Ahles, an actress in his parents' company, and they had eleven
children ; nevertheless Lortzing found time to compose about
the same number of light-hearted *Singspiele*, which can fairly be
counted as the first German operettas.

Ali Pascha von Janina (1824) was unashamedly imitative of
Mozart ; parts of it read like a parody, but the soprano aria
'An Corcyra's reizende Gestanden' was the real thing. This was
followed in 1832 by three very short one-act trifles — *Der Pole und
sein Kind, Andreas Hofer* and *Der Weinachtsabend*. A drinking-song
from *Der Pole* has been a provident source for lesser composers.

Next came two pieces which still hold the stage in Germany — *Die
beiden Schützen* (1835) and *Zar und Zimmermann* (1837). The
Mozartian flavour, though still perceptible, was less positive ; the
melodies retained the same character but the accompaniments often
comprised wearisome chord-repetitions or stale arpeggios. As
time went on, Lortzing's operettas became more pretentious and by
the same token less acceptable — in retrospect at any rate — for
his talent was ill-adapted to anything more ambitious than light
comedy. Of his later works *Der Wildschütz* (1842) was the best ;
in the last of all — *Die Opernprobe* (1850) — he returned to parody,
this time at the expense of Rossini.[1] *Undine* (1845) and the other
'romantic' operas, which the composer took very seriously, have no
place in our story.

Lortzing and his large family waged a continuous struggle
against poverty and disease ; the political troubles of 1848 and 1849
engendered near-starvation. But personal distress was nowhere
reflected in his music ; *jollity* was its most endearing characteristic.
It bubbled happily as operetta-music should — cider rather than
champagne, but rarely leaving a bad taste behind. The addiction
to Mozart and the typically conventional treatment of agreeable

---

[1] The parody was not confined to the overture, as some commentators have
implied ; it was maintained throughout.

but undistinguished melody can be separately illustrated by two quotations from *Casanova* (1841).[1]

In Germany (where there is no lack of bibliography) Lortzing's worth has perhaps been overrated ; from a detached standpoint his stature appears comparable with Adolphe Adam's. Judged solely as a composer he may lead his Parisian contemporary by a short head, but he cannot claim the same historical significance. *Le Chalet* and *Le Postillon de Longjumeau* heralded the era of operetta ; *Casanova* and *Der Wildschütz*, though belonging to the same category, merely betokened the impending disappearance of *Singspiel*.

Lortzing's only direct successors worthy of note were AUGUST CONRADI (1821–1873) and FRANZ GENÉE (1823–1895). The former followed the *Singspiel* tradition in half a dozen colourless operettas from *Der Rübezahl* (1849) to *Das Wunderhorn* (1871). He also produced a few *Possen* ('burlesques'), of which *Der Goldonkel* (1862) was an innocuous affair largely in *Ländler* rhythms, and *Das schönste Mädchen im Städtchen* (1868) showed that he knew his Offenbach. Genée, a Danziger of French parentage, was musical director at the municipal theatres of Reval, Danzig itself, Riga, Cologne, Düsseldorf, Aachen, Elberfeld, Mainz and Schwerin in

---

[1] It should be noted that Lortzing, always a lone fighter, wrote his own libretti.

turn. During the course of his travels he wrote a handful of operettas, including *Der Geiger aus Tirol* (1857), *Die Generalprobe, Der
Musikfeind* (both 1862) and *Rosita* (1864) ; an 'ariette' from *Der
Musikfeind* — 'Das ganze Leben ist Musik' — displayed a facility in
modulation which Conradi or even Lortzing might well have
envied. In 1867 Genée settled permanently in Vienna, and his
name will crop up again during the course of the next two chapters.

OTTO NICOLAI (1810–1849) was a composer of higher calibre.
He was eleven years older than Conradi, thirteen years older than
Genée, and died before either of them was heard of ; but he was far
more progressive in outlook and approach. Inevitably regarded as
a 'one-work man', Nicolai's output was certainly small, but he
crowded plenty of activity into a short career. Born at Königsberg,
he studied in Berlin, and between 1833 and 1847 divided his time
between Rome and Vienna, where he made his mark both as
organist and conductor. In 1847 he was appointed director of the
Court Opera in Berlin, and it was there that in 1849, two months
before his sudden death, he produced *The Merry Wives of Windsor*
(libretto by S. H. Mosenthal after Shakespeare), which immortalised
his name. It is still played regularly on the continent ; in this
country it has occasionally been included in the Carl Rosa repertory,
but to most British listeners the overture alone is familiar. This is
a matter for regret, for *The Merry Wives* is a first-rate operetta. The
comic scenes are lightly handled ; elsewhere the music owes something to Weber and a little, perhaps, to the Wagner of *Rienzi*.[1]

Nicolai reconciled the unassuming characteristics of *Singspiel* with a
large measure of cosmopolitan sophistication acquired during his

[1] Wagner later returned the compliment, for the 'Künstlermotiv' (which figures
prominently in the duet between Walther and Sachs in Act III of *Die Meistersinger*)
is lifted from the 'second subject' of the *Merry Wives* overture.

travels abroad. He was ahead of his time, and his influence on Offenbach, Johann Strauss, Sullivan and even aged Verdi cannot be overlooked. Readers who possess or can borrow a vocal score should
reflect that the penultimate chorus 'Fasst ihn Geister nach der Reih''
was written nine years before *Orphée* ; 'Wie freu ich mich' from
Act II twenty-five years before *Die Fledermaus* ; 'Ihr Elfen, weiss
und roth und grau' from Act III thirty-three years before *Iolanthe* ;
the wives' opening duet 'Nein, das ist wirklich zu keck' forty-four
years before *Falstaff*.

The Merry Wives stands in isolation. One is tempted to say that
it is the only really important German operetta ever written (German as distinct from Viennese). Such an assertion would admittedly leave out of account two border-line cases — *The Barber of
Bagdad* (1858) by PETER CORNELIUS (1824–1874) and *The Taming
of the Shrew* (1874) by HERMANN GOETZ (1840–1876). *The
Barber of Bagdad* was operatic comedy rather than operetta, and I
shall not attempt to trace its chequered career from the fiasco of its
first performance under Liszt's direction at Weimar through a series
of revisions to eventual condensation in one act. Ernest Newman
told the whole sorry tale in *Opera Nights* (1943), and incorporated an
inimitable appraisal. Suffice to record here that it was original in
its conception, sparkling in its humour, and contained a few passages
of rare lyrical beauty.

The career of Hermann Goetz was coincidentally similar to
Nicolai's. Both were natives of Königsberg ; both died in their
thirties ; both are remembered solely for their connection with a
Shakespearean comedy which they set to music shortly before their
deaths. Goetz's tunes were not as good as Nicolai's (or Cornelius's)
but, leaving aside a few scenes which were dramatically superfluous
and musically trivial, *The Taming of the Shrew* (*durchkomponiert*,
adaptation by J. V. Widmann) was a well-balanced, competently
written and attractive work. Some of the concerted pieces, notably
the chorus 'Nun ist es aus', showed Mozartian refinement, but
more often the manner was reminiscent of Mendelssohn — Mendelssohn not quite at his best. Goetz was fond of using *Leitmotive*, not
in the comprehensive Wagnerian fashion but merely to endow
self-contained scenes with unity. Ex. 77, for instance, after being

subjected to symphonic development in the overture, provided a
thematic basis for Act III, Scene 4, and reappeared momentarily in
Act IV, Scene 2. The composer would have been surprised to learn
that forty years later a painstaking analyst (Eduard Kreuzhage)
would solemnly identify it as 'Petruchios Rücksichtslosigkeitmotiv'.

Ex.77 Maestoso con brio

We must now jump back a hundred years or so to Johann
Schulz, one of the first exponents of eighteenth-century *Singspiel*,
who after roaming all round Europe between 1762 and 1787 was
eventually appointed musical director at the court of Copenhagen.
At that time the Danes were struggling to develop a characteristic
Singspiel of their own ('*syngespil*'), but though plenty of literary
talent was available there was a paucity of composers. Music had
hitherto been provided by two earlier immigrants, Paolo Scalabrini
(an Italian) and Ernst Hartmann (a Silesian). Neither the former's
Love Rewarded (1758) nor the latter's *Death of Balder* (1773) had
escaped incongruity in the setting of Danish words, although Hartmann in *The Fishermen* (1780) had written the tune which still
serves as the Danish National Anthem. Schulz was more adaptable :
with *The Harvest Home* (1790) and *Peter's Wedding* (1793) he so
closely identified himself with the aspirations of his adopted country
that he soon came to be regarded as a native composer. So too did
three younger compatriots who followed him to Denmark —
Friedrich Kunzen, Christoph Weyse and Friedrich Kuhlau. Kunzen's pieces adhered to the Hiller pattern and bore ballad-operatic
titles like *Love in the Country* (1810); Weyse with *The Sleeping-
Draught* (1809) and Kuhlau with *The Enchanted Harp* (1817) inclined to local folk-legend. Presently, however, responsibility for
keeping native stage-music alive devolved upon the Danes themselves : Andreas Berggreen, Johann Peter Hartmann (a grandson
of the German-born composer of *The Fishermen*) and his son-in-law
Niels Gade — the most important figure of the three — all played
their part. But neither Berggreen's *Picture and Statue* (1832), nor

Hartmann's *Little Christina* (1846) nor yet Gade's *Mariotta* (1850) were operettas, and Denmark can claim only two-and-a-half recognised composers in that genre — LUDWIG SCHYTTE (1848–1909), AUGUST ENNA (1860–1939) and SOPHUS DANNING (1867–1925). Schytte, a distinguished pianist, is the 'half'; his *Mameluk* (1903) and *Student von Salamanca* (1909) were *Viennese* operettas — both unsuccessful — written long after he settled in the Austrian capital at the age of thirty-nine. Enna, on the other hand, remained at home except for a short period of study in Germany, and his earliest known composition was a genuine Danish operetta — *A Village Tale* (1880). Thereafter he tackled more ambitious subjects, and of the rest of his considerable output only *The Little Matchseller* (1897) and *The Princess and the Pea* (1900) — both after Hans Andersen — qualify for mention here. Much of Enna's music was an unsatisfying combination of real or spurious folk-melody and sickly sentimentality. For *The Little Match-seller*, for instance, he covered a wholesome plain cake with thick pink icing and topped it with tinsel angels; only when he ran out of sugar could the true flavour (as in Ex. 78) be appreciated.

Ex. 78
Allegretto semplice

Danning was best-known as a conductor, and I cannot claim first-hand acquaintance with his compositions. He carried his baton round Europe without forfeiting his nationality, and his only operetta — *Columbine* (1912) — was produced in his home town, Copenhagen.

During the eighteenth century Sweden produced as few composers as did Denmark, and in the absence of cultural ties with northern Germany the native *Singspiel* ('*sångspel*') depended mainly upon folksong. It is true that from about 1770 onwards French *divertissements* and Austrian *Singspiele* were frequently played in Stockholm, where Dalayrac and Dittersdorf were especial favourites, but this was something apart; *sångspel* itself was not affected,

except that in order to maintain a contrast with the popular impor-
tations a stress on the 'folk' element soon became obligatory rather
than, as hitherto, merely a hallowed custom. So *sångspel* developed
into *sågospel* ('saga-play'), with the inclusion of folk-music taken for
granted. Even the operas and operettas of JOHANN SÖDERMAN
(1832–1876) and IVAR HALLSTRÖM (1826–1901), which came much
later, were based on folklore, though some of the music was newly
fashioned. Söderman is mainly remembered for his 'Peasant's
wedding-song', an inseparable part of Swedish nuptial celebrations,
long after his one *sågospel*, *The Devil's first lessons* (1856), was
forgotten. Hallström in *The Enchanted Cat* (1869), *The Mountain
Troll* (1874) and *The Snares of the Devil* (1900) emphasised Scandinavian characteristics ; he never tried to disguise them with Teutonic
titivation as did his Danish counterpart Ernest Enna. It is hardly
necessary to point out the stylistic resemblance of Ex. 79 (from *The
Mountain Troll*) to Ex. 78, but whereas with Enna such a simple
exposition was exceptional it came as second nature to Hallström.

So *Singspiel*, an unpretentious form of entertainment originated
by Hiller and brought to perfection by Mozart, found its last
resting-place in Scandinavia. It was swept from the land of its
origin by a wind of change, when the intoxicating rhythms of the
waltz and the polka danced their irresistible way from the banks of
the Danube to the shores of the Baltic. Wagner remained immersed
in his tetralogy and Brahms went on writing symphonies, but
German operetta, for which Lortzing and Nicolai had provided a
foundation, bowed to the storm. Driven willy-nilly into an
Anschluss with its up-and-coming Viennese counterpart, it soon lost
all national identity.[1]

---

[1] Some individual examples of Germany's contribution to the *Anschluss* will
come under review towards the end of Chapter XV, 'The Strauss Legacy'.

XIII

THE INCEPTION OF VIENNESE OPERETTA

SOME of the seeds from which Viennese operetta was to blossom were sowed by Joseph Lanner and Johann Strauss the elder, but neither lived long enough to witness its ultimate flowering, for their mortal careers (like those of Bellini, Chopin, Mendelssohn and Nicolai) were confined within the limits of the first half of the nineteenth century. Born in the slums of Vienna — Lanner to a glovemaker and Strauss to a publican — each taught himself the violin and in youth earned a living by playing in local beer-gardens and *Weinhallen*. They were creative, too, and by the time they were thirty their marches and dance-music had brought them undreamt-of fame ; soon afterwards, as violinist-conductors, they were sharing the directorship of the Vienna court balls.

In their compositions both felt the waltz-impetus of Weber's *Invitation to the Dance*. Lanner, the more conservative of the two, favoured also the *Ländler* and other traditional measures ; spiritually he belonged to Beethoven's 'Lustiges Zusammensein der Landleute'. Strauss, on the other hand, kept his finger on the public pulse and cultivated above all a rhythmic sprightliness ; into such things as the *Donaulieder* waltz and the *Radetzky March* he infused a sparkle which Vienna could not resist. Thus while Lanner enjoyed success Strauss nearly always capped it. In their private affairs neither escaped the wagging tongue of scandal. Lanner, though modest and clean-living, was an alcoholic. Strauss was a teetotaller, but he was uncommonly aggressive — and a notorious libertine. Small wonder that their rivalry was personal as well as professional ; when Strauss learnt that his wife Anna had attended one of Lanner's concerts his fury knew no bounds. About the same time (1841) he openly took as mistress a young lady bearing the unromantic name of Trampusch. Anna divorced him in 1844 and thereafter lavished all her love on her three sons, Johann, Joseph and Eduard. Maternal affection was rewarded ; whatever their faults, they always treated her better than their father had.

But it was no member of the Strauss family, nor indeed any native of Vienna, who wrote the first Viennese operetta. That distinction belonged to FRANZ VON SUPPÉ (1819–1895), who was born at Spalato (now Split) on the Dalmatian coast. His father was Belgian by origin and Italian by inclination. Nothing was left to chance when his child was baptised Francesco Ezechiele Ermenegildo Suppe Demelli. Although showing precocity in music he was sent to Padua to study medicine, but on the sudden death of his father in 1835 he gladly accompanied his mother, an Austrian, to Vienna. He soon perfected his German and secured employment as a flautist, later as an orchestral conductor. Meanwhile he found time to write burlesques and *Singspiele*, which owed as much to *opera buffa* (see page 163) as they did to Lanner and Strauss the elder. *Poet and Peasant* (1846) had an overture which has since swept the world, but it was *Das Mädchen vom Lande* (1847) and *Des Teufels Brautfahrt* (1849) that earned his contemporary recognition.

The year 1858 was marked by another Suppé triumph — *Paragraph 3* — but was more noteworthy for Offenbach's first visit to Vienna (see page 26). He brought with him a selection from the Bouffes-Parisiens repertory comprising five of his own one-act operettas and Delibes' *Six demoiselles à marier*. The impact was terrific and its subsequent effect incalculable.[1] Yet at the time Suppé was the only composer to realise it : during the early sixties he turned out a dozen one-act buffooneries, all obviously inspired by Offenbach, in which he attempted, with some success, to combine Parisian *savoir-faire* with Viennese *Gemütlichkeit*. He could justly claim that *Das Pensionat* (1860), despite its pseudo-Spanish atmosphere, was the first Viennese operetta, but *Zehn Mädchen und kein Mann* (1862) and *Flotte Bursche* (1863) were more favourably received and have therefore acquired greater historical significance. *Zehn Mädchen* included burlesque, both Italian and British ('Bella

---

[1] 'But for Offenbach's success in Vienna there might have been no such thing as Viennese operetta.' So wrote Erwin Rieger in his *Offenbach und seine Wiener Schule* (1920).

fiame del mio coro' and 'Jn England schall You drink with me the finest Ale') ; *Flotte Bursche*, a student's frolic, was unequivocally Viennese and was described by Ignaz Schnitzer (page 129) as 'eine Wiener Vollblutsoperette'. In 1864 Offenbach reappeared, and under his influence Suppé produced *Die schöne Galathe*[1] (1865), which was in parts quite dramatic ; curiously it had its *première* in Berlin and did not reach Vienna until two months later. For the next ten years Suppé was comparatively inactive, but eventually *Fatinitza* (1876) and *Boccaccio* (1879) set a seal on his reputation. The half-dozen operettas which he wrote during the eighties and early nineties were less successful, although *Die Afrikareise* (1882) was one of his best efforts, and *Donna Juanita* (1880), *Der Gascogner* (1881) and *Des Matrosen Heimkehr* (1885) were nearly as good.[2]

There was little in Suppé's music to appeal to a fastidious listener, but it was rarely enervating and never pretentious. Vulgar, yes ; but in the quick-march rhythms to which he was so much addicted open vulgarity was preferable to the camouflaged variety. The familiar overture to the one-act operetta *Light Cavalry* (1866) was well-suited to its military *milieu* and typified the composer's uninhibited approach. So did the dinned-in *Motiv* of a march-trio from *Fatinitza*, of which 350,000 copies were sold.

Ex. 80

Vor-wärts mit frisch-em Blut   Lieb ist dein Pa-nier,   Vor-wärts mit küh-nem Muth, Süs-ser Lohn wird dir!

Though it would be unfair to dismiss Suppé as a mere popularity-hunter, it must be admitted that his creative talent was not commensurate with his impeccable background and almost unlimited opportunities. His roots, as we have seen, lay in Italy ; before he came to Vienna he knew every note of Donizetti (an uncle by marriage) and of Bellini. In his thirties he developed an equal admiration for the classic gems of French and German opera and caught

---

[1] This is Suppé's spelling ; *Riemann* favours ' Galathea ', *Grove* ' Galatea ', and *Everyman's Dictionary of Music* ' Galatee '.

[2] According to Otto Keller, in his informative *Operette in ihrer geschichtlichen Entwicklung* (1926), Suppé's last operetta — *Das Modell* (1895) — was completed by Julien Stern and Alfred Zamara (page 135), but there is nothing on the title-page of the vocal score to suggest that it was not all his own work.

the Strauss-waltz infection ; only when he was over forty did he fall
an involuntary prey to the wiles of Offenbach. Not surprisingly his
operettas were a stylistic hotch-potch, but it is worth noting that
polkas, galops, marches and other items in vigorous 2/4 time were
more prominent than waltzes, which occurred with comparative in-
frequency. However, there was a good specimen in the overture
to *Die schöne Galathe* ; the F♮ in the eighth bar jerked the audience
out of complacence —

—and the climax arrived on an unexpected $\frac{6}{4}$ chord of E major.
Spaccamonti's song 'Glimmt ein Feuer irgendwo' from *Der Ban-
ditenstreich* (1867) also showed harmonic initiative ; there was an
unusual modulation from tonic to supertonic (G major to A major),
followed by an equally smooth return *via* the dominant seventh.
But it was in *Boccaccio* that Suppé was at his best. To particularise :
the first-act finale — following his usual practice — was 'concerted'
on Italian lines which were here especially appropriate, but it also
incorporated the Viennese characteristics which were expected of
him. Ex. 82, pure Donizetti, led to Ex. 83 ; and for once a waltz-
tune was satisfactorily established as an architectonic base.

When Suppé indulged in eighteenth-century pastiche, as he often
did, he disarmed criticism. The minuet at the beginning of the
third act of *Boccaccio* was irreproachable ; so was a strain from
Donna Juanita (Ex. 84).

Furthermore, his experience as a conductor enabled him to deploy orchestral forces to good effect, and he always kept an eye on the stage situation. Here is the passage which accompanied the rise of the curtain on the first scene of *Die Afrikareise*.

This was the most satisfying of his later operettas; the 'Blumen duettino' had an innocuous charm, and the amusing trio 'Afrika ist sehr gefährlich' was admirably contrived. If, in summing up, one is tempted to regard him as a mere link between Offenbach and Strauss the younger, Suppé nevertheless deserves recognition for his own sake.

We must now renew acquaintance with FRANZ GENÉE, whom we met in the preceding chapter (page 112). When he arrived in Vienna from Germany he brought with him his latest operetta, *Der schwarze Prinz* (1867), which was no more than an outdated *Singspiel* and could not hope to compete with Suppé's *Schöne Galathe*, let alone with Offenbach's *Belle Hélène* — just then the talk of the town. The versatile Genée, no whit discouraged, turned to the pursuit of literature, and wrote libretti for Suppé or anyone else who came along.[1] He did not give up composition altogether; a good welcome was accorded to his *Seekadett* (1876) and *Nanon* (1877). But *Die letzten Mohikaner* (1878, after Fenimore Cooper)

---

[1] Genée later provided translations for the Vienna productions of *The Mikado* in 1888, *The Pirates of Penzance* in 1889 and *The Gondoliers* in 1890.

was voted a dull affair, and his subsequent operettas had little success. Though Genée's music, except possibly in *Nanon*, rarely exceeded mediocrity, he adapted himself cleverly to his new surroundings — when in Vienna he did as the Viennese did. A tiny ensemble from *Der Seekadett* ('Sie, Kapitän') showed an artist's touch, and three songs from *Nanon* ('Treu blieb ich', 'Jung an Jahren' and 'Anna, zu dir ist mein liebster Gang') were sung everywhere. There were also signs of enterprise in parts of *Nisida* (1880), but according to internal evidence *Rosina*, produced at Vienna in 1881, may well have been a re-hash of the lost *Rosita*, written sixteen years earlier at Mainz, for it lacked Genée's latter-day vivacity and was heavily encumbered with Germanic sentimentality. *Die Piraten* (1886) and *Die Dreizehn* (1887) recaptured the Viennese atmosphere, but most of the music was very trivial.

Only two other composers came into the picture ahead of Johann Strauss the younger. One was the well-remembered Karl Millöcker who started operations in 1864 ; but he did not establish himself until the eighties, and appraisal must be reserved for the next chapter. The other was JULIUS BRANDL (1825–1913), whose *Handwerk* was played in 1869. He soon wrote eight more one-act pieces in the Suppé manner, of which *Des Löwen Erwachen* (1872) was widely praised, but in the event none achieved much success.[1] Thus when Strauss entered the field in 1871 he had to face competition from Suppé who had already staked a claim, from Genée and Brandl who were cautiously feeling their way forward, and from Millöcker who had yet to find his feet. Their subsequent activity was a constantly pricking spur to his vigilance.

[1] In *Die Tochter des Dionysos* (1881) there was a five-verse patter song in the Sullivan manner ('Das dumme Volk erzählet Euch vom Himmel und von Göttern'), which had the added interest of a cello *obbligato*.

XIV

THE STRAUSS ERA

JOHANN STRAUSS the younger was born on 25th October 1825. Despite parental discouragement he adopted the musical profession. He had his first public success in 1844, and for the next twenty-five years was content to follow in his father's footsteps as a violinist-conductor and a prolific composer of dance-music. (He is credited with about 140 polkas, and the number of his waltzes has been variously estimated between 150 and 400.) Even Offenbach's appearances in Vienna during 1858 and 1864 failed to make him shift his ground. 'You ought to write operettas,' Offenbach told him, 'you have all the attributes,' but it was not until after paying a return visit to Paris in 1867 that Strauss actually began one. It was completed by 1869 and was to be called *The Merry Wives of Vienna*. Unfortunately the leading lady whom Strauss regarded as a *sine qua non* — Josephine Gallmeyer — was unable to obtain release from another contract and the whole project was abandoned. However, 1871 saw the first performance of *Indigo und die vierzig Räuber*. It was whispered that a more appropriate title would have been *Strauss und die vierzig Textdichter*, and the witticism pin-pointed a fatal weakness. In the music the influence of Offenbach was very noticeable and there was only one Viennese waltz. But now and again Strauss touched a tender chord of expression rarely realised by Offenbach, notably in Fantasca's two songs, 'Geschmiedet fest an starre Felsenwand' and 'Du Schlummersaft'. In each case a charming tune was sung first in the minor and afterwards in the major ; that was all, and enough was better than a feast.[1] The same restraint was observable in *Der Carneval in Rom* (1873). Ex. 86 is taken from

---

[1] Eduard Hanslick, in an obituary notice, maintained that Strauss told him the words of *Indigo* were written to fit existing music. If that is so, these numbers may originally have belonged to *The Merry Wives of Vienna*.

a duet for soprano and tenor which is typical of Strauss in sentimental mood ; the soaring melodic outlines are skilfully intertwined, but the accompaniment is monotonous and the conclusion unsatisfying. (Whereas Offenbach often contrived a natural and effective cadence — see pages 48-9 — Strauss suffered from an inability to round things off convincingly. In many of his waltzes the introductions were superb, the endings perfunctory.)

Indigo and *Der Carneval in Rom* heightened Strauss's contemporary stature, but today they are forgotten. *Die Fledermaus* (1874) probably never will be. Once again the structure was faulty : although not attributable, like *Indigo*, to *forty* librettists, shares could be claimed by half a dozen or so, for the plot originally formed the basis of a German comedy (*Das Gefängnis*) which reappeared in Paris as a *vaudeville* (*Le Réveillon*) and finally reached Vienna through the agency of Carl Haffner and Franz Genée. Yet with one exception, which we shall come to presently, this was the best libretto Strauss ever encountered. That is not saying much, and producers invariably claim a free hand to alter, add or subtract.

(I am waiting for some enterprising director to use Reginald Arkell and A. P. Herbert's version entitled *Come to the Ball*, which in some respects flouts convention but retains all the essential ingredients and is far better constructed than the original.) *Die Fledermaus* is properly regarded as the apotheosis of Viennese operetta ; it is not so widely realised that of all Strauss's essays in the genre this alone was a true evocation of legendary Vienna. The music is immortal, the composer's exploitation of Offenbachian sprightliness being more fully tempered than in *Der Carneval* with native charm and suavity ; nor would it be fair to overlook the influence of Suppé's *Schöne Galathe*. A quotation is obligatory, but since most of the tunes are well known I have chosen a comparatively unfamiliar excerpt (Ex. 87) to illustrate that flair for a miniature which had first been apparent in *Indigo*.

While all Vienna was whistling 'Mein Herr Marquis' and waltzing to the strains of 'Du, du', Strauss was visiting Italy ; on his return he wrote *Cagliostro in Wien* (1875). In this operetta a cunning commentator has found traces of Verdi's influence.[1] But the instance he cites in support of his contention is a little far-fetched, for it quickly evolves into something like a waltz (Ex. 88). And though the opening of Act III — 'Sag' mir, mein Herz' — had an undoubted Italian flavour, most of the music, as in *Indigo*, derived from Offenbach ; the spirit of *Die Fledermaus*, however, haunted the long, tuneful and rhythmically varied duet 'E dés Lorenza [sic] Sie hier zu finden'. *Prinz Methusalem* (1877) and *Die Blindekuh*, i.e. *Blind Man's Buff* (1878) were failures. From the former a charming allegretto in 3/8 time lives on as a waltz.[2] The most striking number from *Die Blindekuh* was the overture, where an oddly shaped ten-bar phrase came unexpectedly to life when developed in several well-contrasted keys and *tempi*. Taken-by-and large these post-*Fledermaus* operettas added little to Strauss's reputation ; for the moment Suppé, with *Fatinitza* and *Boccaccio*, had things all his own way.

[1] Heinrich Jacob, in his very readable chronicle *Johann Strauss und das neunzehnte Jahrhundert: die Geschichte einer musikalischen Weltherrschaft* (1920).

[2] In 1883 *Prinz Methusalem* was given 102 performances at the Casino Theatre, New York, nearly as many as it has achieved in its whole history on this side of the Atlantic.

In 1862 Strauss had married the opera-singer Henriette ('Jetty') Treffz, generously released by her current 'protector' Baron Moritz Tedesco (whom she had presented with two illegitimate daughters).

Up to a point the marriage had been a happy one, and Strauss's early operettas had benefited from conjugal encouragement. But of late he had been seeking consolation elsewhere, for his wife, ten years his senior and now in her sixties, had lost all attraction for him. When she died in 1878 her widower promptly made an honest woman of Angelika ('Lily') Dietrich. Lily too was a singer, but forty years younger than Jetty. She soon showed a preference for congenial male company nearer her own age, and the doting old husband found himself hoist with his own petard. In the first flush of contentment engendered by this second marriage, however, Strauss wrote *Das Spitzentuch der Königin* (1880), musically his best operetta since *Die Fledermaus*. But the libretto, as usual, was shocking, and *Das Spitzentuch* survives only in the form of a waltz potpourri, *Roses of the South*. Its opening melody, familiar to B.B.C. listeners as the signature-tune of 'Grand Hotel', was first heard as an aria sung by Cervantes (not a casually named hero, but the author of *Don Quixote*). Another strain, equally memorable, was originally part of the 'Truffel-couplet'.

Ex.89 Tempo di Valse Moderato

Stets kommt mir wie - der in der Sinn was einst mich de - lec-tir - te,

Der lustige Krieg (1881) was moderately successful on its own account. It provided the short *Kusswalzer*, but two other numbers in that well-worn rhythm — a duet for soprano and tenor (Ex. 90) and the quintet 'Kommen und geh'n' — were born to be sung.

Ex.90 Allegretto grazioso

VIOLETTA

doch, wenn auch blind, so trifft er ge - schwind,

UMBERTO

doch, wenn auch blind, trifft er ge - schwind

The history of *Eine Nacht in Venedig* (1883) does little credit to its composer and less to its authors. Genée and his colleague Camillo Walzel (pseudonym 'F. Zell'), who wrote libretti for Millöcker as well as for Strauss, had at that time two on their stocks — *Der Bettelstudent* and *Eine Nacht in Venedig*. Strauss read the former and was delighted with it, but Genée and Walzel knew very well that the latter was far inferior and bound to be a failure unless it carried the Strauss imprimatur. With psychological insight they told him that his choice of *Der Bettelstudent* pleased them mightily, because (they said) Millöcker was aching to set the other. Whereupon Strauss, stung to jealousy according to plan, retracted his former decision, insisted that he and he alone should have *Eine Nacht in Venedig*, and dashed off the music without even bothering to read the play! It may have been a coincidence that this was the only one of his operettas which did not have its *première* at Vienna. (It was produced in Berlin.) A few bars may be quoted to demonstrate how Strauss, even when not writing an actual waltz, rarely had the rhythm far from his mind.

Ex.91

He was only once fortunate in his librettist, when in 1885 he collaborated with Ignaz Schnitzer in *The Gipsy Baron*, which put Suppé and Genée (in both his capacities) right in the shade. By now Strauss had divorced Lily and had emerged unscathed from a third wedding ceremony, this time to a thirty-year-old, Adèle Deutsch. With his domestic affairs at last running smoothly, he for once devoted some attention to the constructional details of an operetta. He even took the trouble to write to Schnitzer and make pertinent suggestions for bringing his draft of the 'Marschcouplet' in Act III more into line with a Suppé precedent (see Ex. 80, page 120). They do not seem to have been adopted *in toto*, but the finished article was a satisfactory compromise, sure evidence of mutual respect. Though the music of *Die Fledermaus* justly holds pride of place in popular esteem, *The Gipsy Baron*, thanks to this unwonted degree of co-operation with his librettist, was Strauss's best operetta *per se*. The Hungarian element, which had been dragged into *Die Fledermaus* by the scruff of the neck for the sake of the csárdás, was here exploited more instinctively ; in Ex. 92 the characteristic fits and starts of rhythm were reconciled with a melody which sounded wholly spontaneous, although perhaps not ideally suited to the words.

In *Simplicius* (1887) Strauss failed to profit from the lesson of *Eine Nacht in Venedig*. Victor Léon (who was later to write *The Merry Widow* for Lehár) made a simpleton of him just as Genée and Walzel had ; this time it was not Millöcker but Alfred Zamara (page 135) who was a pawn in the game. Léon was an ambitious youngster, concerned only to have his name coupled with that of Johann Strauss ; his libretto touched the depths of incongruity and bad taste. For instance, a solemn intoning of the Lord's Prayer — not just as 'background' but as an integral part of the proceedings — was followed by a loud shout of 'Schnaps her!', heralding a jolly drinking chorus led by the soubrette. That Strauss should condone all this and put his name to such a deplorable concoction was symptomatic, for he apparently regarded operetta not as an end in itself but as a means whereby he could further the expression of his extraordinary talent for writing attractive dance-music and lively marches. And for the next few years he did indeed return to his earlier habit and concentrate on detached pieces, until in 1892 he inadvisedly attempted a 'komische Oper' [1] — *Ritter Pázmán* — on which I shall not comment. Nor is there any temptation to linger over his subsequent operettas — *Fürstin Ninetta* (1893), *Jabuka* (1894), *Waldmeister* (1895) and *Die Göttin der Vernunft* (1897) — although each

---

[1] *I.e.* 'opéra comique', *not* 'comic opera'.

contained some attractive music.   Whereas *The Gipsy Baron* had had
a Magyar setting, *Jabuka* belonged to Croatia.

The scene of *Waldmeister*, the most successful of Strauss's later works,
was Weber's romanticised Germany ; it might almost have been
intended as a parody of *Der Freischütz*.   But the unusual harmonic
freedom displayed in one waltz must have provided Lehár with
food for thought.

Strauss's death on 3rd June 1899 in the city which had given him
birth and honour was an occasion for national mourning.   He was
buried in the Zentralfriedhof, and the ghosts of Franz Schubert and
Johannes Brahms surely took no umbrage when his mortal remains
were laid to earth close beside their own.

A substantial shelf would be needed to accommodate all the
books written about him ;   their authors, when concerning themselves with his creative art, rightly devoted more space to his dance-
music than to his operettas.   Ernst Decsey, however, gave them a
fair and comprehensive appraisal in *Johann Strauss : ein Wiener Buch*
(1922).   Incidentally he was not far off the mark when he traced
back a phrase from *Die Fledermaus* —

— to Lecocq's *Fille de Madame Angot* (Ex. 56, page 79). As regards the relative merits of the operettas there could be no quibble when Guido Adler, in a memorial booklet, unhesitatingly awarded the palm to *Die Fledermaus*. But Heinrich Jacob (*op. cit.* page 126 footnote) expressed a preference for *The Gipsy Baron*, and another distinguished critic, Richard Specht, had a weakness for *Indigo*. It counts for little in the end, for although Strauss wrote fifteen operettas (sixteen if one includes the unknown *Merry Wives*) they were a by-product of his genius. They were so ill-constructed that nowadays they are always played in revised editions — often prepared by Erich Korngold. Indeed what is advertised as a 'Strauss operetta' sometimes turns out to be a contrived pasticcio like *Die Tänzerin Fanny Elssler* (1903), which was evolved by Oskar Stalla and Alois Melichar.

A revival of *Die Fledermaus* at Covent Garden in 1930, with Bruno Walter conducting, Lotte Lehmann as Rosalinde and Elisabeth Schumann as Adèle, set new standards of production and performance so far as this country was concerned and touched off a Strauss vogue. But no more operettas were played, as such ; instead we had to be content with the fabricated *Casanova* (Coliseum, 1932), which picked plums from *Indigo*, *Die Blindekuh* and elsewhere. This seeming paradox pointed the crux of the matter, for much as we all love *Die Fledermaus*, a mention of Johann Strauss immediately conjures up a recollection of *Tritschtratsch*, *The Blue Danube* or an *item* from some operetta rather than the operetta itself. He deserves to be remembered — and revered — as a composer of dance-music, unrivalled in any age or clime.

Strauss's younger brothers, Joseph and Eduard, both wrote plenty of polkas and waltzes — but never an operetta ; *Die Frühlingsluft* (1903), still played in German-speaking countries, is a Joseph Strauss pasticcio. Apart from Suppé, Johann's most dangerous rival in that field was KARL MILLÖCKER (1842–1899). Like Suppé, Millöcker graduated from the flute to the baton. During his youth he wrote a few short operettas, of which *Der tote Gast* (1864) and *Die beiden Binder* (1865) were played at Graz, *Die keusche Diana* and *Der Raub der Sabinerinnen* (both 1867) at Vienna, *Die Fraueninsel* (1868) at Budapest. They were frank imitations of Offenbach and by no means specifically Viennese. But Millöcker soon had plenty of opportunity to study the methods of Suppé and Strauss, for in the seventies he conducted most of their operettas at the Theater an der Wien. Nevertheless his own next attempt — *Das verwünschene Schloss* (1878) — was a folk-parody. There were large doses of Austrian dialect and much of the music was in the jog-trot *Ländler* manner of 'Ach, du lieber Augustin'. A more up-to-date atmosphere was caught in a charming waltz-song, 'Ob man gefallt', from *Gräfin Dubarry* (1879). *Apajune* (1880) and *Die Jungfrau von Belleville* (1882) did not amount to much, but *Der Bettelstudent* (also 1882), with a libretto that ought to have been set by Strauss (see page 129), brought Millöcker right to the fore. There was an excellent love duet (recalling a melody from *Indigo*), and the big waltz, hovering between F major and F minor, soon had every foot tapping, although the bathos of the 'plugged' verbal catch-phrase aroused censorious comment.[1]

Ex.96
Mässiges Walzertempo

Ach, ich hab'___ Sie ja nur___ auf die Schul - ter ge - küsst, ___ ach, ich

hab'___ Sie ja nur___ auf die Schul - ter ge - küsst!

The lively marches and catchy waltz-tunes of *Gasparone* (1884) kept Millöcker well in the picture, and *Der Feldprediger*, which followed later the same year, found him on top form ; *Der Viceadmiral* (1886) was not quite so good. The poor health which dogged him for the rest of his life militated against the quality of his later operettas, though there were occasional recollections of his heyday in *Der arme Jonathan* (1890) and *Nordlicht* (1896).

Millöcker's polkas and marches were less trivial than Suppé's, but his waltzes could rarely compete with Strauss's. His craftsmanship was professionally sound within its limitations, though the choral writing was always perfunctory — even in the well worked-out second-act finale of *Der Feldprediger*. On the other hand, he

[1] The English translation reads :
' Her fair shoulder I kissed,
'Pon my word that was all.'

K

occasionally showed refreshing unconventionality in his use of harmonic and dynamic contrast, *e.g.* in *Gräfin Dubarry* —

— and there was a touch of genuine poetry in the little duet 'Endlich wieder eine Stunde' from *Der Feldprediger*. Like Strauss, he provided fertile ground for dabblers in pasticcio. Soon after his death Vienna heard *Die Damenschneiderin* (1901), *Jungheidelberg* (1904) and *Cousin Bobby* (1906). London had to wait until 1932 for *The Dubarry*, which fell into the same category since by no means all the music was lifted from the original *Gräfin*.

Among Strauss's other Viennese contemporaries were Kremser, Zeller, Roth and Ziehrer. EDUARD KREMSER (1838–1914) specialised in choral music ; *Eine Operette* (1874) was a new departure for him. Though he wrote three more between 1886 and 1891 he was dissatisfied with the standard of their presentation and returned forthwith to his choir-practice ; his only later essay in the genre was the one-act *Madame Ledig* (1900). KARL ZELLER (1842–1898) held an important post in the Ministry of Education and should perhaps be regarded as an 'amateur' composer. In 1876 he wrote a sentimental *komische Oper* — *Joconde* — which was followed by a handful of operettas in an eclectic style akin to Suppé's. In *Der Vogelhändler* (1891, a great popular success) there was a march-duet — 'Ich bin der Prodecan' — which was better than most of its kind, but *Der Obersteiger* (1894), taken as a whole, was more characteristic. *Der Marquis von Rivoli* (1884) and *Die Lieder des Mirza Schaffy* (1887), by LOUIS ROTH (1843–1901), were piecemeal affairs, foreshadowing a questionable tendency of later practitioners which will be referred to in due course. 'Das ist ja Maienwein' from *Der Nachtwandler* (1886) was also prophetic with its intrusive 'German sixth' ; here waltz-rhythm slipped from vivacity to languishment. Of all Roth's effusions *Die Urwienerin* (1887) alone caught the public fancy ; like Millöcker's *Verwünschene Schloss* it was written in dialect that was tiresome to an outsider — 'Kan Frack, kan Claque, Glâce san verpönt'. CARL ZIEHRER[1] (1843–1922) wrote twenty-two operettas of which *König Jerome* (1878) was the first and *Der Landstreicher* (1899) the best. (The 'Vorspiel' — not an overture but a short opening scene — was particularly accomplished.) His *Deutschmeister* (1888), *Tolles Mädel* (1908) and *Ball bei Hof* (1910) also achieved some success. Ziehrer had better taste than Roth ; his music was trivial but inoffensive.

JOSEPH HELLMERSBERGER (1855–1907) and ALFRED ZAMARA (1863– ?) collaborated in *Der bleiche Gast* (1890) and each wrote ten or a dozen operettas independently. *Der schöne Kurfürst* brought Hellmersberger a measure of popularity in 1886, but he had to wait until 1904 for *Das Veilchenmädel* and *Wien bei Nacht* to amplify it. He took Strauss as his model but had little initiative ; the waltz-song 'Alltäglich durchstreif' ich die Stadt' from *Der schöne Kurfürst*, for instance, was a watered-down version of *Frühlingsstimmen*. Zamara, though Viennese by birth, spent much of his life in Germany and only three of his operettas were produced in Vienna, namely *Die Königin von Aragon* (1883), *Der Sänger von Palermo* (1888) — both immature — and *Der Frauenjäger* (1908). The others, which belonged to Munich or Hamburg, were often artlessly reminiscent of Lortzing, but the opening chorus of *Der Doppelgänger* (1886) was rhythmically original — passages in 7/8 time contributed to the interest. On the other hand RUDOLF DELLINGER (1839–1901), who was born in the Sudetenland and conducted his own operettas in Dresden and Hamburg, always adhered to the Viennese tradition. *Don César* (1885) hovered on the verge of *komische Oper*, especially in the poetic 'Traumscene' (which showed skill in modulation), but *Lorraine* (1886), *Kapitän Fracassa* (1889) and *Jadwiga* (1901) were unquestionably operettas. They stressed the lyrical aspect and were somewhat lacking in vigour.

RICHARD HEUBERGER (1850–1914), though trained as an engineer, was a prominent figure in the musical life of Vienna from the mid-seventies onward. Not only did he distinguish himself,

---

[1] His full name was Carl Michael Ziehrer ; most historians drop the Michael, but Karl Westermeyer in *Die Operette im Wandel des Zeitgeistes* dropped the Carl.

like Kremser, as a choral conductor ; he was music critic of the *Wiener Tageblatt* from 1889 to 1896 and later succeeded Hanslick on the staff of the *Neue Freie Presse*. His comparatively early operetta *Das Abenteuer einer Neujahrsnacht* was given at Leipzig in 1886 ; he also wrote four ambitious *operas* and fancied himself as a ' serious ' composer. But he is remembered for *Der Opernball* (1898), the first of six later operettas. The overture — a classic — was a spirited piece of work ; the middle section incorporated two well-contrasted waltz-tunes — one syncopated, the other succulent. In the play itself both recurred too frequently ; the succulent one, after working overtime in the second-act finale, served as a basis for the third-act prelude and when the curtain rose was hummed in hangover by the hero (who obviously knew his *Fledermaus*). This scene was followed by a duet — ' Wenn bei einer Dame ' — which started with a vivacious passage in 2/4 time that was like a breath of fresh air in a hothouse ; but after two stanzas back came the sultry waltz-rhythm that was apparently almost an obsession. Heuberger's remaining operettas were failures. Anton Bauer, in his *150 Jahre Theater an der Wien* (1952), found them repetitive,[1] but *Ihre Excellenz* (1899) was at least provided with another admirable overture, and the subsequent flood of waltzes was held in check by a gavotte — a good one too, being in contemporary style and not mere pastiche. About the same time HEINRICH REINHARDT (1866–1922) had a great success — which he failed to repeat — with *Das süsse Mädel* (1901). It earned retrospective significance as the ' first Viennese musical comedy ', but in fact was a harmless, pleasant little affair, which hardly deserved such questionable notoriety.

The Hungarians ADOLF MÜLLER (1839–1901) and ALPHONS CZIBULKA (1842–1894) became Viennese by adoption ; each wrote eight or nine operettas. Müller, whose father too had been a composer but who had no connection with the Müller mentioned on page 110, could provide a pretty tune and once at least — in *Der Hofnarr* (1886) — demonstrated a flair for straightforward counterpoint : Ex. 98 might be compared with Ex. 58 (page 82) from Planquette's *Cloches de Corneville*. The best of his later operettas were *Lady Charlatan* (1894) and *Der Blondin von Namur* (1898).

---

[1] ' Sie sind bedeutungslos und erinnern in ihren Melodien an sein Meisterwerk.'

Ex.98 Moderato
(Noch etwas langsamer)

SOPRANOS
Das ist die Lie - be, ja, nur al - lein die Lie - be.

TENORS
Er ru - he, ras-te nicht, bis er sie wie-der fand, die sein-es Le-bens Licht für die sein Herz ent-brannt!

BASSES
Ja, der An - schlag ist ge-lung - en, un-ser Kö - nig ha - ben wir.

The most noteworthy feature of Czibulka's music, despite the fact that he was a military bandmaster, was sympathetic treatment of the human voice. Unfortunately he had little gift for melody — the popular *Stephanie-gavotte* was exceptional — and of his stage-works only *Pfingsten in Florenz* (1884) and *Der Glücksritter* (1887) had any success. The duet 'Ich kenn' seine Lage' from *Pfingsten* reached a fine dramatic climax in the approved manner of Italian opera, but as a rule Czibulka spoke in the accents of his native Hungary. It was that same proud corner of the Empire which produced Franz Lehár, who was the foremost exponent of operetta in his generation and demands pride of place in a separate chapter.

XV

THE STRAUSS LEGACY

THE output of FRANZ (FERENCZ) LEHÁR (1870–1948) was not quite so extensive as a full list of titles would suggest, for no composer has ever been more assiduous in using old material over again. His early opera *Kukuška*, produced in 1896, was revised in 1905 and re-christened *Tajana*. His first operetta *Wiener Frauen* (1902) [1] was staged at various towns in Germany as *Die lieben Frauen*, *Der Schlüssel am Paradies* and *Die Klavierstimmen*. *Der Göttergatte* (1904) underwent little change, other than one of sex, in *Die ideale Gattin* (1913) ; a further metamorphosis produced the slightly less bulky *Tangokönigin* (1921). *Das Fürstenkind* (1909) lived again as *Der Bergprinz* (1932). *Zigeunerliebe* (1910) unexpectedly arrived in new guise at Budapest in 1942 as *Garaboncias*. Nearly all the music of *Endlich allein* (which had its Viennese *première* on an inauspicious date, 2nd August 1914) was repeated in *Schön ist die Welt* (1930), where a fresh pair of librettists made use of the same plot. Finally, Lehár turned the ineffective *Gelbe Jacke* (1923) into the fabulous *Land des Lächelns* (*Land of Smiles*, 1931) by inserting a single additional song for Richard Tauber (see Ex. 99, page 140). After disentangling, we are left with one opera ; one musical play for children — *Peter und Paul reisen in Schlaraffenland* (1906) ; two burlesques — *Mitislaw der modern* (1907), *Rosenstock und Edelweiss* (1910) ; and, as nearly as I can calculate, twenty-five genuinely independent operettas.

Lehár was born in Hungary, but his father, who was of Czech origin, sent him to study music at the Prague Conservatorium. His principal subject was the violin, but he attracted the attention of Dvořák, who encouraged him to compose. At the outset of his professional career he served the German army at Elberfeld and the

---

[1] Strictly speaking it was his second, but I am ignoring the immature *Arabella, die Kubanerin*, which was neither performed nor published.

Austro-Hungarian army at Budapest (and elsewhere) in the capacity
of bandmaster. During this period he wrote some marches and
dance-music and also completed the full-length opera *Kukuška*.
This was an assured piece of work which showed considerable
technical resource where solo voices and orchestra were concerned ;
curious insensitivity in choral writing — a weakness Lehár never
overcame — was already evident. Slav influence was marked (a
trio in the first scene recalled Smetana's *Vltava*) and only the
Peasants' Dance at the beginning of Act III foreshadowed his future
lightheartedness. In 1896 Lehár was transferred to a regiment quar-
tered at Vienna, but six years later the financial rewards of his first
two operettas enabled him to sever the military connection. Thereafter he concentrated on composition, dividing most of his time
between Vienna and his country retreat at Bad-Ischl. Unlike Johann
Strauss, he was content with one wife ; they were a devoted couple.

Lehár's attitude to operetta was unequivocal. For him it was a
distinctive art-form to be taken seriously and not to be debased by
the incorporation of parody or burlesque. As a rule his librettists
— who included Victor Léon, Alfred Grünwald and Robert Bodan-
sky — avoided ingredients unlikely to find acceptance ; the set-
tings were often fantastically romantic, the characters over-glamorised
and the situations in which they found themselves far-fetched, but
nevertheless a plausible basis of reality was maintained. Furthermore,
the 'comic relief' was part of the whole conception ; it was not
extraneous nonsense dragged in for the sake of a cheap laugh.
Despite this admirable consistency of approach Lehár's operettas
varied greatly in artistic merit and — as events proved — in popular
appeal. *The Merry Widow* (1905) has outdistanced all competitors,
with *The Count of Luxembourg* (1909) lying second. *Der Rastel
Binder* (1902) — surprisingly — and *Eva* (1911) — deservedly —
have also done extremely well, but of the post-war works only *The
Land of Smiles* has had comparable success ; a success largely due to
the impact of one song, ideally suited to the expressive vocal
talent of the great artist who was its original interpreter. The first
Lehár operetta in which Tauber appeared was *Frasquita* (1922) where
he sang 'Hat ein' blaues Himmelbett'. 'Gern hab' ich die Frauen
geküsst' from *Paganini* (1925) and 'O Mädchen, mein Mädchen'

from *Friederika* (1928) were specially written for him. So was 'Dein ist mein ganzes Herz', *anglicé* 'You are my heart's delight', which made *The Land of Smiles* ; what a gift it was for a robust tenor![1]

Ex. 99   Allegro ma non troppo

Dein   ist mein schön-stes Lied, weil es al-lein   aus der Lieb-e er bl'üht. Sag mir noch

ein - mal mein ein- zig' Lieb',   o, sag' noch ein-mal nur: Ich hab' dich   Lieb'.

But Lehár's melodic inspiration flowed unsteadily and the stream was continually rising and falling ; although it never dried up completely it sometimes became the merest trickle.

Except in *Wiener Frauen* (which harked back to Suppé) and *Der Rastel Binder* (which had a Slovak setting), seductive Straussian waltz-rhythms were an even more dominating feature of Lehár's operettas than they had been of Strauss's own, but the polkas and mazurkas often reflected his Slav background. In the early days, perhaps, he did not use his technical equipment to best advantage ; the tonic/dominant 'tum-tum' grew inexpressibly tedious. Admittedly the uninhibited tunes of *The Merry Widow* had no need of what Nietzsche called 'titivation', but one feels that even 'Vilja' would have lost nothing and gained a lot if the treatment had been more imaginative. Now and again, however, a happy dramatic contrast was achieved through musical means. This passage from *The Count of Luxembourg* might have owed its origin to *Richard Strauss* (though nothing will tempt me to describe *Der Rosenkavalier* as an operetta).[2]

Ex. 100   Allegretto

Ich denk', wir las - sen die As - tro-no-mie   und schweb-en zur Er - de, Ba-ron.

---

[1] Tauber himself composed the operetta *Old Chelsea* (Princes, London, 1943).

[2] Technicians may compare the 'false relation' (at the word 'und') with the Offenbach example in Ex. 37 on page 51.

Bit by bit, Lehár found it increasingly expedient to bring his technique into play. For instance, he developed a trick of building up lyrical intensity by piling chromatic transitions over a tonic or dominant pedal, as in *Der Mann mit drei Frauen* (1908).[1]

Presently more questionable expositions of harmonic virtuosity intruded themselves. At the climax of the duet 'Sie sehen reizend aus' from *Eva* great blocks of 'augmented sixths' flew simultaneously up and down the gamut in chromatic scales, while in *Die ideale Gattin* a four-note *idée fixe* (*a*) found itself involved with Debussy.

Sometimes these colourful touches were so startling that the whole effect was incongruous, but in a very short duet from *Wo die Lerche singt* (1918) — 'Ein Hauch, wie von Blüten' — a flowing 9/8 melody was undisturbed when the accompaniment suddenly shifted from a $^6_4$ chord of B♭ major to the dominant seventh of E major in root position. A straightforward waltz caught the infection in *Der gelbe Jacke* (Ex. 103), and another Richard Strauss *tic* was absorbed in *Friederika* (Ex. 104).

[1] Despite its title, this work was *not* based on the life of Johan Strauss.

Ex.104
Allegro moderato

Lehár had a sure sense of orchestral values ; after 1910 or there-abouts he inclined to elaborate wood-wind decoration which was often charming and occasionally brilliant. But his touch was at times inappropriately heavy-handed. *Giuditta* (1934), for instance, demanded triple wood-wind, four horns, three trumpets, three trombones, tuba, a minimum of three executants in the percussion department, harp, celesta and a full body of string-players (in places the violins were divided into six parts).[1] It is impractical rather than immoral to use a steam-hammer to crack a nut, but in Lehár's case the disproportion was symptomatic of his injudicious attempts to disguise poverty of ideas with excess of ostentation. With the solitary exception of the one-act *Frühling* (1922), all his operettas from *Die blaue Mazur* (1920) onwards contained long stretches of continuous music, in which snippets of *Leitmotive* were expected to acquire significance through repetition in contrasted *tempi* and thereby heighten the tensity of a dramatic situation. This form of construc-tion, of which Louis Roth (see page 134) was an early exponent, was much favoured by the post-war Viennese school. But it is rarely suited to operetta, for if it is to be effective the tools must be those of a master-builder. Lehár managed quite well in *Frasquita* but the precedent was dangerous ; his other operettas of the twenties and thirties are remembered only for their purple patches, notably the 'Tauberlieder', and seem unlikely to survive intact. Some — though not all — of the earlier ones are also slipping into an ob-scurity which may or may not be deserved. If the beloved *Merry Widow* is to take a companion along the road to immortality it may be neither the uninspired *Zigeunerliebe*, nor the highly charged *Land of Smiles* nor yet, I fear, the sprightly and capricious *Eva*. The *Widow's* most probable escort looks likely to be that other old war-horse, *The Count of Luxembourg*.

[1] *Giuditta*, described as a 'musikalische Komödie', was perhaps a border-line *komische Oper*.

O S C A R S T R A U S (1870-1954) was born in Vienna, which remained his spiritual home until after the 1914-1918 war, but from 1900 till 1927 he lived in Berlin, where most of his operettas were written and many had their *premières*.[1] (Subsequently he settled in New York, but he returned to Austria just before his death.) In his youth he spent much time on ambitious projects — operas and such-like — which brought no tangible reward, and his first operetta, *Colombine*, did not come till 1904. His early essays in the genre were surprisingly French in character and incorporated burlesque *à la* Offenbach ; only *Hugdietrichs Brautfahrt* (1906) was well received. Straus soon changed his tactics, and in 1907 the romantic and characteristically Viennese *Waltz Dream* (libretto by Rudolf Bernauer and Leopold Jacobson) was deservedly a big success. *The Chocolate Soldier* (1908, Felix Dormann and Jacobson) was based on *Arms and the Man* ; therein lay one explanation of its great popularity everywhere in Britain except *chez* George Bernard Shaw. These two operettas were as good as any of Lehár's, and *Das Tal der Liebe* (1909), if it had had a better libretto, might have reached the same level. (The overture was splendid.) Presently, however, Straus's fame went to his head and his artistic standards suffered a corresponding decline. Of the thirty 'operettas' which he produced from 1911 onwards not one was comparable with his *chefs d'œuvre* ; some of them were very trivial indeed, even if judged, as they must be, as 'musical comedies'. For the moment I shall charitably pretend that he gave up composition in 1910 and endeavour to assess his quality on that imaginable hypothesis.

The first thing that strikes one is that in certain respects he was ahead of his time. He brought to a fine art — so far as operetta was concerned — the type of continuity which Roth had essayed (fruitlessly) twenty years before, and which Lehár did not adopt as a habit until ten years later (with only a small measure of success). The simple *Leitmotive* of *A Waltz Dream* and *Das Tal der Liebe* were woven inconspicuously into a tapestry which remained commendably unpretentious. The same treatment would have been

---

[1] *The Little Friend* (1912) and *Love and Laughter* (1913), written to English libretti, were first played in London ; *Riquette* (1925) and *Mariotte* (1928, libretto by Sacha Guitry) in Paris.

less appropriate in *The Chocolate Soldier*, which included a larger proportion of dialogue than the other two, but nevertheless there were some subtle thematic evolutions. In Nadina's aria, beginning with the recitative 'Wie schön ist dieses Männerbild', the short verse-sections may perhaps have sprung from three separate impulses and they were sung in three slightly differing *tempi* ; yet they had a melodic similarity and a rhythmic identity which helped to endow the whole with unity — a unity which was shattered, however, by an incongruous waltz-refrain which is still the housewife's choice.

Straus preceded Lehár, too, in judicious use of harmonic contrasts. The trio 'Ach, was vernehm ich' from *A Waltz Dream* was scarcely more than an ingenuous curiosity ; the three stanzas — call them *x*, *y* and *z* — were presented in succession as follows : *x* in the key of Gb, *y* in Db, *z* in Ab ; then *x* in Ab, *y* in Eb, *z* in Bb ; to round things off, *y* and *z* in F. But the daring example of chromatically descending open consecutive fifths in the bolero from *Das Tal der Liebe* may well have inspired a passage in Lehár's *Zarewitch* (1927), where the process was reversed. Nor did Straus overdo waltz-rhythm ; like Lehár, he was addicted to mazurkas, though it was in quick 2/4 time that he was at his most nimble, *e. g.* in the sextet 'Ach, es ist doch ein schönes Vergnügen' and the quartet 'Wenn ein Mann ein Mädchen kompromittiert', both from *The Chocolate Soldier*. Once at least he emulated Johann Strauss's skill as a miniaturist — in 'Verloren ist mein junges Glück' from

Das Tal der Liebe. Finally one notes that he sometimes had the happy idea of combining two independent waltz-strains ; the potentialities are obvious, yet few other composers have realised them. (Lehár did so once, rather half-heartedly, in *Eva.*) Ex. 106 is taken from *A Waltz Dream* —

Ex.106 Walzertempo

Braus-end und kling - end zieht's durch den Raum, Herz-en be - zwing - end Walz - er-traum!

— and there was another good example in *Das Tal der Liebe* — 'Ach, ein Walzer heiss und süss'.

But Straus did *not* give up composition in 1910 ; on the contrary, popularity spurred him to ill-advised prolificacy. Though his *savoir-faire* was apparent here and there in *Die himmelblaue Zeit* (1914), *Niobe* (1917) and *Eine Ballnacht* (1918), it was soon afterwards lost to sight. *The Last Waltz* (1921) had one or two good songs, — among them an agreeably catchy 'production number' — but the success it enjoyed in Vienna and elsewhere must have been largely due to the fact that the title aroused association in the public mind with *A Waltz Dream*. Actually it belonged to a different world ; much of the music was old-fashioned and might almost have been written by Millöcker. *Teresina* (1925), *Eine Frau, die weiss, was sie will* (1931) and the rest relied on the 'Boston', the 'Slowfox', the 'Shimmy' and the 'Charleston'. Such things may have been all very well in their way ; they were no part of Viennese operetta. (*Eine Frau, etc.* was played in London as *Mother of Pearl*, with a new libretto by A. P. Herbert.)

EMMERICH KÁLMÁN (1882–1953) came from the Lake Balaton district of Hungary and most of his operettas were almost aggressively Magyar in character, even when the setting was inappropriate. Ex. 107 (page 146) is from *Die Csárdásfürstin* (*The Gipsy Princess*, 1915) — where it is only one of many equally stirring evocations—but it could just as easily belong to *Das Hollandweibchen* (*A Little Dutch Girl*, 1920), *Die Herzogin von Chicago* (1928) or *Das Veilchen von Montmartre* (*Paris in Spring*, 1930).

Ex.107 Tempo di marcia lente

Curiously enough the Magyar strain was not particularly noticeable in Kálmán's first operetta *Herbstmanöver* (1909), though it was originally written to a Hungarian libretto.[1] Thereafter, however, wild gipsy rhythms were exploited to the full, and when they ran riot in *Zigeunerprimas* (1912), *Gräfin Maritza* (1924) and *Die Zirkusprinzessin* (1926) audiences gladly surrendered to their magic. Although there were occasional excursions in more lyrical vein, perhaps only in *Das Hollandweibchen* — a very well-balanced work — did they fall naturally into place. Elsewhere the adoption of acquired Teutonic or Viennese manners was apt to make his music sound either affectedly pompous or languishingly sentimental. Hence the comparative lack of effectiveness of *Der kleine König* (1912), *Die Faschingsfee* (1917) and *Die Bajadere* (1921). However, from *Die Faschingsfee*, set in Munich's 'Latin Quarter', the characteristic three-bar preamble to the march-ensemble 'Ging ich in der Früh' must be quoted (Ex. 108). In these little interludes the harmony was often as evocative as the rhythm — see Ex. 109 from *Das Hollandweibchen*.

Ex.108 Allegro moderato

Clar. & Bassoon in 8ves.

Ex.109 Allegretto

---

[1] *Herbstmanöver* was played in London as *Autumn Manœuvres*, in New York as *The Gay Hussars*.

Kálmán never wrote a *Merry Widow*, but he was on the whole a more consistent composer than Lehár, and he too approached operetta from the standpoint of a serious musician. He chose his librettists carefully and was well served, first by Leo Stein and Béla Jenbach, afterwards by Julius Brammer and Alfred Grünwald ; he always insisted that the chorus should be an integral part of the plot. Furthermore, although his operettas of the twenties incorporated an occasional tango or fox-trot, he had a knack of imbuing them with Hungarian verve and never utterly succumbed to insidious contemporary influence. Nor did his compatriot BÉLA SZABADOS (1867–1936), who produced a dozen unassuming Magyar operettas of which *Four Kings* (1890) was the first, *Fair Ilonka* (1906) the most successful and *Bridal Warfare* (1923) the last. According to all reports they were very popular in Budapest, but they went no further afield.

If Lehár, Oscar Straus (by virtue of his pre-war work) and Kálmán are the only three twentieth-century exponents of Viennese operetta — or should it be called Austro-Hungarian operetta ? — who can be awarded first-class honours, LEO FALL (1873–1925) heads the list of those who must rest content with a 'second'. A native of Olomouc in Moravia, he wrote about twenty operettas, including several short one-act pieces. *Der fidele Bauer* (1907) established his reputation in Vienna, but elsewhere he is mainly remembered for *The Dollar Princess* (also 1907), *Die geschiedene Frau* (*The Girl in the Train*, 1908) and *Madame Pompadour* (1922). Others to cross frontiers were *Die schöne Risette* (1910), *Der liebe Augustin* (1911, played in Britain as *Princess Caprice*) and *Die Sirene* (1912). *The Eternal Waltz* (also 1912) was written to an English libretto.

Der fidele Bauer stands apart from the rest. It had a vigour suited to the subject and abounded in healthy songs with a rustic flavour — 'Ich bin nix wie a Bauer' (that dialect again !), 'Jeder trägt sein Pinkerl' and 'Ich kenn' wohl ein Dirndl'. In Fall's more sophisticated works the fluent charm of the melodies did not always save the music from lapsing into sugary sentimentality. Now and again a number would be lifted right out of the ordinary by graceful orchestral figuration—*e.g.* the duet 'Will meine Schülerin' from *The*

Dollar Princess (Ex. 110)—but there were many depressions due to the narrowness of the composer's harmonic outlook ; tonic pedals and drone basses were ubiquitous. Nevertheless Fall had one valuable attribute — a greater realisation than many of his fellows of the potentialities of the human voice as a medium for musico-dramatic expression. He gave his singers plenty of opportunity to make the most of his melodies and at the same time display their own talents to good advantage. This flair was of immense value in the concerted numbers. Ex. 111 is the conclusion of a quintet from *Die Sirene* ; the counterpoint will not stand academic analysis but is adequate for the purpose, and there is a praiseworthy attempt at characterisation. (The only essential feature of the orchestral accompaniment — here omitted — is a drone on the open fifth E-B, which persists throughout.) Fall often used this device of successive vocal entries in canon ; for instance, it added a touch of colour to one of his best waltzes — 'Küssen könnt' ich heute so heiss' from *Madame Pompadour*. In their construction most of his operettas adhered to the straightforward tradition of early Lehár. When he adopted the principle of the spasmodic *Leitmotiv* in *Der heilige Ambrosius* (1921) and *Die spanische Nachtigall* (1924) his technical deficiencies were all too apparent. The overture to *Die geschiedene Frau* — for Viennese operetta an almost unique specimen in sonata form — was an exceptional effort ; unfortunately it set no precedent.

Next in importance to Fall, though a long way behind, come the Hungarian GEORG JARNO (1868–1920), the Viennese ROBERT WINTERBERG (1884–1930) and the Bohemian OSKAR NEDBAL (1874–1930). Jarno's *Förster-Christl* (1907) coincided with Fall's *Fidele Bauer* ; it belonged to the same category and was nearly as popular. *Das Musikantenmädel* (1910) and *Die Marine-Gustl* (1912) also did well in Vienna, but his later works — including *Mein Annerl* and *Junger Sonnenschein* (both 1918) — were produced at Berlin. Except in *Der Förster-Christl* Jarno tried to emulate Lehár ; so too did Winterberg, whose three best operettas all appeared in 1911 — *Ihr Adjutant* at Vienna, *Die Dame in rot* (which had an English setting) at Berlin, *Madame Serafin* at Hamburg. In the trio 'Ich nehm' mir mein Lebtag kein Blatt vor den Mund' from *Ihr Adjutant* gavotte- and waltz-rhythm were effectively set side by side, and the

second-act finale of *Madame Serafin* was well worked up in the approved manner of his predecessors. Nedbal was a viola-player and later became conductor for the Czech Philharmonic Society at Prague, but for several years he lived in Vienna, where he produced five operettas. Of his *Polenblut* (1913) Otto Keller (*op. cit.* page 120 footnote) wrote : 'This is the most praiseworthy operetta I have heard for a long time'. Nedbal's taste was impeccable but he lacked a gift of melody ; apart from *Polenblut* only *Die Winzerbraut* (1916) had any success.

EDMUND EYSLER (1874–1949), Viennese born and bred, wrote operettas unceasingly. *Bruder Straubinger* (1903), which had a dull first act but improved as it went along, contained at least one tune that caught the public fancy — 'Küssen ist keine Sünd''. *Die Schützenliessen* (1905) — with the 'Mutterlied' and 'Süsse, süsse' — and *Künstlerblut* (1906) — with 'Kommt dann plötzlich' — consolidated his popularity ; *Der Frauenfresser* (1911) and *Der lachende Ehemann* (1912) augmented it. The cheerful old-fashioned style, often reminiscent of Suppé or even Lanner, was much appreciated by unsophisticated Austrian burghers who were apt to find Lehár's music decadent and Kálmán's alien. None the less, in Eysler's post-war works — *e.g. Das Land der Liebe* (1925) and *Das Strumpfband der Pompadour* (1930) — he followed the example of Oscar Straus and introduced jazz-rhythms. Not even a second political cataclysm deterred him from composing ; his one-act *Hochzeitspräludium* was played at Vienna in 1946 and his swan-song, appropriately entitled *Wiener Musik*, in 1947. Although many of his sixty-odd operettas and musical comedies had success abroad, especially in Italy,[1] he himself rarely left his birthplace. VICTOR HOLLÄNDER (1866–1940) was less prolific but more widely travelled and more versatile. Born in Silesia, he earned his living as conductor, pianist and music-teacher at Hamburg, Budapest and London in turn ; later he emigrated to the United States and he died in Hollywood. He occupied his spare time with composition and during a long career wrote about fifteen operettas in a straightforward manner akin to Eysler's. *Der rothe Kosak* (1901), *Der Sonnenvogel* (1904), *Die Prinzessin vom Nil* (1915) and several others

[1] *Die schöne Mama* had its *première* at Rome in 1921 as *Bella Mamina*.

enjoyed modest success. Holländer had a marked inclination to minor keys, and many of his ensembles were well constructed. More recently, some features of the Eysler tradition have been kept alive by the Swiss, PAUL BURKHARD (1911–   ) in a handful of agreeable trifles ranging from *Hopsa* (1935) to *Spiegel, das Kätschen* (1956). Best known is *Der schwarze Hecht* (1939), which is often revived in Switzerland and has also been played in Germany as *Feuerwerk* and at the Bristol Old Vic as *Oh! my papa!*

VICTOR JACOBI (1883–1921) was a native of Budapest, where his *Marriage Market* — written to a Hungarian libretto — had its first performance in 1913. Like *Sybil* (Vienna, 1919), it later did well in both London and New York. So did several operettas by his younger compatriot PAUL ABRAHAM (1892–   ); they included *Viktoria und ihr Hussar* (1930), a curious mixture of Kálmán, jazz and ingenuous *chinoiserie*.

With the unimportant exceptions of Holländer and Burkhard, the composers who have so far passed under review in this or the preceding chapter were all born within the confines of the old Austro-Hungarian Empire, but many of their operettas were also popular in Germany. Ironically enough three Germans, Lincke, Gilbert and Künneke (along with Oscar Straus), must bear a large share of responsibility for the eventual degeneration of Viennese operetta into musical comedy or revue. PAUL LINCKE (1866–1946), an out-and-out Berliner, started as a bassoonist and presently became a conductor. He wrote some twenty-five pieces for the stage, described as operettas, burlesques or revues, and though his style was basically Viennese he was prone to vulgarities which it might not be unfair to describe as Teutonic. He featured local colour and topicalities, as may be judged from such titles as *Eine lustige Spreewaldfahrt* (1897), *Berliner Luft* (1904) and *Berlin so siehste aus* (1908). (*Wenn die Bombe platzt* was probably funnier in 1906 than it would have been some forty years later.) Lincke is remembered for the attractive waltzes from *Venus auf Erden* (1897) and *Frau Luna* (1899), for the sprightly 'Norddeutscher Lloyd polka' from *Nakíris Hochzeit* (1902), and above all for the fetching 'Gluhwürmschen' ('Glow Worm') song from *Lysistrata* (also 1902). After *Pst! pst!* (1917) he devoted most of his time to a publishing business, but in 1940 he broke a long silence with a final operetta, *Ein Liebestraum*.

JEAN GILBERT (1879–1942, real name Max Winterfeld) called most of his concoctions operettas and they had certain Viennese characteristics, but only the early specimens — e.g. *Die keusche Susanne* (1912, anglicé *The Girl in the Taxi*) — could be considered plausible representatives of the genre. *The Lady of the Rose* (Daly's, London, 1921) incorporated a measure of continuity on Lehár lines, but the rest were trivial to the point of fatuity.[1] EDUARD KÜNNEKE (1885–1953) also slipped from early promise — the light opera *Robins Ende* (1909) — into a welter of jazz, repetition and cheap sentimentality. Only in the whimsical *Vetter aus Dingsda* (*The Cousin from Nowhere*, 1921) did he appear to any advantage. This had a pretty 'theme song', 'Ich bin nur ein armer Wander-gesell' (which in the English version became 'I'm only a strol-li-ing va-ga-a-bond'), and one or two of the vocal ensembles were charming, besides being accomplished in their workmanship.

It was left to two fertile purveyors of Weimar-Republic musical comedy — a morbid growth, which combined nostalgia with affected sophistication — to deal Viennese operetta its most crippling blow. In 1931 the Austrian ROBERT STOLZ (1886–   ) joined forces with the German RALPH BENATZKY (1887–1957) at the *White Horse Inn* (*Im weissen Rössl*), with its evocative background of the Weissensee and the Bavarian alps. One gladly concedes that its uninhibited *bonhomie* was infinitely preferable to the sultry introversion of Stolz's *Peppina* or the sham glitter of Benatzky's *Cocktail* (both 1930). Artistic unity might count for little (slapstick jostled 'romance'), the tunes might be trivial and the intellectual appeal negligible, but none could deny that the *décor* was sumptuous. In an age of frustration, unease and much living-near-the-bone, *Im weissen Rössl* was adjudged *kolossal*. The spectacular 'musical' had arrived ; genuine Viennese operetta was now a thing of the past.

---

[1] I was introduced to Gilbert at one of his British *premières*. Trying to be polite, I commented favourably on his orchestration, only to be met with the disconcert-ingly candid rejoinder that 'he was always too busy to attend to such details himself'!

XVI

THE SLAVS [1]

FROM 1620 (the battle of the White Mountain) until the emergence of an independent Czechoslovakia after the 1914–1918 war Bohemia and Moravia were politically, though not ethnographically, part of Austria. A tradition of native song and dance persisted in Bohemia's woods and fields, but for two centuries it played little part in urban culture. It was an unheard-of innovation when in 1823 Weigl's *Schweizerfamilie* (see page 110) was produced at Prague *in Czech*. The instigator was the composer-conductor František Škroup. He followed up with a *Singspiel* of his own contriving — *Dráteník* (1826) — which Rosa Newmarch in her *Music of Czechoslovakia* (1942) tactfully described as 'pleasantly uninspired'. Škroup's subsequent works — e.g. *The Marriage of Libuša* (1834) — showed that he had too cosmopolitan an outlook to be capable of fulfilling national aspirations, but nevertheless he had given the lead. That it was not promptly followed was due partly to lack of talent and partly to political dissuasion. Not till 1866 was Czech opera put on the map with Smetana's *Brandenburgers in Bohemia*, which had been written three years previously.

BEDŘICH SMETANA (1824–1884) did not take his next stage work very seriously, however : 'I composed it without ambition, straight off the reel, in a way that beat even Offenbach himself

---

[1] Perhaps I ought to identify passages from works reviewed in this chapter by quoting from the original texts in every case; but not many of my readers will be any more conversant with the Russian, Polish and Czech languages than I am myself. Very few Slav operettas have been translated into English ; the better-known ones, however, have often been played in German. To avoid threefold inconsistency, therefore, I shall disregard the rare English adaptations and compromise by using the accepted German version whenever there is one. But a few small doses of Slav philology will be unavoidable.

hollow.' In its original form *The Bartered Bride* (1866, libretto by Karel Sabina) was certainly a very unassuming affair, with only two short acts and eight detached musical numbers. For a revival in 1869 Smetana added the drinking-chorus 'Wie schäumst du in den Gläsern', the dance of the comedians, and Mařenka's aria 'Wie fremd und todt is alles umher'. Later the same year the whole was reconstructed in three acts, the furiant being inserted in Act I and the polka in Act II. Finally, for a production at St. Petersburg in 1870, dialogue was replaced by recitative. Whatever Smetana himself may have thought of it, *The Bartered Bride* remains his masterpiece.[1] Every bar is redolent of the Bohemian countryside, but the music has a universal appeal by reason of its spontaneity, tunefulness and well-balanced alternations between rustic humour and tender sentiment. Though the composer was an ardent national-ist, he was also a travelled and cultured musician, and he proved it in the superbly amusing trio 'Gekommen wär er mit mir so gerne' and the expressive sextet 'Noch ein Veilchen' no less than he did later in his symphonic cycle *My Country*.

Two Widows (1874, libretto by F. Züngl) was also in the first instance built on *Singspiel* or *opéra-bouffe* lines, but Smetana was furious when an indiscreet critic turned his own reference to Offen-bach into a boomerang. To make his intentions perfectly clear he wrote a new *durchkomponiert* version and rearranged two acts into three ; in this form *Two Widows* has survived. Though less imme-diately attractive than *The Bartered Bride*, it is lively and entertaining. A constructional weakness is the perfunctory treatment of the chorus, which makes only three conventional appearances — at the begin-ning of Act I and at the ends of Acts II and III ; it might just as well have been left out altogether. The overture, following Smetana's usual practice, is in sonata form and incorporates a *fugato*. There is also an excellent polka, and the music is spirited throughout ; a few bars from a patter-quartet — part of the second-act finale — will demonstrate its quality. (Is there not a foreshadowing here of the ensemble ' Quell'otre! quel tino! ' from Act I, Scene 2 of Verdi's *Falstaff*?)

---

[1] The English title is inapposite, for the heroine is neither a 'bride' nor 'bartered'. The French *Fiancée vendue* is a literal translation of the original.

All Smetana's stage-works were founded on national tradition, but except for *The Bartered Bride* and *Two Widows* the subjects were historical or romantic rather than humorous, and the touch was sometimes heavy-handed : *Dalibor* (1867) and *The Kiss* (1876) were not innocent of Wagner's influence. *The Secret* (1878) and *The Devil's Wall* (1882) were less pretentious and might almost rank as operettas. (In the latter there was a sparkling vocal ensemble which echoed Ex. 112 ; the time signature was 9/8 and once again the key was A major, one of Smetana's favourites.)

Smetana was the precursor of ANTONÍN DVOŘÁK (1841–1904), the only indisputably great composer since Mozart to distinguish himself in operetta (or its contemporary equivalent) as well as in choral works, symphonies, concertos and chamber music. His world-wide reputation owes little to his operas and operettas, which are not played often enough, even in his own country. Yet they are truly representative of his genius. With the modesty of greatness he was conscious of the public attitude — and slightly aggrieved by it. 'People see in me only a writer of symphonies,' he wrote, 'but for many years I have demonstrated my liking for dramatic composition.' And again : 'I do not write opera from a desire for glory, but because I consider it the most beneficial for the people'.[1] Altogether Dvořák wrote ten 'operas'. They were all conceived as continuous music, rather than as a succession of songs, ensembles and dances connected by recitative, but many of the short scenes were self-contained. With one exception — the unpublished *Alfred* (1870) — they were based on Slav history or legend, and four of

[1] Quoted by his biographer Otakar Šourek.

them were sufficiently light and fanciful to accord with our definition of operetta. Though not of equal merit, each deserves a paragraph to itself.

In 1871, at the age of twenty-nine, Dvořák invited Smetana's candid opinion on *King and Collier*; Smetana returned the score without comment, and the officials of the Czech Theatre in Prague were lukewarm in theirs. Whereupon, Dvořák, who never lacked persistence, set *King and Collier* all over again — not repeating a single phrase of the music; the new version had its *première* in 1874. (For many years it was believed that the manuscript of the original had been burnt, but it was re-discovered in 1929, and some devoted admirers arranged a performance for the edification of connoisseurs. Their enthusiasm was perhaps misguided; the libretto was poor enough anyway, and the pseudo-Wagnerian treatment of it utterly inappropriate.) The second *King and Collier* had a lively overture on classical lines, displaying to perfection that unconventional approach to key-relationship which was to be such a marked feature of the composer's later work. The tonic was F♯ minor, but the most memorable melody (one might call it the 'second subject') appeared in E major and C major (about as far away as anybody could get) before satisfactorily rounding things off in F♯ major. The opening chorus characteristically contrasted an *allegretto scherzando* in 3/4 with an *allegro vivo* in 2/4, and presently there was an attractive song largely in five-bar rhythm.

Ex.113 Andantino molto tranquillo

Later the interest died away somewhat, and the second act was perfunctory; here, perhaps, reaction against Wagnerian affectation went too far. But Act III brought its compensations. Jeník's song 'O jak touzím k to bé' and the penultimate ensemble led by the King — and helped on its way by 'imitative' interpolations from oboe and cello — showed Dvořák, if not at his best, then certainly in promising form.

So far as I know, no historian has stressed that *The Pigheaded Peasants* (written in 1874, produced 1881) was a one-act curtain-raiser, Dvořák's only essay in that form. Yet the fact has its importance ; the action is so swift and the music bubbles along so cheerfully from start to finish that one hardly has time to notice that now and again it lapses into something like triviality. As in Smetana's *Two Widows*, the chorus is a superfluity, being dragged in for the last scene alone. Whatever its shortcomings, however, *The Pigheaded Peasants*, considered as a whole, is a charming little work. The overture — again in sonata form, with the second subject in the sub-mediant this time — sets the pace, and Lenka's aria 'Wie ist denn mir' is a melodic gem.

The Peasant a Rogue (1878) is one of the best operettas ever written. Here Dvořák found a good libretto (by J. A. Veselý), and as for the music, Karl Hoffmeister, in his review of the composer's achievements, did well to claim that it combined the best features of *Figaro* and *The Bartered Bride*. With an *embarras de richesse* to choose from, I shall content myself with one quotation. (Notice the impact of the B♮ in the third bar.)

Ex.114 Allegro moderato

Reconciliation of melodic inspiration with harmonic initiative was also demonstrated in two splendid ensembles — 'Dort wo im trauten Schatten' and 'Aufgeputzt schön das Haar'. And if the quartet 'Lass dir doch' brought echoes of 'Gekommen wär er mit mir so gerne' from *The Bartered Bride* there was no harm in that ; it was merely symptomatic of Dvořák's indebtedness to his predecessor. Furthermore in *The Peasant a Rogue* there was greater assurance than hitherto in the musical build-up : *Leitmotive* were absorbed without disturbing either instinctive ebullience or acquired realisation that in opera and operetta the singers, rather than the orchestra, should hold pride of place.

These three works all belonged to Dvořák's thirties — the period of the Stabat Mater and the early symphony in F major which later became 'no. 3'. Not until he had completed a further vast quantity of symphonic music — and visited the New World — did he again turn his hand to operetta. There was no negro influence in *The Devil and Kate* (1899, libretto by Adolf Wenig) ; on the contrary, it depended even more than *The Peasant a Rogue* on native folk elements. Hell was neither Dante's inferno nor Offenbach's travesty ; as Sourek (page 155 footnote) pointed out, Dvořák's devils were just 'good fellows'. The overture, like that to *King and Collier*, was in F♯ minor, and unusual in being largely based on two tunes which did not recur in the operetta itself. The first was a quasi-folksong.

Ex.115 Allegro

(The other, a suave cantabile, was introduced in the 'relative' A major and recapitulated in its dominant, E major.) The first two acts of *The Devil and Kate* were well contrasted, the elaborate thematic evolutions being the product of Dvořák's full maturity. Act I, lyrical and lively by turns, played very fast ; Act II was more sombre in character and mostly in slow *tempi*. Act III was less interesting than the others, but the long monologue for the Queen ('Wie traurig rings-um'), with a cor anglais prominent in the background, was a sincere expression of feeling.

The Czech nation has never produced a *specialist* in operetta, though at one moment VILÉM BLODEK (1834–1874) looked a likely candidate. His *In a Well* (1867) rivalled the original *Bartered Bride* in contemporary popularity, but the composer died before completing *Zitek*, its projected successor. KAREL KOVAŘOVIC (1862–1920), who belonged to the next generation, wrote several youthful operettas — including *The Bridegrooms* (1884) and the one-act *Way through the Window* (1886) — but he is better remembered for his instrumental music and the serious 'national' opera *Psohlavci* (*The*

Dogs' Heads, 1898). Later still the introspective VITĚZSLAV NOVÁK (1870–1949) rather surprisingly gave birth to *The Imp of Zvikov* (1915) and *A Night at Karlstein* (1916). His contemptuous casting aside of such an old-fashioned convention as a key-signature had no significance ; these two operettas were patchy, but not atonal. *The Imp* had a prose libretto, set in satirical vein ; there were no detachable arias and continuity was preserved by the use of simple — often trivial — *Leitmotive*, which were subjected to repetition rather than development. *A Night at Karlstein* was more lyrical, and the third-act prelude stood out as a finely wrought entity.

Though KAREL WEIS (1862–1944) spent all his life in his native land and composed Czech operas, he chose German libretti for his two operettas — *Die Dorfsmusikanten* (1905) and *Der Revisor* (1907, after Gogol). They incorporated the customary native dance rhythms, but alien trends were also noticeable. Weis wrote pretty tunes, his handling of choral forces was expert, and his orchestration appropriately delicate ; the duet 'Welch reizend junger Mann' from *Der Revisor*, for instance, was enlivened by some charming instrumental decoration. (The first four bars of the melody were almost identical with Sullivan's 'When our gallant Norman foes' from *The Yeomen of the Guard*.) Less praise is due to JAROMÍR WEINBERGER (1896–   ), who in *Schwanda the Bagpiper* (1927), and elsewhere, crushed unassuming and typically Bohemian melodies under a heavy load of Teutonic erudition and vulgar pretension. Prophecy is a dangerous game, but surely *Schwanda's* success will prove to have been ephemeral. One is at least entitled to hope that it has established no precedent.

We must now cross the Carpathians to make the acquaintance of STANISŁAW MONIUSZKO (1819–1872). During the whole of the nineteenth century historic Poland was partitioned between Czarist Russia, Hohenzollern Prussia (later Hohenzollern Germany) and Habsburg Austria ; consequently topographical references, if they are not to be misleading, may well become involved. Moniuszko was born under the Russian flag in a province which had once been part of Poland and afterwards became the short-lived independent republic of Lithuania ; several of his early operettas were produced at Lemberg (now Lwów) in the Austrian sector, and he died at Warsaw, then a German outpost. The fact remains that he was a Pole and proud of it, doing all he could to revive the tradition of national opera which had been inaugurated by Joseph Elsner with *Leszek Bialy* (1809) and Karol Kurpiński with *The Palace of Lucifer* (1812). Moniuszko's greatest success was the 'tragic' opera *Halka* (1847), but as a rule he concentrated on comedy. Probably the output of his teens and early twenties was not taken very seriously (*The Bureaucrats* was dated 1834), but he had written ten operettas by the time he was thirty. All but three of them — *The New Preciosa* (1841), *The New Don Quixote* and *The Lottery* (both 1843) — were in one act. *Verbum nobile* (1860) and *The Haunted Manor* (1865) represented his maturity. The music was vigorous and healthy, often recalling the manner of Glinka, and there was nothing aggressively nationalistic about it. A *dumka* from *Verbum nobile* — 'Jak tu ująć żal na wodze' — was authentically Polish, but there was also plenty of internal evidence that Moniuszko had an awareness of French and German models. One did not need to be a Pole to appreciate the cosmopolitan *bonhomie* of *The Haunted Manor*.

Ex.116 Allegretto

The tradition of Polish operetta was maintained by the German-born ADOLF SONNENFELD (1837–1914) with *A Warsaw Milliner* (1878) and other comic pieces; later by WLADYSŁAW MILLER the younger (1862–1929) with a round half-dozen that included *The Almond King* (1890) and *Fern Flower* (1895).

Farther east operetta was adventitious, although several distinguished Russian composers made tentative essays. The privately performed *Mandarin's Son* (1859) by CÉSAR CUI (1835–1918) is said to have been 'quite in the style of Auber'. (One of the leading parts was sung by Modest Mussorgsky.) ALEXANDER BORODIN (1833–1887) incorporated parodies of Meyerbeer and Rossini in his *Valiant Knights* (1867), but much of the music was

spontaneous.[1] PAVEL BLARAMBERG (1841–1907) wrote two
'comic operas' — *The Mummers* (1881) and *Russalka Maiden* (1887)
— and NICOLAI LISSENKO (1842–1912), an ardent collector of
folksong from his native Ukraine, exploited its characteristics in
several branches of original composition, including half a dozen
operettas. Most of them were written for children, but *A Night in
May* (1882) was adult. Rimsky-Korsakov's more colourful setting
of the same Gogol story (1880) was in a different category ; like his
posthumous and immortal *Golden Cockerel* (1909) it belonged to a
world of extravagant fantasy. Under the Soviet régime Russian
composers adopted a different approach, and the youngsters — as
they then were — DMITRI SHOSTAKOVICH (1906–   ) and
MARIAN KOVAL (1907–   ) — introduced sophisticated satire to
their respective *Nose* and *Dipsomaniac* (both 1929).[2] A more favourable reception was accorded to a series of musical comedies initiated
in 1923 by CONSTANTIN LISTOV (1900–   ) with *The Queen
is Wrong* and *The Ice House*, while among the later productions of
SERGE PROKOFIEV (1891–1953) one notes *Betrothal in a Monastery*
(1941) — based on Sheridan's *Duenna* — which has been played in
the U.S.S.R. and elsewhere, though not yet outside the Iron Curtain.
A correspondent to *The Times* (23rd May 1961) referred to 'its
constantly engaging melody, its unremitting humour, its indiscriminate eclecticism of idiom'.

Turning now to the southern Slav states or provinces which
were later to form Yugoslavia, we find that DAVORIN JENKO
(1835–1914), a native of Slovenia, settled in Belgrade at the age of
twenty-seven and subsequently wrote several light pieces for the
stage, mostly based on Serbian folklore. Among them were *The
Fortune-teller* (1882) — a genuine operetta — and *Djido* (1892) —
more of a *Singspiel*. Jenko's contemporary Ivan Zajc, from Croatia,
wrote over fifty 'operas', many of which were evidently frivolous in

---

[1] M. D. Calvocoressi in *A Survey of Russian Music* (1944) recorded the discovery
of the manuscript in 1930 and a revival six years later.

[2] In a critico-biographical study of Shostakovich published in 1959 the author,
D. Rabinovich, devotes nearly three pages to a discussion of *The Nose*. After com-
menting on 'the deliberate cacophony and complete neglect of the natural melodious
element', he concludes that the composer 'used images borrowed from the past
to direct the spearpoint of his satire against the monstrosities of petty-bourgeois
philistinism.'

intent, but their style was Italian (Zajc had studied music in Milan) and they cannot be regarded as representative specimens. After the unification of the country in 1918, however, the Croat composers IVO TIJARDOVIĆ (1895–   ) and JAKOV GOTOVAC (1895–   ) each had great success in more characteristic ventures: notably the former with *Little Floramye* (1924) and the latter with *Ero the Joker* (1935).[1] Meanwhile MATIJA BRAVNIČAR (1897–   ), a Slovene, did nearly as well with his *Scandal in the Saint Florian valley* (1930). Today the most prolific exponent is IVO LHOTKA-KOLINSKI (1913–   ), son of Fran Lhotka who was of Czech origin and a pupil of Dvořák but for more than fifty years has been an important figure in the musical life of Zagreb. According to a Yugoslav commentator Lhotka-Kolinski in his latest offerings 'develops a happy vein of melodic recitative accompanied by a chamber orchestra and enlivened by satire that approaches the grotesque'.[2]   One therefore suspects that *The Journey* (1957) and *The Button* (1958) may owe more to Shostakovich in his youth (*The Nose*) than to Smetana in his maturity (*Two Widows*), but at least it is good to know that a semblance of Slav operetta is still kept alive.

[1] The Zagreb Opera brought *Ero the Joker* to London in 1955.

[2] Mrs. Djurić-Klajn, in a contribution to *Die Musik in Geschichte und Gegenwart*, edited by Friedrich Blume and still in process of publication, volume by volume, at Basle.

XVII

ITALY AND SPAIN

FOR over three hundred and fifty years Italy has been the land of opera, and from the start the Italians have recognised two separate varieties — the serious and the comic. Jacopo Peri's *Dafne* (1597), usually accounted the first-ever opera, was '*seria*' ; Orazio Vecchi's *Amfiparnaso* (possibly written in the same year) was rated by Burney as '*opera buffa*'.[1] For two and a half centuries *opera seria* and *opera buffa* flourished side by side, and most exponents of classic 'Italian opera' distinguished themselves in both categories ; the differentiation was never so much one of style as of character. Their formal construction — separate arias connected by *recitativo secco* with an occasional chorus thrown in for good measure — remained unchanged until about the beginning of the eighteenth century, when Alessandro Scarlatti, Leonardo Vinci and Leonardo Leo brought to *opera buffa* the added interest of the 'concerted finale', usually a succession of vocal ensembles building up to a climax. It was not until later that the same convention was adopted in *opera seria*, where for long 'it was regarded as gross impropriety for one personage to interrupt another'.[2]

When operas were too short to occupy a whole evening, audiences were given a 'natural break' by the interpolation of self-contained *intermezzi*, usually in one or two scenes. They were well described in Wright's *Travels in Italy* (1730).

> The *intermezzi*, or intermediate performances, which they have at some of their smaller theatres between the acts, are very comical in their way, which is somewhat low, not much unlike

[1] Charles Burney, *General History of Music* (1789). Some authorities date *L'Amfiparnaso* as early as 1594.

[2] Edward J. Dent, *Alessandro Scarlatti, his life and works* (1905).

the farces we sometimes see on our stage. They laugh, scold, imitate other sounds, as the cracking of a whip, the rumbling of chariot wheels, and all to Music. These *intermezzi* are in *recitativo* and song, like the operas. But such entertainments, similar in manner but different in subject, seem to interrupt the unity of the piece itself.

Soon afterwards the Italians themselves came round to Wright's way of thinking, and from 1740 or thereabouts *intermezzi* were dispensed with. In 1752, however, Eustachio Bambini and his company took with them to Paris a handful of the best-known specimens, including Pergolesi's *Serva padrona* (written in 1733) ; the impact on subsequent developments in France has been recorded in Chapter II. In Italy native composers like Baldassare Galuppi, Nicola Piccinni, Giovanni Paisiello, Domenico Cimarosa and Antonio Salieri continued to cultivate *opera buffa* in a manner which reflected the spirit of their age, but the genre was brought to a fine art by a foreigner — W. A. Mozart (see pages 109-10). Gioacchino Rossini and Gaetano Donizetti carried the tradition into the nineteenth century with such masterworks as *The Barber of Seville* (1816) and *Don Pasquale* (1843).

From the death of Donizetti in 1848 until the emergence of Puccini in the mid-nineties, Italian stage-music was dominated by the operas of Giuseppe Verdi. *Opera buffa* wilted ; as for operetta, while it was already blooming in France and beginning to flower in Vienna, the seed sown by FEDERICO RICCI (1809–1877) with *Il marito e l'amante* (Venice, 1852) never took root in Italy.[1] Federico's nephew, LUIGI RICCI the younger (1852–1906), is credited with *Un curioso accidente* (1871), *Per un cappello* (1884) and *Il frutto proibito* (1888), but his lead was never followed. One is driven back to Verdi, but though any single scene from *Falstaff* (1893) might qualify as a self-contained operetta *par excellence*, the scale of the whole conception precludes it from being accommodated to our terms of reference. Of the few composers who ventured to adopt the same approach on a smaller scale none was completely successful,

---

[1] Ricci's *Marito*, as *Une Fête à Venise*, reappeared twenty years later in Paris, along with his *Folie en Rome* (1869) and *Docteur Rose* (1872) which were both given at the Bouffes-Parisiens. And see page 161 for a reference to the Croat composer Ivan Zajc.

JOHANN STRAUSS the younger (1825–1899)

FRANZ LEHÁR (1870–1948)

though a word of praise is due to ATTILIO PARELLI (1874–1944), who in the one-act *Dispettosi amanti* (first played at Philadelphia in 1912 as *A Lover's Quarrel*) applied the *Falstaff* treatment to embryos both tuneful and singable. Here and there the derivation was all too obvious ; Donna Angelica's 'Il mio consiglio segue', for instance, was a variation on Ford's 'C' è Windsor una dama'. On the other hand, a fragment of melody assigned to Florindo (the tenor) —

Dol-ce Ro-sau-ra, di-let-ta spo-sa, va-ga qual te-ne-ro boc-ciol di ro-sa

— led to an ensemble which was developed along Verdi lines but whose impulse was unquestionably spontaneous.

ERMANNO WOLF-FERRARI (1876–1948) made a brave attempt to bring *opera buffa* up to date. In his operettas (let us call them that) the story was carried on by means of 'accompanied' rather than *secco* recitative, and at times the composer was apt to affect a comparatively modern idiom, but they captured the authentic eighteenth-century atmosphere. They were given unity by the repetition of snatches of *Leitmotiv* which, incidentally, sometimes had a Teutonic rather than an Italian ring about them.[1] Here are two 'snatches' ; the first is from *Le donne curiose* (1903, after Goldoni), the second from *L' amore medico* (1913, after Molière).

O, — la sign-or-a Ele-o - nor- a!

---

[1] Wolf-Ferrari's father was German by birth, and several of his operettas had their *premières* at Munich, where he had previously been a pupil of Joseph Rheinberger.

M

Apart from the overture to the one-act *Segreto di Susanna* (1909) and two attractive orchestral interludes from the otherwise rather repellent 'tragic' opera *The Jewels of the Madonna* (1911), Wolf-Ferrari is best-known in this country by his *Quattro rusteghi* (1906, libretto by G. Pizzolati after Goldoni), anglicé *School for Fathers*. Here only a quartet where the tenor's *cantabile sostenuto* 'Vago sembiante amabile' prompts the others to *staccato* interjections shows him on top form ; thereafter the catchy little melody that forms the basis of a popular entr'acte recurs with inartistic frequency. Though Wolf-Ferrari had a gift for quaint expression and a sure sense of the stage — both of which attributes he exploited to full advantage — there is in much of his music something faintly distasteful, as there might be in a glass of Asti spumante from a bottle opened several hours previously. FELICE LATTUADA (1882–   ), adopted his methods in the one-act *Preziose ridicole* (1929), which was enlivened by a fugal overture and several amusing ensembles.

Gianotto Bastianelli, biographer of PIETRO MASCAGNI (1863–1945), made no mention of *Si* (1919) and did not even include it in what purported to be a comprehensive list of compositions. *Si,* which failed utterly, was an ambitious operetta in three acts, incorporating waltzes and mazurkas *à la* Lehár. The full-blooded 'seduction duet' was typical Mascagni, and there were several crudely vigorous expositions in the manner of Alfio's song from *Cavalleria rusticana*. *La Rondine* (1917) by GIACOMO PUCCINI (1858–1924) was a hyper-sentimental operetta, redeemed only by a scene in the second act which momentarily introduced a quite uncharacteristic waltz-tune. Played on a full orchestra the effect was startling.

Ex.120   Tempo di Valzer col massimo slancio (♩.=58)

It is a pleasure to turn next to what was perhaps Puccini's finest work — the one-act *Gianni Schicchi* (1918, libretto by G. Forzano, a long way after Dante). Many admirers were surprised by the harmonic dissonances (they hadn't yet heard *Turandot*), but they were rewarded with 'O mio babbino caro' and 'Addio, speranza bella'. In this comic masterpiece the hand of genius was apparent on almost every page ; never more so, perhaps, than in the magnificent ensemble beginning at figure 60 with the words 'Ecco la cappellina', where melodic inspiration was coupled with a superb sense of humour and backed by an astonishing display of technical resource.

Gianni Schicchi has influenced several younger composers, among them FRANCESCO MALIPIERO (1882–   ) and CARLO MENOTTI (1911–   ). In the former's 'three Goldoni comedies' — *La bottega de caffè, Sior Todero Brontolon* and *Le baruffe chiozzotte* (all written about 1920 and produced in 1926) — his customary austerity was tempered by a Puccini-like fluency in the vocal writing, and the entry of the Chief of Police in Menotti's clever *Amelia al ballo* (1937, his own libretto) would have come as no shock (musically, that is) to the sorrowing relatives of Buoso Donati. *Amelia*, in parts, was overloaded with detail, but there were some unassuming passages — for instance, the trio 'Chi può, saper' for the heroine, the husband and 'the lover'. It was the last work that Menotti wrote to an Italian libretto, and like Parelli's *Dispettosi amanti* it was translated into English for a first performance at Philadelphia. Another equally amusing one-act operetta, *The Telephone*, was produced in 1947 at the Metropolitan Opera House, New York, as a curtain-raiser to his stark opera *The Medium*. (Menotti, while retaining his nationality, now lives in the U.S.A.) Finally, an Italian composer of lesser repute : IGINIO RANDEGGER (1880–1918), nephew of the singing-teacher Alberto Randegger. During the last few years of his life he wrote half a dozen trifling operettas, of which *Il ragno azzurro* (Milan, 1916) and the posthumous *Sua eccelenza Belzebù* (Rome, 1919) enjoyed some local popularity.

Clearly, Italian influence on the development of operetta was indirect. The intrinsic merits of *Le donne curiose* and even of *Gianni Schicchi* are of less significance than the fact that French *opéra bouffe* derived ultimately from the *intermezzo*, and that, thanks to

Suppé the Viennese school, in its early days at least, was imbued with the spirit of *opera buffa*. Furthermore, it was an Italian who wrote the first *Spanish* operetta, and the chain of circumstances which led to this curious eventuality must be briefly recounted. The primary instigator of stage music in Spain was the dramatist Pedro Calderón de la Barca, who in 1657 produced *El Golfo de las Sirenas*, the first *zarzuela*, *i.e.* a play interspersed with songs and dances.[1] Though the music of the early *zarzuelas* was more often traditional than original, several were 'composed' by Juan Hidalgo, José Marin and Sebastián Durón in the late seventeenth century, by José de Nebra, Rodríguez de Hita and others during the first half of the eighteenth. From about 1760 onwards, however, Italian opera became increasingly popular in the peninsular, and *zarzuela* soon vanished from the scene. As compensation there sprang up the *tonadilla* or singing interlude, Spanish equivalent of the *intermezzo*; its foremost exponents were Jacinto Valledor, Blas de Laserna and Manuel García.[2] But when Spain was rent by war and revolution Italian domination was consolidated, and by about 1815 the *tonadilla* had followed the old *zarzuela* into oblivion. In the mid-thirties the poet Manuel Bretón de los Horreros prompted a national renaissance, but ironically — like Jean Monnet in Paris eighty years before (see pages 7-8) — he was driven by lack of native talent to choose as collaborator a young Italian immigrant. This was BASILIO BASILI (1820–?), whose father was director of the Milan Conservatorio; a cosmopolitan, as Duni had been, he exploited to the full the song and dance rhythms of his adopted country in *El novio y el concierto* (1839), *El ventorillo de Crespi* (1841) and *Los solitaros* (1843). Their success was not stupendous, but it was sufficient to augur a promising future for Spanish operetta.

For *El novio* Bretón de los Horreros revived the designation *zarzuela* which had been in disuse for seventy years. Although the historian Soriana Fuertes (who later became director of the Teatro del Liceo at Barcelona) described several similar pieces for which

---

[1] The origin of the term was fortuitous; anyone interested should read Chapter VI in Gilbert Chase's *Music of Spain* (1941).

[2] García's son was a celebrated teacher of singing in Paris and afterwards in London, where he died in 1906 at the age of one-hundred-and-one.

he arranged the music in 1844 and 1845 as *tonadillas*, '*zarzuela*' proved more acceptable, and Madrid granted the genre permanent status when its new Teatro de la Zarzuela was opened in 1857. The nineteenth-century *zarzuela*, at its best, was a colourful affair, introducing the villainous bandits, glamorous bull-fighters, starving beggars, well-padded prelates and other picaresque oddities that have always been part of the Iberian scene. In formal construction it resembled French operetta and might be in one, two, three or even four acts ; but in character there were several points of divergence. For one thing *zarzuela* was not necessarily light-hearted ; it ranged from the frivolity of burlesque to the intensity of tragedy. There was also a tendency to rely on traditional airs and dances ; only an expert on Spanish folk-music could determine the precise extent in any particular instance. Another distinctive feature was the loose manner of presentation : the audience was expected to join in the fun, not merely by singing the choruses but by indulging in cross-talk with the actors and actresses.

In mid-century the foremost practitioners were Hernando, Gaztambide, Oudrid, Barbieri, Inzenga and Arrieta. RAFAEL HERNANDO (1822– ?) started operations in 1848 with *Colegiates y soldados*, but the crucial year was 1849, when JOAQUÍN GAZTAMBIDE (1822–1870) established himself with the 'cómica ópera' *La mensajera*, CRISTÓBAL OUDRID (1829–1877) with *La Paga de navidad*, and Hernando had another success with *El duende*. FRANCISCO BARBIERI (1823–1894) did not lag far behind with his *Gloria y peluca* (1850) nor JOSÉ INZENGA (1828–1891) with *El campanento* (1851).[1] Neither Hernando nor Inzenga realised their early promise : Hernando soon faded out of the picture and Inzenga's name is now connected solely with his 'Ecos de España' (a collection of folksongs published in 1874). Gaztambide was a more important figure. His first few attempts were immature, but the concerted numbers of *El valle de Andorra* (1852) showed sound musicianship and *El estreña de una artista* (also 1852) was for many years a great

---

[1] A very detailed account of this phase was incorporated by Emilio Cotarelo in his unfinished *Ensayo histórico sobre la zarzuela*, serialised from 1932 to 1936 in the quarterly *Boletín de la Academia Española* which ceased publication shortly after the outbreak of the Spanish civil war.

favourite. He put some of his best work into *Catalina* (1855), *Los Magyares* (1857) and the one-act *Una vieja* (1860). Notice the rhythmic inflections in this melody from *Catalina*.

Ex.121 Allegretto grazioso

A   la can-ti - ne-ra ve nid   y com - prad, el   ri-co a guar-dien te y el dul__ ce   pa-nal.

The specialist Oudrid was extremely prolific; he wrote over a hundred *zarzuelas* but was essentially a dealer in triviality and acquired no lasting reputation. Barbieri, by contrast, was an erudite musicologist. He never fulfilled his great ambition which was to write a Spanish *opera*, but to operetta he brought a measure of scholarly distinction. His *Jugar con fuego* (1851), *Mis dos mujeres* (1855), *Pan y toros* (1864) and *El barberillo de Lavapies* (1874) rank as classics.

So long as a *zarzuela* contained a sufficient proportion of segui-dillas, boleros, jotas and so on, stylistic individuality counted for little, and it was by no means unusual for two or more composers to co-operate. For instance, Hernando, Gaztambide and Inzenga all contributed to *El segreto de la reina* (1852), and in *Don Simplicio* (1853) they were joined by Barbieri. One who stood apart from the rest was EMILIO ARRIETA (1823–1894, Barbieri's dates exactly). The soaring 9/8 melodies and 'concerted finales' of *El dominó azul* (1853) and *Marina* (1855) betrayed his Italian upbringing (he had been educated at Milan) and were viewed with suspicion by his enthusiastically nationalistic colleagues.[1] Yet much of *La guerra e la muerte* (also 1855) was typically Spanish, as were occasional items in his other operettas — *e.g.* the bolero 'La niña de mis ojos' from *De tal Pola, tal Astilla* (1864).

Barbieri's operatic aspirations were eventually brought to fruition by his staunch supporter TOMÁS BRETÓN (1850–1923), to whom Arrieta's Italianisms were anathema. Bretón came closer than any-one else to the ideal of Spanish opera in *Los amantes de Teruel* (Madrid, 1889) and *Garin* (Barcelona, 1892), and in his *zarzuelas* he applied

---

[1] Not that even Barbieri deliberately shunned 'concerted finales': there was a very well constructed one in *El tributo de las cien doncellas* (1872); but it was based on typically Spanish embryos.

considerable technical resource to the evolution of hereditary conceptions. *La verbena de la paloma* (1894) and *El caballo del señorito* (1902) still hold the stage. In one number from *La verbena* there were several characteristic — and charming — examples of 3/4–6/8 ambiguity.

Bretón's contemporaries FERNÁNDEZ CABALLERO (1835–1906) and RUPERTO CHAPÍ (1851–1909) also turned their hands to opera, but did better with their *zarzuelas*, which were not entirely free, however, from French and Italian influence. Caballero is remembered for *El dúo de la Africana* (1893) and *Gigantes y cabezudos* (1898) ; Chapí for *La tempestad* (1882), *La bruja* (1887), *La revoltosa* (1897) and *El puñao de rosas* (1902). JOAQUÍN VALVERDE the elder (1846–1910) and FREDERICO CHUECHA (1846–1908) were second-rate purveyors who achieved little on their own account but had a big popular success when they collaborated in *La gran vía* (1886). So did FERNÁNDEZ ARBÓS (1863–1939), better known as a conductor, with *El centro de la tierra* (1895).

Although Isaac Albéniz and Manuel de Falla each wrote a *zarzuela* or two almost as a matter of course, credit for the maintenance of the Gaztambide-Barbieri-Bretón tradition in the first three decades of the twentieth century must go to AMADEO VIVES (1871–1932), a versatile musician of considerable experience. He was Catalonian by birth and learnt his trade at Barcelona. Carl van Vechten, whose *Music of Spain* (1918) was enlivened throughout by a dry wit, graphically described his subsequent wanderings, which brought him (temporarily) to the lowest depths of degradation.

He became an acolyte in a church and his first compositions were written under the influence of the organ music which he heard. From Barcelona he strayed to Malaga where he became a conductor, and from there he went to Madrid where he played in churches and cafés indifferently, it would seem. At times he was even reduced to peddling in the streets and writing musical criticism.

Time's whirligig eventually landed Vives as professor of composition at the Madrid Conservatorio ; in his spare time he wrote a few operas as well as about sixty *zarzuelas*, of which *Don Lucas del Cigarral* (1899), *Bohemios* (1920) and *Doña Francisquita* (1923) were the most successful. They were all characteristically Spanish, but Vives was less hidebound than many of his contemporaries in the same field : he realised the importance of adequate orchestral support for his melodies. Here is an example from *La villana* (1927).

Among Vives' more serious-minded colleagues one should mention JESÚS GURIDI (1886–   ) — of Basque descent — for the sake of *El caserío* (1926) ; JOSÉ SERRANO (1873–   ), sometime director of the Teatro de la Zarzuela in Madrid where he produced *La*

canción del olvido in 1917 ; RAOUL LAPARRA (1876–1943) who was born at Bordeaux but bestrode the Pyrenees in 1929 with *Las Toreras*. Meanwhile the honoured name of *zarzuela* was being dragged in the dust by JOAQUÍN VALVERDE the younger (1875–1918) and others who shall be nameless ; their multifarious effusions were 'an indiscriminate mixture of musical ingredients ranging from the bubbling froth of Viennese operetta to the synthetic hooch of tin-pan alley'.[1]

Although the infectious rhythms of the bolero, the habanera, the tango and the rest have fascinated composers all over the world and have often been incorporated in their music, it would be unrealistic to claim that Spanish operetta, as such, has ever acquired more than local significance. The *zarzuela*, like the bull-fight, is a revealing manifestation of the national quintessence — and remains indigenous.

[1] Gilbert Chase, *op. cit.* page 168 footnote.

§

BRITISH OPERETTA

XVIII

ORIGINS; EARLY EXPONENTS

HISTORIANS of music, even those who are true-blue Britons, find it hard to dilate with enthusiasm on the creative aspects of the art in this country during the two centuries or so which followed the death of Purcell in 1695. The true-blues are justified in laying claim to Handel, who settled here permanently in 1712 at the age of twenty-seven, but thereafter their task is ungrateful. A favourite early landmark, *The Beggar's Opera*, will however serve as a convenient take-off point for that corner of the field — its most fertile corner, as it happens — which it is our present purpose to explore.

The original *Beggar's Opera* (1728) was the classic example of a type of entertainment almost as popular in London — though not by then so well-established — as the contemporary fairground *vaudeville* in Paris (see page 7). Under the first two Georges such 'ballad-operas' comprised merely a string of topical songs written by anybody and traditional songs written by nobody. They were as loosely constructed as their French counterparts — and nearly as irreverent. They ridiculed the brawlings of Italian opera-singers rather than opera itself, and satirised the foibles and follies of the age with biting intensity by equating the courts of royalty with the cells of Newgate.[1] We have already seen how in France reputable impresarios like Monnet and Favart discarded the licentiousness associated with *vaudeville*, brought new life to the old *comédie à ariettes*, and with the aid of accomplished musicians introduced a measure of artistic unity to their unassuming but often charming

---

[1] The music was of less consequence than the words, which were often extremely witty. Alexander Pope played an occasional hand ; the 'regulars' were Charles Coffey, Colley Cibber and (most important of all) John Gay, who wrote *The Beggar's Opera* at the instigation of Jonathan Swift.

productions. So in Britain did ballad-opera graduate to respect-
ability under the guidance of the librettist Isaac Bickerstaffe and the
composer Thomas Arne. Unlike *The Beggar's Opera* and its fellows,
Thomas and Sally (1760) and *Love in a Village* (1762) were innocent
of scurrility; here satire was tamed to gentle raillery. Although
Arne sometimes permitted interpolations from extraneous sources,
they were carefully chosen to fit the bulk of the music, which
was his own. These little pieces were therefore not ballad-operas
in the strictest sense of the term, but they were so closely related
that it would be pedantic not to conform with the acceptable
convention which accords them the same designation. In character
they displayed a rather self-conscious artificiality, 'like actresses
masquerading prettily as milkmaids dabbling in the dew' (to borrow
an apt simile from Eric Blom [1]), but much of their music can still
be listened to with pleasure.

The parallel with France holds good thus far — but not much
further. The *divertissements* of Philidor, Grétry and Dalayrac led
to the *opéras comiques* of Méhul and Boïeldieu, which were direct
progenitors not only of *Le Postillon de Longjumeau, Orphée aux enfers*
and *Les Cloches de Corneville* but of *Fra Diavolo, Carmen* and *Manon*.
In Britain, on the other hand, there was no corresponding process
of evolution. Arne's successors improved on *Thomas and Sally*, but
they were lonely, unpretentious standard-bearers until they fell out
of the ranks in the early eighteen-hundreds, leaving a relatively scant
legacy for the future. Among them were Thomas Linley (best
remembered for *The Duenna*), Samuel Arnold (*The Maid of the
Mill*), William Shield (*The Flitch of Bacon*) and Stephen Storace
(*No Song, no Supper*). The most prolific and by far the most
versatile was Charles Dibdin — author, actor, theatrical manager,
singer, pianist, composer. He had a stronger gift of natural melody
than the others (we all remember 'Tom Bowling') and he raised
ballad-opera to its highest plane with *Lionel and Clarissa* (1768),
The Waterman (1774) and *The Quaker* (1775). But perhaps because
he had an ungracious personality and a quarrelsome temperament
his subsequent career was chequered and he eventually fell on evil
days; *The Round Robin* (1811) — his final chirrup — fell on deaf ears.

[1] *Music in England* (1942).

So did the last few works of Shield, who survived until 1826, for by then ballad-opera had withered and died : in a garden where no roses had bloomed for several generations even a modest violet could no longer draw sustenance from the barren soil.

Elsewhere the first half of the new century was an era of musical giants. At its outset Haydn in ripe old age was still astonishing the world with his perennial youthfulness, Cherubini was in full flower, Beethoven had just written his first symphony and eight more were in the offing. Fifty years later Weber, Schubert, Donizetti, Bellini, Mendelssohn and Chopin (a meteoric galaxy, since only one out of the six reached his forties) had come, conquered and gone ; Rossini was comfortably installed in retirement as an elder statesman ; Glinka, Berlioz, Schumann and Liszt had attained maturity ; Wagner and Verdi were already forces to be reckoned with. To this golden age the British contribution was negligible, and many of the native-born composers whose names *are* remembered spent much of their time abroad ; some became naturalised citizens of foreign countries. S. S. Wesley — who plays no part in our story — and Henry Bishop were praiseworthy exceptions. The latter, therefore, should not be upbraided for 'Home, sweet home', which may have been a gentle lark at the expense of the wandering boys. His 'bel canto' operas, along with those of the Irish roamers Michael Balfe and W. V. Wallace, were pale copies of their Italian models but they were tuneful enough to be popular, and they bridged the chronological gulf between ballad-opera and operetta without having much in common with either. Balfe was the most gifted of the group. He and Sterndale Bennett (who ploughed his own Mendelssohnian furrow) may be considered — *faute de mieux* — as the foremost British composers of their day.

The comparatively obscure JOHN HULLAH (1812–1884) creeps into this chapter unostentatiously, but under his own steam. He was born at Worcester, educated at the Royal Academy of Music, and at twenty-four collaborated with Charles Dickens (same age) in the one-act *Village Coquettes* (1836). These two inexperienced young men, who were perhaps trying to adapt ballad-opera, now defunct, to contemporary requirements, unwittingly perpetrated something very like an operetta. The libretto, one of Dickens's earliest surviving efforts, was an ingenuous rather than ingenious burlesque of current sentimentality — so ingenuous that the unsophisticated audience probably took 'the ivy clinging to the old garden wall' quite seriously, and wept quietly when it heard how 'withered autumn leaves lie strewn around me here'. The music was self-effacing, but it showed attention to detail. Hullah soon afterwards wrote two more short operas — *The Outpost* and *The Barbers of Bassora* — but they are lost and forgotten, maybe because their *authors* did not later distinguish themselves. Their composer devoted the remainder of his life to writing songs, singing them, and encouraging others to do likewise — by precept as well as example.

The Village Coquettes can be regarded either as an attempt to rekindle a flame from the dead embers of ballad-opera or as a premature flash in a new pan — premature because more than twenty years were to elapse before the emergence of a British school of operetta. That such a school eventually did emerge had little to do with Hullah. It was due to the enterprise of THOMAS GERMAN REED (1817–1888), a musician turned impresario, who deliberately set out to cater for that vast section of the mid-Victorian public which liked to be diverted but sincerely believed that to enter a theatre was the first step on the road to damnation. Reed did not share that view (he had worked in theatres all his life) but he had a keen eye for business. In 1855 he rented St. Martin's Hall in Long Acre, where by coincidence Hullah was already giving recitals with his pupils. Reed joined in with a succession of innocent entertainments to which no possible exception could be taken on moral grounds. His artistic standards, too, were beyond reproach, and the 'entertainers' over a period of years were neither amateurs nor inexperienced professionals striving to establish themselves. Among them were Charles Santley (with ballads), Charles Dickens (readings), George Grossmith ('*Piano and I*') — of whom more in Chapter XX — and Mrs. German Reed (impersonations). The last-named, born Priscilla Horton, was a distinguished actress, but as that word held unholy associations she soon announced a tactful retirement from 'the stage' — while continuing to grace the boards of St. Martin's Hall. There followed an immediate upsurge in the box-office receipts, and in 1858 her husband was obliged to seek

ARTHUR SULLIVAN (1842–1900)

EDWARD GERMAN (1862–1936)

larger premises. In the 'Gallery of Illustration' at the lower end of Regent Street — and later in St. George's Hall at its top end — he had such success that he was able to strengthen his company in all departments. Short musical plays — and some not so short — were soon the outstanding feature of his repertory ; he thus became midwife to British operetta.

The infant inherited a few traditional characteristics from its ancestor the ballad-opera, transmitted through the agency of *The Village Coquettes* (therein alone lies Hullah's significance) rather than of better-known contemporary works like Bishop's *Fall of Algiers*, Balfe's *Siege of Rochelle* and Wallace's *Matilda of Hungary* (which were hardly more British in character than they were in topography). In some features the new baby bore a marked resemblance to its French cousin *opéra bouffe* (already a precocious youngster), but thanks to Reed it was nurtured in a very different atmosphere. If a bourgeois, almost puritanical upbringing retarded adolescence it went far to ensure healthy manhood. Our Victorian forefathers, so often a target for ridicule, were in fact neither fools nor knaves. Before we laugh off as naïveté or condemn as hypocrisy their reluctance to go to a 'theatre' while readily taking their womenfolk and children to 'illustrative gatherings' in a 'gallery' or 'hall', let us remember that to their minds the word 'theatre' evoked the unbridled licence of such notorious institutions as the Empire Music-hall and the Bouffes-Parisiens, which they regarded — with some justification — as being before all else a breeding-ground for prostitution. They knew they were safe with Reed, who insisted that nothing should be said or done 'which would bring a blush to the cheeks of the most discreetly brought-up young person'. It was a policy which paid dividends (as Gilbert and Sullivan later discovered to their enrichment). In this country at least it continues to do so : one need not be a prude to note with satisfaction that the welcome accorded here to *Oklahoma!* and *My Fair Lady* (see pp. 248-9) has owed nothing to impropriety, whereas other transatlantic productions, superficially of comparable calibre but suggestively 'blue', have been relative failures. As for *Salad Days* (page 235), it is right in the German Reed tradition — except that it requires two pianos instead of the one piano and one harmonium

N

which were normally *de rigueur* at the Gallery of Illustration and St. George's Hall.

The 'German Reed Entertainments' continued until the death of Alfred German Reed, son of Thomas, in 1895.[1] Thomas himself composed musical sketches as well as directing them : *He's coming* was played at the Gallery of Illustration in 1871 and half a dozen others at St. George's Hall between 1873 and 1879, of which *Three Tenants* was published posthumously in 1898. GEORGE MACFARREN (1813–1887) provided *Jessy Lea* (1863) and *The Soldier's Legacy* (1864), which were apparently intended as parodies of Bishop or Balfe, and another early contributor was Arthur Sullivan (see page 190). From time to time Reed also employed Caldicott, Clay and the brothers Cellier. ALFRED CALDICOTT (1842–1897), like Hullah, was a native of Worcester. Despite indoctrination at the Leipzig Conservatorium, he was never cured of an apparent inability to find inspiration in any time-signature other than 6/8. His slight talent was therefore better exhibited in detached ballads than in his operettas (most of which came later), but *A Fishy Case* (1885) and others no doubt appealed to the juvenile audience which he obviously had in mind. Clay and Alfred Cellier were much more important figures.

FREDERIC CLAY (1838–1889), though sometimes airily dismissed as the perpetrator of popular songs like 'She wandered down the mountain side', was an accomplished composer who wrote about fifteen operettas, several of which had considerable merit. *Out of Sight* (1860), leaving aside one indiscretion with a cornet *obbligato* was a commendable effort for a young man barely twenty-one. The overture took the unusual form of a bolero, there was some mild burlesque of grand opera, and the barcarolle 'My bark is ready, the wind is fair' was charming. This little work earned him widespread recognition, and presently he wrote *Court and Cottage* (1862) and *Constance* (1865) for Michael Costa at Covent Garden. (*Constance* had a libretto by T. W. Robertson and included an excellent comic trio.) In *Ages Ago* (Gallery of Illustration, 1869) Clay collaborated for the first time with W. S. Gilbert. The latter's

[1] Subsequently St. George's Hall was the magicians' Mecca (*Maskelyne's Mysteries*, etc.) ; it was destroyed by enemy action in 1941.

fertile imagination was already foreshadowing the ghosts' scene from *Ruddigore*, for among the characters was an array of ancestors who stepped down from their picture-frames ; musically the best item was a typical ballad, 'Moments so fleeting'. Gilbert and Clay scored again with *The Gentleman in Black* (1870) and *Happy Arcadia* (1872) but Clay's *Cattarina* (1874) marked a temporary break in the partnership. They came together again with *Princess Toto* (1876) which was unremarkable except for an extremely good waltz-song for coloratura soprano. This was the end of their alliance, for by then Gilbert had found a more illustrious confederate, and Clay's *Golden Ring* and *Merry Duchess* (both played around 1880 but possibly written earlier) were terribly hampered by poor libretti. He had himself to blame, indirectly, for Gilbert's desertion. Having dedicated the score of *Ages Ago* to Sullivan — a lifelong friend — he introduced him to Gilbert at one of the rehearsals. Moving as they did in circles which converged, the two men were almost bound to meet sooner or later, but as Clay alone was the loser thereby one is glad to give him credit for having 'started something'. For himself, he was born with a genuine melodic gift not unlike Balfe's, and his approach was that of a cultured musician. This waltz from *Don Quixote* (1876) owes more to Chopin or Brahms than it does to Offenbach or Johann Strauss.

Ex.124 Tempo di Valse

But though much of Clay's music was both pretty and refined it conformed too closely with the requirements of a Victorian drawing-room to survive in a more virile atmosphere ; it was curiously lacking in dynamic energy.

ALFRED CELLIER (1844–1891) and his brother François (see page 200) had French blood in their veins but were Londoners born and bred. Alfred started his career as an organist, and betweenwhiles contributed to the German Reed repertory : his *Charity begins at Home* (1870) was a firm favourite at the Gallery of

Illustration. In 1873 he was appointed musical director of the Princes Theatre, Manchester. It was there that he secured the production of his first three full-blown operettas — *The Sultan of Mocha* (1874), *The Tower of London* (1875) and *Nell Gwynne* (1876). *The Sultan* reached the capital in 1876 and the composer did not lag far behind, for 1877 marked the beginning of a long association with the Comedy Opera Company and its successor the D'Oyly Carte. After conducting 'Gilbert-and-Sullivans' at the Opera Comique and the Savoy for five years, Cellier was chosen by Carte and Sullivan to represent their interests in the United States — and later in Australia. All this activity left little time for composition and from 1877 until 1886 (when he came back from his long tour) he wrote only a few one-act trifles, several of which served from time to time as curtain-raisers for *The Sorcerer*, *H.M.S. Pinafore* and *The Pirates of Penzance*. On his return to London, however, he revised *Nell Gwynne*, and to avoid confusion with Planquette's work of the same name (see page 83) re-christened it *Dorothy*. At first it made no impact, but it was rescued from the clutches of George Edwardes at the Gaiety by Howard Leslie, a chartered accountant who acted as 'business adviser' to various theatrical managements. He engaged young Marie Tempest and Ben Davies for the two leading rôles and shrewdly allowed the Gaiety's blue-eyed boy, Hayden Coffin, to remain with the company. At the Prince of Wales' and afterwards at the Lyric *Dorothy* settled down to break all records. Cellier's good fortune did not turn his head. He knew, though many in the audience did not, that *Dorothy* had been a hurried re-hash of an earlier work, and though naturally delighted — and enriched — by its unprecedented success he was not insensible to the experience he had gained during the intervening ten years. He now had higher standards than before, as well as a fuller sense of his responsibilities. He could not know that he had only two years to live, but none the less he put all he knew into *Doris* (1889) and *The Mountebanks* (produced posthumously in 1892). It was not to be expected that they would emulate the fantastic, almost freakish success of *Dorothy* — 931 performances — but each notched 200 or more.

In *Dorothy* and *Doris* Cellier's collaborator was an experienced and prolific but very uneven librettist named B. C. Stephenson ;

they were among his better efforts. *The Mountebanks* was by Gilbert, and it was one of his private pets. For years he had tried to foist it on Sullivan in some guise or other, but the latter had always raised objections to the magic-philtre *motif* which had already done duty in *The Sorcerer*, besides being repelled by the merciless mocking of middle-aged womanhood unendowed with sex-appeal. This was always one of Gilbert's less lovable traits and here he allowed it to transgress all bounds. Cellier was either less sensitive or less fussy than Sullivan and took it all in his stride. In any case there were compensations, for though two scenes at least left a very nasty taste in the mouth, the libretto of *The Mountebanks*, taken as a whole, was vintage Gilbert, and Cellier rose to the occasion.

Though he lacked Clay's melodic fluency and many of his tunes sound rather forced, Cellier had a knack of showing them off to good advantage. His orchestration was always apt and occasionally brilliant, he rarely lapsed into harmonic clichés, and in course of time his straightforward copybook style of writing came to acquire a certain individuality. Furthermore he was blessed with an adaptable sense of humour which, when coupled with technical skill, enabled him to give added point to verbal quips by little twists of rhythm. In his early works the concerted numbers were somewhat elementary in construction, but in this respect more than any other his D'Oyly Carte experience stood him in good stead. *Doris* contains several admirable ensembles : 'What do you lack ?', in which the chorus is divided into four groups (fathers, wives, daughters, apprentices), is as good as anything of its kind in any operetta. So is the long *durchkomponiert* section in the second act of *The Mountebanks* which ends with the haunting waltz-tune 'An hour, 'twill rapidly pass', one of his happiest inspirations.

Ex.125

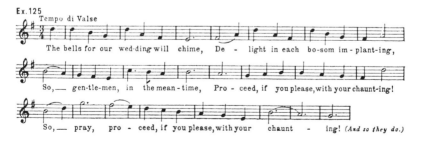

Cellier was only forty-seven when he died. Had he lived longer, *Doris* and *The Mountebanks* might have ranked as the first two works of a mature 'second period'. Leaving aside hypothetical speculation, and at the risk of appearing ungenerous to his memory, one is bound to regard them in retrospect as nine-day wonders and to judge him, rather, by his comparatively prolific output in the seventies. Those early operettas which he wrote for German Reed and for Manchester showed the touch of a talented craftsman with a sure instinct for the stage, but no more than Clay's could they hope to face the competition that was shortly to be forthcoming.

XIX

SULLIVAN

OUTSTRIPPING his compatriot rivals by a far greater margin than did the leaders of the continental schools, ARTHUR SULLIVAN stands head and shoulders above any other British composer of operettas. Of the twenty-one which he wrote (including three one-act pieces) nine or ten can still be relied upon to draw capacity audiences almost anywhere in the English-speaking world. W. S. Gilbert — with whom he collaborated in fourteen — has of course had a lot to do with it, not merely because of the excellence of his libretti in themselves, but because he had the knack of writing verses which Sullivan enjoyed setting to music and which consequently brought out the best in him. Their joint success — possibly unique in the annals of art — was largely due to the fact that their talents were ninety-five per cent complementary. Their temperaments were conflicting ; though their close association spanned a quarter of a century and for long periods brought them into almost daily contact, they rarely saw eye to eye and never really became friends. (The familiar use of Christian names was not so widespread then as it is today, but Sullivan's letters to his musical directors always began 'My dear Alfred' or 'My dear Frank', his soubrette was always 'My dear Jessie' and for all I know to the contrary the Prince of Wales may have been 'My dear Ted'. One therefore notes with interest and regret that his librettist, even when in good favour, had to be content with 'My dear Gilbert', and more often than not with a terse 'Dear G.'.)

During his lifetime Sullivan submitted too gracefully to the adulation of sycophantic admirers, and after his death a reaction set in which in some quarters passed the bounds of reason. Balance was restored by Thomas Dunhill in his admirable little book *Sullivan's Comic Operas* (1929). Yet perhaps he and other equally discriminating scholars of recent years have tended to play down Gilbert's share in the proceedings. It is easy enough to pick holes in his work if one adopts the high standard which he himself strove to maintain, but one should remember that as a general rule the libretto of an operetta is a mere peg on which to hang the music, and that the literary merit is often so negligible that the author does not demand the critical appraisal which must be accorded to Gilbert. On the purely musical side, which is our present concern, the G. & S. operettas are noteworthy for their classical refinement ; for the unobtrusive assurance of the composer's technique in harmony, counterpoint and orchestration ; for the variety — rather than individuality — of his melodies ; above all for the originality of his approach to the problems of rhythmic accentuation in word-setting. I have essayed detailed analysis of these qualities in another book (*The Music of Arthur Sullivan*) and I do not propose to in-trude on that ground again, except where it may be desirable to point comparison with other composers. Instead, I shall merely outline very briefly the background and build-up of each operetta in turn, hoping thereby to demonstrate its significance as a representative of the genre. A biographical survey on the scale vouchsafed to Offenbach would also, I feel, be superfluous here, but note will be taken of a few salient features in Sullivan's career and character to the extent that they affected his music.

Born in London on 13th May 1842, he received his training at the Chapel Royal, the Royal Academy of Music and the Leipzig Conservatorium. His early works — which included a cantata, a symphony, and a cello concerto — were rather mixed in quality and style (the best of them owed much to Schubert and a little to Mendelssohn) but nearly all were favourably received. Being present in 1867 at a private performance of Offenbach's *Deux aveugles* his thoughts turned to operetta, and he quickly dashed off a musical adaptation of Maddison Morton's farce *Box and Cox* — lyrics and reversal of the title by F. C. Burnand. A glance through the original vocal score — rather than the truncated version used nowadays — leaves no doubt as to the source of inspiration. In its formal design the Offenbach model was followed in so far as successive items were devoted to parody, to 'ra-ta-plan' and to 6/8 balladry. The 'ensemble de perplexité', however, was replaced by a 'gambling duet' and the 'chanson à boire' by a lullaby over the breakfast bacon ; histrionic considerations (fortunately, perhaps) determined the omission of a can-can. Stylistically, too, there was indebtedness to the same quarter, and Ex. 126 could fittingly be set beside Ex. 19 (page 44) from *Ba-ta-clan*, though Sullivan had not yet learnt to use conventional devices in Offenbach's deceptively artless manner.

Cox and Box, after a private try-out, was played in public at a charity matinée ; obviously suited to the Gallery of Illustration, it was soon added to the repertory there. It was also for German Reed that Sullivan later in the same year wrote *The Contrabandista* (libretto again by Burnand). The music was in the *Cox and Box* vein, which was hardly strong enough to carry it through two acts, but several of the unassuming numbers were quite accomplished ; 'From rock to rock' foreshadowed some of the better-known patter-songs. (Although Reed did not transfer his regular company to St. George's Hall until 1873, he rented it during the autumn of 1867 for full-scale operatic productions, one of which was *The Contrabandista*. But an orchestra of forty proved too great a strain on his resources ; the venture was abandoned after a few months, and consequently Clay and the rest had to persevere with their piano and harmonium.) *The Contrabandista* was never revived in this country, but in 1879, equipped with a new and up-to-the-minute Americanised libretto, it found appreciative audiences in Connecticut, Rhode Island, Massachusetts and New Hampshire.[1]

Sullivan's next work for the stage — his first with Gilbert — saw the light in very different surroundings : the old Gaiety theatre, managed by John Hollingshead, a specialist in pantomime and irreverent burlesque. The music of two numbers alone has survived from *Thespis* (1871) — one was transferred to *The Pirates of Penzance*. It is mainly remembered because it failed to live up to the high standards of presentation which Gilbert and Sullivan (emulating German Reed) afterwards set for themselves ; some of the 'male' parts were actually played by shameless young ladies wearing tights !

Four years later, at the instigation of Richard D'Oyly Carte, the two men joined forces again in the classic curtain-raiser *Trial by Jury*. This had no dialogue and needed none, but a splendid precedent was set when the chorus was made an organic part of the dramatic scheme. Not everywhere did Sullivan succeed in avoiding triviality, but the Usher's song was only one of several self-contained sections which proved clearly that his realisation of witty Gilbertian conceptions was far more apt than Frederic Clay's. To *Trial by Jury*

---

[1] Most of the words and music of *The Contrabandista* were subsequently incorporated in *The Chieftain* (see page 197).

the generic term 'comic opera' might for once be appropriately applied, for it really is comic from start to finish. *The Zoo* (also 1875) was an indiscretion. Sullivan could do little with the fatuous libretto (not by Gilbert), but a few bars may be worth quoting from one graceful duet with a typically sentimental cadence.

The Sorcerer (1877) did more credit to Gilbert than to the composer. There were four or five good numbers and the character of Mr. Wells was uncommonly well portrayed, but there was too much 'Farmer Giles', too much sentimentality, and not enough of the constructive skill which helped to make *Trial by Jury* evergreen. *H.M.S. Pinafore* (1878), however, established Sullivan beyond all doubt as a master of operetta. *La Vie parisienne* had been as French — almost — as the rue de Montmartre ; *Pinafore* was as British — almost — as the British Navy. It was composed during a period of considerable physical suffering, but listening to the music one would never suspect it. Good rousing tunes with a nautical tang were the order of the day ; and although tricks of the trade that gladden the musician were less in evidence than usual, *Pinafore* included one of the most delightful of Sullivan's many excellent 'double choruses'.

This sort of thing does not just 'happen' ; it may require hours of mental toil before it sounds, as here, completely spontaneous. Compare Ex. 47 on page 68, where Jonas's effort, while deserving appreciative comment in its surroundings, looks shoddy beside Sullivan's.

The Pirates of Penzance (1879), like The Sorcerer, did not show Sullivan at his best. By Pinafore standards the music of Act I was uneven and parts of Act II (despite some amusing parodies) were rather crude. But no single item from the contemporary operettas of other composers — nor indeed from Pinafore itself — achieved the melodic purity of 'Ah, leave me not to pine' or surpassed the humorous artistry of 'When a felon's not engaged in his employment'.

For many years Sullivan had been showing increasing sensitivity to French influence — that of Bizet especially — and by 1880 it was fully assimilated. This partly explains why the music of Patience (1881) was both more subdued and more subtle than that of its predecessors. The first act, considered as an entity, was an exceptionally fine achievement, but the second tailed off badly after reaching a climax with the infectious comic duet 'So go to him and say to him'. No such criticism can be applied to Iolanthe (1882), which of all Sullivan's larger works is the most consistent ; there is hardly a single lapse into triviality. Many musicians hold it as their favourite and it is easy to see why : Sullivan had by now overcome his teething troubles and had not yet utterly succumbed to certain vexatious mannerisms that were to plague the possibly more sparkling works of his full maturity. Another feature which helped to lift Patience and Iolanthe to a level beyond the reach of lesser mortals was the remarkable flair for group-characterisation shown in both. In Sullivan's previous operettas there had been charming choruses for pretty girls, but the participants had remained anonymous : there was nothing to distinguish the bridesmaids of Trial by Jury from the Major-General's daughters in The Pirates, who themselves had been thespians in a previous incarnation. The composer now took good care, however, that the fairies of Iolanthe should not be confused with the love-sick maidens of Patience, and the distinction between Peers and dragoons was even more astutely delineated. It was during the run of Patience, incidentally, that D'Oyly Carte's company moved from the Opera Comique in Wych Street (on part of the site now occupied by Bush House) to the newly built Savoy Theatre just off the Strand, where *Iolanthe* and all Sullivan's subsequent operettas had their *premières*.

Princess Ida (1884) stands rather apart from the rest. It is the only one in three acts (the second is much the best) ; the only one with blank-verse dialogue (lifted from an old Gilbert play) ; the only one burdened with two principal tenors and three tenor arias (two of which are excellent). The music, unlike that of *Iolanthe*, is unequal in quality ; it is also varied in style. On the one hand are frequent echoes of Sullivan's youth when his primary allegiance was to Schubert — at times the contrapuntal texture almost suggests chamber-music. On the other are some startlingly rumbustious outbursts which drive contrast to a pitch of incongruity. For all that, and perhaps because it is outside the ordinary run, many of us find *Princess Ida* most enjoyable, but its successor *The Mikado* (1885) is nearly always at the head of the popularity polls. The melodies are indeed as immediately memorable as those of *Pinafore*, and probing musicologists will find a far greater hidden store of rhythmic ingenuity, harmonic charm and orchestral brilliance. They will also note, with less satisfaction, that the aforementioned mannerisms are beginning to get out of hand.

Sullivan was no proverbial prophet, for he found nearly all his honour in his own country. *The Mikado* is the only work that has had its due success outside Britain, the Commonwealth and the United States ; it is still played in Germany and Switzerland. The failure of the French to appreciate his gifts is surprising, and possibly dates from 1886, when Richard Dauntless's song from *Ruddigore*, 'I shipp'd, d'ye see, in a revenue sloop', was taken by our neighbours on the other side of the channel as a reflection on the fighting qualities of the French Navy. It is hard to see how the misapprehension arose ; one would have expected that the London representative of any Parisian journal would be sufficiently familiar with our usage to realise that the sole target of Gilbert's shaft was British boastfulness. But Arthur Pougin (whom we met earlier as a fervent admirer of Adam and Maillart) could not control his fury. Nor was it just a case of rushing impetuously into print ; in a revised edition of the

Clément-Larousse *Dictionnaire des opéras*, published as long after the event as 1897, he quoted the offending verses in a misleading and provocative translation, underlined their enormity, and then launched one of the most ill-natured attacks that can ever have found place in a standard reference-book. (Were it not there for all to read, one would scarcely credit a reputable critic with the concluding sneer at a man who all his life had been a lover of France and the French.)

> It is well to remember that Messrs. Gilbert and Sullivan have long tried — in vain — to foist one of their operettas on Paris ; this may be their revenge out of spite. Should they be tempted to renew their efforts after making such a charming 'joke', it is to be hoped that they will be even less successful than heretofore. Take note, too, that Mr. Arthur Sullivan is a Chevalier of the Legion of Honour ; nobody seems to know why.[1]

Now all this happened many, many years ago, but so far as I am aware no recantation has ever been issued, no apology uttered. Such prejudices die hard, no less when they are founded on entirely false premises. (Debussy, however, an honourable exception among French musicians, expressed a keen admiration for Sullivan.)

Leaving aside 'I shipp'd, d'ye see' (which is merely competent imitation-folksong-cum-sea-shanty) and a few recollections from *The Sorcerer* which sound rather out of place, *Ruddigore* marked a further step forward in Sullivan's development. Melodic inspiration was not flowing quite so smoothly as usual, perhaps, but his technique had emerged stronger than ever from the travail of *The Golden Legend*, which he had recently completed. If there had been no *Golden Legend* (which can be saluted, while we pass by, as far and away the most satisfying of his 'serious' works) there would have been no ghost's song as we know it, and if there had been no ghost's song at its boiling-point a revival of *Ruddigore* in 1921 might not have been the success it was. If since then its career has been unchequered most of the credit must go to Sullivan, for here Gilbert was not at his best, and whatever expedient is adopted to round off the second act (three have been tried) the final curtain always falls on a wretched anti-climax.

---

[1] He was *Sir* Arthur Sullivan by then, but let that pass.

For years Sullivan had been urging Gilbert to write him a
'grand opera', but the latter — wisely — had never agreed to do so.
Partly as a sop to his colleague, however, and partly because he
always fancied himself as a romanticist, he came forward with
The Yeomen of the Guard (1888), which might well be dubbed an
opéra comique.   Sullivan was delighted, and threw himself with
enthusiasm into the task of composition.   During the preparation
of *The Yeomen* their personal relationship remained unusually cordial,
and at first they both regarded it as the best thing they had done
together.   Sullivan — who always kept a keen eye on the box-office
— changed his mind when in the event it ran for only 423 performances, a very good score by normal standards but well behind
Pinafore (with 700), *The Mikado* (672) and *Patience* (unexpectedly
high in the list with 578).   In *The Yeomen*, as in *Ruddigore*, the music
was the dominating feature ; Gilbert was floundering in waters too
deep for him and Sullivan had to wade to the rescue.   The plot,
though sound enough dramatically, teemed with inconsistencies
which would have been of no consequence in the topsy-turvy world
of the author's customary imaginings but could not pass muster in
a story of real-life characters whose human emotions the audience
was asked to share.   And while it can gladly be conceded that several
lyrics and a few passages of dialogue carried a rare touch of almost
poetic distinction, grim Gilbertian pleasantries — supportable enough
as absurdities in *The Mikado* or *Ruddigore* — sounded shockingly
distasteful against the sombre background of the Tower, the torture-
chamber and the headsman's axe.   The composer, too, occasionally
lost his footing, for the exciting situations were not all adequately
dealt with, and once or twice he stumbled into the commonplace.
But the music, taken as a whole, carried more conviction than the
words.   Much of it combined geniality with dignity, and the
orchestration throughout was unusually warm and glowing for
Sullivan, who again drew on his *Golden Legend* experience to good
purpose.

After these experimental excursions, worth-while though they
were, a return to the earlier manner was overdue and doubly welcome when it came.   *The Gondoliers* (1889) cast inhibitions aside.
Savoy audiences once more found themselves revelling in the

perpetual sunshine and song of that never-never land where sense makes nonsense, nonsense sense, where

> Every flower is a rose,
> Every goose becomes a swan,
> Every kind of trouble goes
> Where the last year's snows have gone.

Gilbert's harshest critic, his partner, found *The Gondoliers* a 'perfect book'. Gilbert can indeed be praised for an excellent piece of work, and Sullivan too was on top form ; here and there he succeeded in capturing an unwonted rhythmic *élan* more typical of Offenbach. Even the formal opening of the overture throws out a hint of the treats in store, and there are at least half a dozen separate items which represent him at his very best. Because Sullivan was in the main a specialist in gaiety and *The Gondoliers* the gayest of his operettas, one likes to think of it as being also the most characteristic. But if the assessment is just it is also equivocal, for it must be admitted that there are some characteristic lapses. Dunhill (*op. cit.* page 187) rightly stigmatised one number in the first act as being 'scarcely tolerable to the musical ear', and there are two in the second that descend almost to the same level. One has to draw attention to these indiscretions — and there are others, though less blatant — if only to emphasise the validity of a previous assertion that *Iolanthe* was the most consistent (*i.e.* most consistently *good*) of these operettas.

In 1890 the partnership of Gilbert, Sullivan and Carte was rent by a violent quarrel.[1] While the break lasted the composer satisfied his inner urge by writing a grand opera (*Ivanhoe*, 1891) and *Haddon Hall* (1892), which bore superficial resemblances to *Ruddigore*. Though Sullivan worked hard for a new and relatively inexperienced collaborator, sparing no pains to make the venture a success, the libretto was wishy-washy and much of the music boring. Eventually Carte lured Gilbert back to the fold, and *Utopia Limited* (1893) was heralded (metaphorically) with a flourish of trumpets. *Gilbert* deserved it, for *Utopia*, despite minor faults of construction, was one of his most brilliant achievements ; had Sullivan risen to the occasion

---

[1] The accompanying publicity adversely affected box-office receipts ; *The Gondoliers* had been expected to reach 600 performances at least, but it was withdrawn after 554, the fourth longest run in the series.

their ever-faithful supporters might have been rewarded with a second *Mikado*. But the music failed to arouse enthusiasm. The composer's mine of melodic inspiration was nearly worked out, and neither a continued ready flow of rhythmic devices nor impressive displays of technical resource could disguise the fact. Next — from Sullivan — came a re-orchestrated and expanded version of *The Contrabandista*. The additions, which included two attractive Spanish dances, fitted surprisingly well into the 1867 framework, but Carte was clutching a straw if he cherished hopes that *The Chieftain* (as it was now called) would make a favourable impression in 1894/5. Of *The Grand Duke* (1896) only two things need be said: that if everybody did not already know that W. S. Gilbert was its propagator the conditions laid down on page 3 would here preclude a mention of his name, and that though Sullivan endured his labour pains with stoicism it was all of no avail in the end, for their fourteenth and last child was a weakling and died in infancy. Its parents never spoke to one another again.

The composer's misfortunes were not yet over, for *The Beauty Stone* (1898), a species of *opéra comique* provided by Comyns Carr and Arthur Pinero (distinguished but unhelpful colleagues), was another dismal failure, though certainly a better work of art than *The Grand Duke*. The music was in good taste but curiously restrained, and with Sullivan restraint led to tedium. *The Rose of Persia* (1899), on the other hand, was light-hearted to the point of frivolity. (The libretto, overburdened with puns, was by Basil Hood — one of the less anaemic of Gilbert's imitators.) Though not all the tunes showed Sullivan's customarily refined approach, the music had more vitality than anything he had written since *The Gondoliers*. Here and there, too, were passages in a surprisingly up-to-date harmonic idiom. Elsewhere a veneer of sham orientalism could not hide the poverty of the material, and there were occasional lapses into a slovenly style of writing already becoming associated with 'musical comedy'. Although the duet 'Oh, what is love' was by no means devoid of charm, one regrets that innumerable dealers in triviality should have been able to find in its opening bars (Ex. 129) a Sullivan precedent for one of their favourite and most threadbare clichés. The harmonic progression (*a*) is the essential feature, but

O

in 'Through the long night I dream' from *Chin-chin* (page 217)
Ivan Caryll also reproduced the initial *melodic* phrase in identical
rhythm — though in a different key.

Ex.129 Allegretto

Sullivan's share in *The Emerald Isle*, on which he started work a few
months before his death, was so small that this composite operetta
can more conveniently be considered in Chapter XXI when we
come to review the achievements of Edward German, who was
responsible for its completion.

Not even Sullivan's most fervent admirers have been able to
deny the infirmity of the music which he wrote during the last ten
years of his life. Neither they nor his most carping critics need be
blind to the causes of deterioration. It was due partly to the with-
drawal of the Gilbert stimulus, but since *Utopia* followed the same
trend one must look for a further explanation : it will be found in
Sullivan's health-chart. Ever since the mid-seventies he had been
subject to recurring attacks of a chronic and extremely painful
kidney complaint. Three times they nearly killed him : once on
New Year's Eve 1883, a few days before the production of *Princess
Ida* ; again in 1887, when he was on his way to Berlin to conduct
a gala performance of *The Golden Legend* in honour of Kaiser
Wilhelm I's eightieth birthday ; thirdly in 1892, while he was engaged
on *Haddon Hall*. This last attack was a crippling blow. Thereafter,
while high living and a tendency to self-indulgence continued to
take their toll, Sullivan was obliged to have increasing resort to
opiates in order to carry on at all. Towards the end he was a
pathetic figure, full of neuroses and seemingly with as little directive
control as the pilot of a rudderless vessel. In company he would be
as gracious as ever one moment, unaccountably tetchy the next.
When composing, he would concentrate fitfully, chain-smoking for
a few hours — and then as likely as not tear up in disgust what he had
written. The closing stages of his long fight against a cruel disease

had landed him in an equally distressing mental conflict between the two sides of his personality. It was partly resolved in the late summer of 1900; relaxing in September sunshine on the grassy slopes fringing Lake Lucerne he found peace of mind and a measure of relief from physical pain. But by the time he returned to London autumnal mists were again gathering round, and he had neither heart nor strength to resist a renewed onslaught from his implacable old enemy. Death came on 22nd November, and surely came as a friend.

Had Sullivan died in 1879 after completing *The Pirates*, his work would even so have been a pedestal for British operetta, though in that unhappy event the structure might only have attained significance as a mausoleum. His achievements of the eighties did in fact raise it to the proportions of an *arc de triomphe*. What of his position *vis-à-vis* the leading exponents of the other national schools? Here in Britain we are better acquainted with Offenbach and Messager, with Johann Strauss and Lehár, than the French or Viennese with Sullivan. Increasing familiarity with his rivals may quicken our admiration for them, but it also entitles us to make comparisons. And that many of us would rank *Pinafore*, *Iolanthe*, *The Mikado* and *The Gondoliers* just above *La Belle Hélène*, *Véronique*, *Die Fledermaus* and *The Merry Widow* is not due in the very least to patriotic sentiment or insular prejudice. (In matters musical our people have rarely been guilty of either.) At the risk of being accused of 'British boastfulness' I put forward in all seriousness the proposition that thanks to Arthur Sullivan we have developed greater artistic sensibility, so far as operetta is concerned, than our friends on the continent who know him not.

XX

IN SULLIVAN'S WAKE

THREE names closely associated in one connection or another with the Gilbert and Sullivan series are Clarke, Grossmith and Cellier. Because HAMILTON CLARKE (1842–1912) 'put together' the overture to *The Mikado* and possibly had a hand in one or two others, it has been overlooked that he was a composer in his own right. (He sometimes used the pseudonym 'Yvolde'.) Although he specialised in anthems and part-songs he also wrote half a dozen pretty little operettas for children. They bore titles like *The Daisy Chain* (1892) and *Hornpipe Harry* (1894) ; the music was in accord.[1] GEORGE GROSSMITH (1847–1912) is now only remembered as having been what Anna Russell calls 'the little man who sings the patter-songs', but as an entertainer at the piano he was a lineal progenitor of the Norman Longs and B. C. Hilliams of our own day. He showed his versatility, too, by writing both words and music for the one-act *Cups and Saucers* (1878) — which for a few months shared the bill with *Pinafore* — and he actually collaborated with Gilbert in *Haste to the Wedding* (1892), an adaptation of Labiche's farce *Le Chapeau de paille d'Italie*. Such an undertaking was really beyond his capabilities, but some of the jollier numbers were reminiscent of Sullivan at his lightest (except in their orchestration) and there was even a 'double chorus'. FRANÇOIS CELLIER (1849–1914), who succeeded his brother Alfred as musical director at the

[1] Short musical plays suitable for performance by children in a schoolroom or even a nursery were a by-product of German Reed's venture at St. George's Hall. Since Clarke's there have been hundreds more. Their composers could rarely expect the music to receive serious appraisal, but credit for artistic essays must go to Hope Temple (afterwards Madame André Messager), George Jacobi (see page 204), Florian Pascal (page 203), Arthur Hinton, Nicholas Gatty, Gustav Holst (page 227), Frederic Norton (page 225), Thomas Dunhill (page 229), Harry Farjeon, Victor Hely-Hutchinson and Ian Whyte. Such pieces, however, are not operettas in the normally accepted sense of the term and will henceforth be disregarded.

Savoy, was also allowed to try his hand at a curtain-raiser from time to time. The ensembles, at any rate, of *Captain Billy* (1891) and *Old Sarah* (1897) were an echo of his master's voice.

Two other imitators, OSMOND CARR (1857–1916) and ERNEST FORD (1858–1919), were more ambitious, and on a larger canvas their weaknesses were plain for all to see. Carr's standards must have been thrown out of gear by the failure in 1892 of *Blue-eyed Susan* after the success in 1891 of *Joan of Arc*. The former is the only one of his works in which I can spy merit : a touch of artistry is discernible in the *buffo* trio 'We are three scamps' and the duet 'Why should you live in poverty ?' But *Joan of Arc*, which found a much more appreciative audience, was a truly deplorable burlesque in which both words and music matched the tastelessness of the full title — *Joan of Arc, or The Merry Maid of Orleans*. *Morocco Bound* (1893) was comparatively 'straight', but there was little attempt to recapture the mood of *Blue-eyed Susan*. In *His Excellency* (1894) Carr made a sorry shambles of a Gilbert libretto that would have been manna from heaven to Clay or Alfred Cellier, and the rest of his output — *In Town* (1892), *Go Bang* (1894), *My Girl* (1896), etc. — is not worth criticising ; a succession of comic songs plus an occasional jog-trot chorus will not add up even to a musical comedy, let alone an operetta. Carr's close contemporary Ernest Ford had loftier ideals and greater potential, but he had an inordinate admiration for Sullivan which blunted initiative : *Daniel O'Rourke* (1884), *Joan* (1890) and *Jane Annie* (Savoy, 1893) were surely not intended as the laboured parodies of his idol that they appeared to be.[1] In fairness to Ford it must be added that he was a competent conductor and a respected pedagogue ; two years before his death he was

---

[1] In Bernard Shaw's notice on *Jane Annie*, published in *The World* (24th May 1893), only 100 out of the 1500 words were devoted to a discussion of the music, and the composer's name was not mentioned. Shaw was more interested in the librettists. 'If I ask Messrs. [J. M.] Barrie and [A.] Conan Doyle whether I am to regard their reputations as founded on Jane Annie or Jane Annie on their reputations, I have no doubt they will hastily declare for the second alternative. And, indeed, it would ill become me, as a brother of the literary craft, to pretend to congratulate them seriously upon the most unblushing outburst of tomfoolery that two responsible citizens could conceivably indulge in publicly.' In their hearts Barrie and Conan Doyle must have agreed with him ; they afterwards kept very quiet about *Jane Annie*.

appointed professor of composition at the Guildhall School of Music.

Among those who strove to emulate Sullivan during his own heyday the most accomplished, apart from Alfred Cellier in his brief maturity, was EDWARD SOLOMON (1853–1895). During a short career he wrote a few little pieces for German Reed and about a dozen full-length operettas. Unfortunately most of them suffered from bad libretti and only *Claude Duval* (1885), *The Nautch Girl* (Savoy, 1891) and *The Vicar of Bray* (1892) made much impression. In one respect they recall Offenbach — they tended to conform with a pattern ; for instance each had its stereotyped — and usually commonplace — 'patriotic' song, while more often than not the first act ended with a big waltz-tune broadening out into a concluding *allargando*. It must be placed to Solomon's credit that he rarely lapsed into cheap sentimentality ; most of the 'serious' numbers were merely dull, and he was obviously more at home in 'pattery' stuff. Exceptionally, the duet 'In a vale, midst softest breezes' from *Polly* (1884) was both graceful and well-contrived, and the rousing 'King of the king's highway' from *Claude Duval* achieved vigour without vulgarity. *Lord Bateman* (1883) contained some amusing burlesque of Italian opera, and the composer's sense of humour served him even better in *Pickwick* (1889, a skilful adaptation of the Bardell imbroglio by F. C. Burnand). Here Solomon was at his best, though the posthumous trifle *Jealousy* (published in 1898) must be commended for a rhythmic sprightliness which was all too often lacking in his music. His technique was adequate, but when he tried to escape from allegiance to Sullivan he was apt to fall into mannerisms whereby he was perhaps subconsciously hoping to display originality — *e.g.* snippets progressing chromatically in contrary motion such as occur in this passage from *Virginia and Paul* (1883).

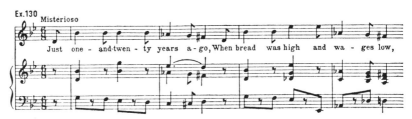

It is to be feared that the twenty-odd operettas of FLORIAN PASCAL (1850–1923) brought him neither fame nor fortune. Though he aspired to *opéra comique* in the promising *Cymbia* (1883), his only public success — which came two years later — was a frank burlesque dignified with a title that epitomised the pun-conscious wit of the eighties — *The Vicar of Wide-a-Wakefield, or The Miss-Terry-ous Uncle. Gipsy Gabriel*, an attempted repetition of *Cymbia*, achieved professional production at Bradford in 1887, but thereafter Pascal concentrated on short pieces which usually saw the light in very obscure surroundings. There was never any difficulty about arranging *publication* however, for 'Florian Pascal' was the pen-name of Joseph Williams, life-member and sometime managing director of the well-known firm of music-publishers which still carries on the good work under the same name.[1] From his long catalogue of trifles *Eyes and No Eyes* (1896, libretto by Gilbert), the pseudo-Japanese *Jewel Maiden, Tempests in tea-cups* (both 1898), *Sally* and *Wooing a Widow* (both 1903) deserve mention. Though he occasionally exploited a humorous situation with happy effect, Pascal's music suffered from an addiction to cloying sentiment and an inability to throw off the four-bar habit. His main weakness, however, was poverty of invention ; he was thoughtful but un-inspired. The careful imitative figuration, for instance, might have been an attractive feature if the melodies so treated had had point or charm of their own — but often they hadn't. The 'duelling song' from *Wooing a Widow* found him in unusually assured mood. The first verse was in G major throughout ; the second and third in the successively unrelated keys of A♭ major and B♭ major. Each verse, therefore, required a contrasted return to the tonic refrain, and in his handling of a device initiated but not patented by Sullivan Pascal here showed considerable finesse. His music for *A Sensation Novel* (1912), written to another Gilbert libretto after the author's death, introduced the novel sensation (in an operetta) of coquetry with Debussy's whole-tone scale.[2]

---

[1] Since these words were written the firm has been acquired by Messrs. Augener.

[2] *A Sensation Novel* and *Eyes and No Eyes* were not products of Gilbert's later years. The former had been given in 1871 at the Gallery of Illustration with music by Frederic Clay, the latter in 1875 at St. George's Hall with music by German Reed.

Before closing this somewhat melancholy chapter a few kind words must be spared for those spirited cosmopolitans WILHELM MEYER-LUTZ (1822–1901) and GEORGE JACOBI (1840–1906), even though they were not native to these shores. Meyer-Lutz was a Bavarian organist who came to England at the age of twenty-eight. For more than thirty years he followed his chosen profession at Roman Catholic churches and cathedrals in Birmingham, Leeds and London. During this period he wrote a handful of operettas, including *Blonde or Brunette* (1862) and *Zaïda* (1868), and his music plumbed the depths of mid-Victorian balladry. ('Pure as Angel's breath the love should be That lights the flame in maiden's breast.') His style underwent a change when at the age of sixty he became a music-hall conductor and contributed his share to a series of burlesques bearing mirth-provoking titles like *Faust up-to-date* (1888), *Ruy Blas and the blasé roué* (1889) and *Cinder - Ellen up-too-late* (1891). Meanwhile he wrote two more operettas — *Frankenstein* (1887) and *Miss Esmeralda* (1888). The former's first-act finale was an accomplished essay in the Donizetti manner, and in the duet 'Cupid hath long my heart enchained' from *Miss Esmeralda* the independent vocal lines were skilfully interlinked. George Jacobi — no connection with Victor Jacobi (page 151) — was born in Berlin, studied in Brussels and then for a time conducted at the Bouffes-Parisiens, but he soon moved to London. Long before Hervé — who was not personally popular in this country — became musical director at the Empire (see page 71), Jacobi had settled in as uncrowned king at the rival music-hall round the corner — the Alhambra — where he made many good friends. As a composer he did not amount to much, though he occasionally gave rein to a flair for harmonic and rhythmic enterprise. His first operetta — *Mariée depuis midi* (Bouffes-Parisiens, 1874) — was perhaps his best, but it was in London that he made his mark. He wrote innumerable ballets as curtain-raisers — or curtain-droppers — and was expert at cooking the music of other composers to suit Alhambra tastes. *La Poule aux œufs d'or* (1879) was a typical *ragoût* to which he did not fail to add a garnish of his own concocting ; here is the recipe as published in the programme :

Music selected from Rossini, Hérold, Shield, Offenbach, Lecocq, Gevaert, Bucalossi, Chabrie [*sic*], Planquette and A. Sullivan. New Songs, Marches and the whole of the Original Ballet Music composed by Mr. G. Jacobi.

One suspects that Mr. G. Jacobi did not demur when given a disproportionate share of the credit for these ingenious composites, but apart from his Parisian venture he wrote at least two operettas all on his own — *Venice* (1879) and *The two Pro's* (1892) — as well as the second act of *The Black Crook* (1881), a work which had been started by Frederic Clay.

Thus far operetta in Britain presents an unbalanced appearance. In other national schools the leaders were kept on their toes by competitors who were close on their heels. In Vienna, for instance, the achievements of Suppé and Millöcker spurred Johann Strauss to further efforts, while in France the supremacy of Offenbach, Delibes and Lecocq was challenged first by Hervé and Jonas, later by Audran and Planquette. This healthy state of affairs did not prevail in Britain. Though it would not be far-fetched to regard Alfred Cellier as the British Audran and Solomon as the British Planquette, on the same basis one would have to agree that Sullivan was the British equivalent of Offenbach, Delibes and Lecocq rolled into one, with bits of Bizet and Chabrier thrown in for good measure. Nobody but Cellier and Solomon came into the picture alongside. By the mid-nineties, when the disciples were dead and the master a worn-out shadow of his pristine self, native operetta was in desperate straits. As no composer of Sullivan's calibre came forward to identify himself with the genre there was never a complete recovery, but the old plant survived longer than might have been expected (see Chapter XXI), and meanwhile there sprang up beside it a new but not wholly unrecognisable variant — Edwardian musical comedy (which must wait until Chapter XXII).

XXI

STEADYING INFLUENCES

BEFORE proceeding further into the twentieth century we must glance backward for a moment to mid-Victorian days, when British music — except perhaps for the first stirrings of operetta — was still in a state of suspended animation. The only full-length opera whose name, even, has survived from the fifties, sixties and early seventies is Julius Benedict's *Lily of Killarney*, which was produced in 1862 (nearly twenty years after Balfe's *Bohemian Girl* and Wallace's *Maritana*) and was virtually the last of its tribe. Meanwhile the contemporary oratorios and cantatas of J. F. Barnett, John Stainer — and Sullivan himself — sported fashions that soon became outworn. The eighties and nineties, however, saw an overdue national renaissance with which Barnett and Stainer could not keep pace and Sullivan (now following a profitable line of his own) found himself out of sympathy. Its missioners, in age order, were Mackenzie, Parry and Stanford, three men who were not only distinguished composers but also held honoured posts as Principal of the Royal Academy of Music, Director of the Royal College, and Professor of Music at Cambridge University. That in 1899 Elgar's *Enigma Variations* put all three in the shade so far as composition was concerned is here beside the point.

In that field, without in any way disparaging the good work of Mackenzie and the splendid work of Parry, a dispassionate judgment must concede more lasting significance to the achievements of CHARLES VILLIERS STANFORD (1852–1924). Apart from anything else he remains a rare example of a near-great composer who, so far from considering that operetta was beneath him, devoted as much care to *Shamus O'Brien* (1896, libretto by G. H. Jessop after Le Fanu) as he had to the cantatas and symphonies on which his reputation at that time largely depended. His flow of spontaneous melody surpassed that of either of his two colleagues, and in the best of *Shamus* — as in so many of his songs — he used unpretentious methods to evoke that typically Irish mood in which laughter is often akin to tears and tears are never far removed from laughter. (Need it be added that he had been born in Dublin ?) For instance, a charming melody which the heroine on her first entrance sang to the words ' Where is the man that is coming to marry me ' was later accorded diatonic treatment in impeccable style.

Ex.131 Andante

And Stanford displayed, throughout, that rhythmic facility in word-setting which he shared with Sullivan and developed with greater consistency of purpose, even if he did not so regularly astonish us with a startling flash of brilliance.

Although a younger generation of composers (some of whom are still happily with us) owed a great deal to Stanford the professor, both at Cambridge and later at the Royal College of Music, one is nevertheless inclined to regret that he devoted so much time to academic pursuits, for in creative art his immense store of learning eventually became a two-sided attribute. Instead of being content to relax and let inspiration have its fling, he too often strove — unconsciously perhaps — to emulate the masters whom he had studied so carefully and whose virtues he was continually expounding and hoping to inculcate ; unproverbially Nature, driven out with a tuning-fork, did not always come running back. This is not the place for a comprehensive exposition of the argument, but certain features of *Much Ado about Nothing* (1901) require a comment, because had the approach been more intuitive this could have been a first-rate *opéra comique* (without dialogue). Julian Sturgis had his faults as a librettist, but as an adapter of Shakespeare he here showed the skill of a Boito ; it availed nothing, for Stanford was at his most wayward. There were a few fine, deeply felt passages (especially in the last scene of all) but there were others which were rather laboured essays in a heavy Brahmsian style, and by contrast some of the choral writing in Act I was a throwback to the more perfunctory manner of Meyerbeer or early Wagner. The Dogberry scenes have been highly praised and may be effective in performance, but the only humour that emerges from the printed page is Shakespeare's own ; odious comparison with *Falstaff* is inescapable, and it must be confessed that the music does not identify itself with the characters as Verdi's does so superbly with Bardolph, Pistol and Doctor Caius. In *The Critic* (1916, libretto by Cairns James after Sheridan) Stanford's outstanding talent was again misapplied ; it was a *tour de force* with minimal appeal. Some of the jokes (like Sheridan's) were simple to the point of crudity ; others, less well-matched with the burlesque of the original, were sufficiently abstruse to strain the mental capacity of a Doctor of Music. It was all exquisitely done, of course, but *cui bono* ? It meant nothing to the audience at the Shaftesbury Theatre, and many musicians will be relieved to learn that Scott Goddard (who was erudite enough to catch all the allusions but too modest to admit it) 'felt as though he were a street urchin looking through a window at the goings-on among the gentry in the big house'. Had Stanford written a couple more *Shamuses* instead of falling prey to eclecticism in *Much Ado* and to intellectual esoterism in *The Critic*, he might now be recognised as an all-rounder to be mentioned in the same breath as Dvořák. He had the potential, but circumstances prevailed against him.

Hubert Parry — 'that dear, good fellow' as Elgar called him — was as competent, sincere, high-minded and painstaking a composer as ever lived. He was not endowed with genius, and in default a combination of those estimable qualities goes far to explain the apparent paradox that his music often sounds simultaneously inspired and machine-made. He never attempted operetta or anything like it, and one rather wishes that ALEXANDER MACKENZIE (1847–1935) had exercised the same restraint. Mackenzie was an important — a very important — figure in his day ; his music (like his personality) had a healthy down-to-earth-and-no-nonsense grain, which may have been antipathetic to admirers of the more earnest Stanford and the more fastidious Parry but was nevertheless a valuable corrective. On occasion, however, he came down to earth too abruptly, and his operettas (by contrast with Stanford's *Shamus*) added little to their composer's reputation. The first — *Phoebe* (1894) — achieved neither publication nor performance, and Mackenzie himself cannot have taken *His Majesty* (Savoy, 1897) very seriously. When he heard a brass band playing a 'selection' two years later he apparently failed to recognise it, for he remarked to his companion (Granville Bantock) : 'You know, Sullivan does write some jolly good tunes'. This was a backhanded compliment to his contemporary, for although much of *His Majesty* derived from that source — notably a tenor 'serenade' and the chorus-number 'The mistress we adore' — there were few signs of comparable fluency or constructive skill. Admittedly the lyrics can have given the composer no incentive to exert himself, for most of them were deplorable (though written by a versifier who elsewhere in these pages has been commended). Musically the most original item was an ensemble where the distinctive styles of various composers were parodied in turn. Mackenzie's third and last operetta, the one-act *Knights of the Road* (1905), contained some agreeable 'background music', but the well-featured 'locket song' was an unworthy lapse into triviality.

EDWARD GERMAN (1862–1936), whose real name was Edward German Jones, was a native of Whitchurch (Salop). Owing to ill-health he had to leave school at an unusually early age ; he devoted much of his youth to the study of music and became especially proficient on the violin. He entered the Royal Academy in 1880, and in 1888, after several years' experience as an orchestral player, was appointed musical director of the Globe Theatre. Meanwhile he had begun to compose : his *Rival Poets* (St. George's Hall, 1886) showed a refreshing — and prophetic — individuality.

Ex.132 Allegro

With love___ in her boat Like a flag_____ un-furled, She can keep___

(*continued over*)

For the next fifteen years, however, German concentrated on incidental music for Shakespearean productions (much of which still retains its popularity) and on more substantial symphonic works which were similar in style to the early compositions of Elgar (who remained a staunch friend and admirer). In 1901, shortly after Sullivan's death, German was chosen — curiously, perhaps, in view of his limited experience in operetta — to undertake completion of *The Emerald Isle*. He faced a horribly difficult task : Sullivan had left little beyond a few melodic sketches, so that those numbers for which he was given credit in the vocal score lacked the customary final polish and German, not surprisingly, failed to make them sound spontaneous. Inevitably the overall effect was one of heterogeneity ; moreover neither the librettist nor German (nor possibly Sullivan himself, despite Irish parentage) was capable of evoking a genuine Celtic atmosphere. *Shamus O'Brien* had been the real thing ; *The Emerald Isle* was spurious. It did sufficiently well, however, to be closely followed by the more characteristic *Merrie England* (1902) and *A Princess of Kensington* (1903). As all three pieces were played at the Savoy under the management of Rupert D'Oyly Carte (who by now had succeeded his father), their composer soon became widely regarded as the new wearer of Sullivan's mantle. But the box-office receipts were discouraging, and in the event German wrote only two more operettas — *Tom Jones* (1907, after Fielding) and *Fallen Fairies* (1909).[1]

---

[1] *Fallen Fairies* was a resuscitation of one of W. S. Gilbert's early sentimental plays written in blank verse, an ailing and therefore favourite child. The author had at various times offered the libretto in vain to Sullivan, Elgar, Messager, Massenet, Liza Lehmann and Mackenzie, and in consequence German found him in unusually docile and co-operative mood. The others had been shrewder judges of literary merit ; the absence of a male chorus, sometimes adduced as a fatal flaw, was probably immaterial.

In his light music German inclined to a mannered style intended to typify the merriness of England in the days of Henry VIII, Elizabeth I, Charles II, George III or Victoria impartially ; this has been described unkindly but not altogether inappropriately as 'olde-englyshe-tea-shoppe'. Certainly the overfondness for 6/8 'country dance' rhythms and for stereotyped progressions of 'secondary sevenths' became very irritating (particularly in *Tom Jones*) and made the composer easy game for a parodist. (So easy that when in 1934 Vivian Ellis — page 234 — attempted the far trickier task of parodying Sullivan in the revue *Streamline* he found himself willy-nilly imitating German most of the time.) Yet no one should deny the true flair for melody. Although *Merrie England* was ineffective in the theatre, it was not long before every soprano in the land was warbling 'Who shall say that love is cruel', every contralto 'O, peaceful England', every tenor 'Dan Cupid hath a garden', every baritone 'Who were the Yeomen'. After sixty years these songs, when well sung, still draw deserved applause, and there must be many members of amateur operatic societies who have enjoyed giving their support to the big tune from the first-act finale.

Ex.133 Allegro grandioso

These items went down so well with the public that German did his best to reproduce one of each type — so far as circumstances allowed — in his subsequent operettas. The later examples, taken in detachment, were equally meritorious, but they told one nothing new : only the waltz-song from *Tom Jones* found the same favour as its prototype. Here and there, however, a new note was struck ; for instance the excellent first-act finale of *A Princess of Kensington* was based on an infectious tune with a rhythmic vigour worthy of Offenbach —

Ex.134 Allegro giocoso

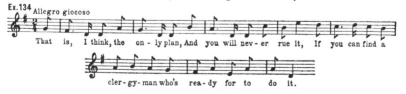

That is, I think, the on - ly plan, And you will nev - er rue it, If you can find a cler - gy- man who's rea- dy for to do it.

— and the opening chorus of Act II from *Fallen Fairies*, with its long drawn-out modulation to the mediant, had an almost voluptuous appeal.

Ex.135 Andantino

Although German's harmonic and rhythmic resource fell short of Sullivan's he showed his predecessor's skill — that is to say *great* skill — in the handling of limited orchestral forces. (A case in point is the march-chorus 'God save Elizabeth' from *Merrie England*.) Furthermore he surpassed him in sympathetic treatment of that most delicate of instruments, the human voice ; with vocalists he is understandably the more popular composer of the two. It was partly the fault of his librettists that his operettas, being ill-constructed, lacked solidity, but as Nietzsche said of Offenbach's each had its 'moments of wanton perfection'. He never fulfilled the expectations of those who at one time accounted him an outstanding exponent of operetta, but the refinement and restraint of his approach was a splendid example to others in the same field.

SIDNEY JONES, according to most authorities, was born at Leeds in 1869, but the fifth edition of *Grove* says London and 1861. However that may be, he earned his living first as a clarinettist, later as a conductor. The experience served him well, for his first two operettas — *A Gaiety Girl* (1893) and *An Artists' Model* (1895) — showed few signs of immaturity. The melodies were attractive, the workmanship consistently economical (reminding one of Lecocq) and at times expert ; passages which might otherwise have sounded trivial were often given added interest by unexpected vocal entries in canon, delicate orchestral figuration or other such tricks of the trade. Some of the choral writing, too, was accomplished ; here is an example from *A Gaiety Girl*, in which the sudden rhythmic unison (*a*) effectively emphasises the climax.

Ex.136 Allegro moderato

The contemporary popularity of these pieces, fully deserved, was surpassed by that of *The Geisha* (1896, libretto by Owen Hall) which, though palpably inspired by *The Mikado* (not such a bad source of inspiration), remains Jones's *chef d'œuvre*. 'A goldfish swam in a big glass bowl', 'Chin-chin-Chinaman' and the rest still have their power to charm or amuse, and the leading tenor — who so often comes off badly in operetta — had a ballad of unusual distinction in 'Star of my soul'. *A Greek Slave* (1899) was a comparatively mediocre affair, although the 'Invocation' was both picturesque and dramatic. *San Toy* (also 1899) enjoyed the same success as *The Geisha*, but the composer's China resembled his Japan too closely and the music, often repetitive, does not wear so well. *My Lady*

P

Molly (1903), which had a less exotic setting, was a more polished piece of work, though rather mixed in style. The ensemble 'Kiss, lad, and never tell' recalled a similar number from *An Artists' Model*, and Mendelssohnian lightness in the tiny, exquisite chorus 'Here's a nice to-do' — and elsewhere — was incongruously contrasted with hearty pastiche. ('To you, Sir Miles' was a genial parody of 'The Vicar of Bray'.) A few bars of a waltz-duet from this operetta will demonstrate how a clever craftsman like Jones could breathe life into the simplest alternation of tonic and dominant harmonies.

Ex.137 Tempo di Valse

When we were chil-dren, I and you, Of course you re-col-lect? Of course I re-col-lect.

See-see (1906) was yet another excursion to the Orient, much less rewarding than its predecessors. (The *verse*-section of the best song — 'Maid on a screen' — was a gem, but the refrain was tarnished.) The composer's attributes were better displayed in *The King of Cadonia* (1908) ; few operettas contain a more evocative piece of tone-painting than the elaborately constructed barcarolle, which is indeed beyond praise. An adequate quotation would take up far too much space, but anyone who doubts Jones's quality should procure a vocal score and study this item at leisure.

Disappointed perhaps by the failure of *The Persian Princess* (1909), which was redeemed from dullness only by the graceful chorus 'Gliding through the waters blue', Jones subsequently relaxed his efforts. He never again wrote an operetta all on his own, although he collaborated with Paul Rubens (page 219) in *The Girl from Utah* (1913) and *The Happy Day* (1916). The polyphonic opening to the former was quite brilliant ; the scene was a fashionable tea-shop where two separate parties gossiped away amongst themselves against a background chorus of waitresses, and Jones could carry off that sort of thing as well as anyone. In these composite works, however, he hardly lived up to the standards he had set for himself twenty years earlier, and presently he gave up composition altogether. Modest by nature, although touchy when his capabilities were questioned, he found his talents ill adapted to the requirements of the jazz-mad twenties and was glad to retire into the obscurity from which he had emerged. Sidney Jones's death in 1946 passed almost unnoticed, and he has never yet been given full credit for his achievements. Round the turn of the century he alone played as positive a rôle in operetta as that other Jones who preferred to be known as Edward German, and for a decade or so they jointly led the field. Their contemporaries were indeed hard put to it to keep up with the Joneses.

XXII

GO AS YOU PLEASE

THE gradual withering of British operetta and the simultaneous flowering of musical comedy can be typified in some measure by a brief summary of the career and achievements of IVAN CARYLL (real name Félix Tilkin) ; even the successively contrasted environments of his birth, maturity and death have symbolic significance, for he was born in 1861 at Liège, flourished in Edwardian London and died in 1921 in New York.

Caryll studied music in Belgium. In his early twenties he came to England, where he soon made himself useful by adapting French operettas to suit local requirements, notably Audran's *Cigale et fourmi* in 1890 and Lacome's *Ma mie Rosette* in 1892. Nor did he neglect composition on his own account, for his first operetta, *The Lily of Léoville*, came in 1886 and *Little Christopher Columbus* (1893) set him firmly on his feet. There was nothing specifically 'continental' about these early efforts ; indeed they persistently explored a vein of Victorian sentiment almost reminiscent of Frederic Clay. The turning-point came in 1894 when Caryll became musical director at the Gaiety Theatre just at the moment when George Edwardes was about to launch *The Shop Girl*. He seized the opportunity with both hands and wrote the bulk of the music *ex officio*. Although not the *first* musical comedy, *The Shop Girl* went a long way towards establishing the essential features of this comparatively new form of stage entertainment. Edwardes, the instigator, believed in 'teamwork' and employed an assortment of script-writers and composers, thus anticipating the methods of the film magnates of the next generation. Theoretically this militated against artistic unity, but 'the Guvnor' was quite capable of attending to that side of affairs himself. The barest minimum of boy-gets-girl romance for a plot ; sumptuous scenery and dresses ; lively hummable tunes ; no boring 'ensembles'; a couple of good comedians; above all a bevy of the prettiest young ladies imaginable: this was the 'unity' asked for by *flâneur* and tired business-man alike, and Edwardes saw that they got it. Caryll, being on his permanent staff, had the whip-hand over other contributors to the music of *The Shop Girl* and its successors, nearly all of which, during the next fifteen years or so, enjoyed enormous popularity. Among them *The Toreador* (1901) deserves a mention because it was the last production at the 'old' Gaiety before it was pulled down, *The Orchid* because it was the first at the new theatre which rose from the rubble in 1903.[1]

Caryll trod on dangerous ground when he tried to parody *Carmen* in the 'grand march and chorus' from *The Toreador* — but for the most part the music he turned out for the Gaiety served its purpose admirably. It was stereotyped, adequately lilting and catchy, and made no demands on an audience that seemingly never tired of the monotonous 'dotted' rhythms or the almost unrelieved tonic/dominant tum-tum of the accompaniments. For other theatres he went on writing operettas — often described with pardonable vagueness as 'musical plays' — which revealed that a perfunctory style was now becoming second nature. The least trivial were *The Gay Parisienne* (1896), *The Lucky Star* (1899), and *The Duchess of Dantzic* (1903, libretto by Henry Hamilton), but *The Girl from Kay's*, *The Earl and the Girl* (both also 1903) and *The Cherry Girl* (1904) were equally successful. However, *The Little Cherub* (1906), *Chin-chin* and *Nelly Neil* (both 1907) were failures, and as by this time Caryll was less happy at the Gaiety — where he at last found himself deservedly playing second fiddle to Lionel Monckton (see page 218) — he presently took himself to the United States. His first piece in new surroundings — *The Satyr* (1910) — made little impression (it was later played in this country as *The Pink Lady*), but he eventually established a reputation in New York with *The Little Café* (1912). *The Girl behind the Gun* (1919) found special favour back in London, where just then most people wanted to forget about guns and it was accordingly re-christened *Kissing Time*.

[1] This was the age of the fabulous 'Gaiety Girl' who by tradition usually married into the peerage. With curious lack of foresight George Edwardes had allowed the personifying title to be used for Sidney Jones's operetta (see page 213), which he himself had produced — not at the Gaiety but at the Prince of Wales'.

Caryll displayed slightly more enterprise (musically) in America than he had in Europe. There were a few welcome touches of harmonic initiative in *The Satyr* (notably in the charming duet 'When love goes a-straying'), while ragtime rhythms played their part in *The Little Café* and in the first-act finale of the otherwise unexciting *Oh! oh! Delphine* (1913). A fox-trot entitled 'Don't fall in love with me' from *The Girl behind the Gun* made it clear that the composer was not falling behind the times, and had he lived longer he would doubtless have continued to follow changing fashions.

LIONEL MONCKTON (1861–1924) was a more talented musician, but he never fully realised his potentialities, which in any case were developed rather late in life. Even during his thirties he still had to be content with adapting French operettas and writing single numbers for inclusion in other people's musical comedies. Later he found himself enmeshed in the web of collaborations that bedevilled the industry and he rarely escaped into the open. Leaving aside two unimportant early essays, he can be credited with only four operettas of his own. (His own, that is, bar the occasional but almost inevitable 'interpolations'.) They were *A Country Girl* (1902), *The Cingalee* (1904), *The Quaker Girl* (1910) and *The Dancing Mistress* (1912). Meanwhile, however, he was gradually overhauling Caryll as the predominating partner in George Edwardes's Gaiety series ; he certainly played a more conspicuous part in *Our Miss Gibbs* (1909) where Edwardian musical comedy reached a pinnacle. The same year gave birth to *The Arcadians*, the first of three operettas which he wrote in conjunction with Howard Talbot (see page 220). This had a triumphant career, but *The Mousmé* (1911) and *The Boy* (1917) — which can only by courtesy be described as an operetta — were less successful. Though Monckton contributed to several war-time revues, he was an Edwardian *par excellence* and his spirit faded with the age. Despite all entanglements he was quite capable of completing a satisfactory operetta off his own bat. His patter-songs were acceptable imitations of Sullivan's, and though he failed to achieve commensurate skill in ensemble work (the 'double chorus' from *The Quaker Girl* was a poor affair) he was quite happy when following a more spontaneous lead, as in the delightful '*Tip-toe, tip*-toe' (also from *The Quaker Girl*). Now and again, too,

there was an unexpected touch of characterisation : a plagal cadence
(*a*) from *A Country Girl* brought a soft western burr to the delivery,
conjuring up, perhaps, a momentary vision of rosy cheeks and the
taste of rough cider.

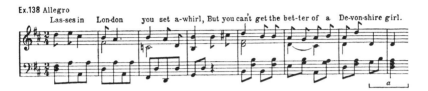

Ex.138 Allegro
Las-ses in   Lon-don   you set a-whirl, But you can't get the bet-ter of a De-von-shire girl.

Moreover, Monckton wrote some memorable tunes : if 'Moon-
struck' from *Our Miss Gibbs* ('I'm such a silly when the moon
comes out') is always associated in the public recollection with his
wife Gertie Millar (afterwards the Countess of Dudley) that fact
need not blind one to its rhythmic verve and classical symmetry.

PAUL RUBENS (1876–1917), like Monckton, was the product of
a public school and Oxford University, and though he was junior
by fifteen years their active careers marched side by side. He won
his spurs with *Three Little Maids* (1902) and *Lady Madcap* (1904), in
which he set himself a precedent by writing his own libretti ; the
only positive attribute of his music, up to date, was a certain Gallic
élan in the rhythm. The most successful of his subsequent works —
which showed considerably more polish — were *Miss Hook of
Holland* (1907), *The Sunshine Girl* (1912), *Tonight's the Night* (1914)
and *Betty* (1915, libretto by Frederic Lonsdale). It need hardly be
added that Rubens also made frequent contributions to operettas
and musical comedies for which Sidney Jones, Caryll or Monckton
were primarily responsible ; among other composers with whom
he entered into collaboration was Haydn Wood (*Tina*, 1915).
Though he abominably overworked facile harmonic progressions
of the type for which Sullivan had to be taken to task in Ex. 129
(page 198), he now and again showed an artist's touch in moods
both sentimental and vivacious, and he had a sure sense of the theatre.
Nothing could be better of their kind than two contrasted items
from *Miss Hook of Holland* : the barcarolle 'By the side of the sleepy
canal' and the bewitching 'Little Miss Wooden-shoes', both most

effective in their context.   It was in *Miss Hook*, rather than in the
more pretentious *Balkan Princess* (1910) that Rubens was at his best,
but *Dear Little Denmark* (1909), though not a big favourite, was
almost as good.   In particular there were two excellent chorus-
numbers — the entry of the Grand Duke in Act I and 'We are
servants low and humble' in Act II.   The mêlée of actresses and
students in *After the Girl* (1914) was another admirable ensemble,
and indeed Rubens, though less gifted than Monckton, was a more
accomplished craftsman.   He even indulged in an occasional
madrigal or glee — there were two, both virtually unaccompanied,
in *My Mimosa Maid* (1908) — and when he chose to take a little
trouble he could startle with an unexpectedly charming modulation.
Ex. 139 is from *Miss Hook of Holland*.

Ex.139   Andante

Now the   moon,   Sil - ver   white,   Bids   us   bask   *etc.*

HOWARD TALBOT (1865–1928) was born in New York, his
real name being Richard Munkittrick.   He came to this country as
a young man and studied music with Hubert Parry, to whom in
1893 he dedicated an appropriately academic curiosity entitled
A Musical Chess Tournament which was given three times at Oxford
and three times at King's Lynn.   A more conventional stage piece,
Monte Carlo (1896), had almost as short a life.   (Granville Bantock
wrote an interpolated item, 'Who'll give a penny to the monkey?'
— surely a rather tactless allusion to Talbot's true patronymic.)   But
while all London was raving about *San Toy* (at Daly's) and *The
Runaway Girl* (current attraction at the Gaiety), a long provincial
tour was testing the worth of a new and more ambitious effort by
this enterprising recruit to the ranks of operetta.   One would have
thought that *The Geisha* and *San Toy* had surfeited audiences with
oriental burlesque and pidgin English — but not a bit of it.   *A
Chinese Honeymoon*, first played at Hanley in 1899, broke records

when it reached the capital in 1901 ; viewed in retrospect this was a
freak triumph comparable with that of *Dorothy* fifteen years earlier.
George Dance (lineal descendant of Charles Favart and H. B. Farnie)
was the producer and author, but the competent libretto was in no
way remarkable.   Nor were there any specially good tunes, and
from any standpoint the best number was a comic ensemble in the
Victorian music-hall tradition — 'Martha spanks the grand pianner'.
Talbot's subsequent output more faithfully reflected both his ability
and his limitations.   His melodic inspiration rarely flowed as freely
as Monckton's (he was prone to barely disguised repetitions) and he
had not the instinct which enabled Rubens to exploit a stage situation
to advantage.   But Royal College training had endowed him with
a distrust of utterly vacuous accompaniments, and his workmanship
had a professional look about it.   Like Sidney Jones, he was addicted
to simple canons, and his choral writing was particularly skilful.
In this respect the first-act finale of *The Blue Moon* (1905, partly by
Rubens) and the opening chorus of *The Girl behind the Counter* (1906)
could hardly be bettered.   An ingenious rhythmic overlap from
The Belle of Brittany (1908) demands quotation.

Thanks to his technical resource and good taste (by the standards of
the present chapter), Talbot was a healthy influence when called on
to collaborate : in *The Arcadians* he was a useful foil for Monckton,
who was more fluent but less well-equipped.   Though the latter
stole most of the limelight with 'The pipes of Pan' and 'I love
London', Talbot made a thoroughly good job of the 'shower

chorus' in the Ascot scene, where his treatment matched the exceptionally clever rhymes of Arthur Wimperis, one of the few talented librettists of the period :

> See our dresses — every *one* done
> By the foremost firms in London,
> All their handiwork is *undone*,
> 　　Every shred !
> Swan from Edgar swims asunder,
> Stagg has got her Mantle under,
> Pooles in puddles slip and blunder,
> 　　Hope has fled.

In his later works — *e.g.* the musical comedies *Mr. Manhattan* (1916) and *Who's Hooper?* (1919) — Talbot made no attempt to attune himself to a changing world. But he went on composing to the end, and died too soon to hear performances of *Her Ladyship* or *The Daughter of the Gods*, both written during the last year of his life. In any case, they belonged to a vanished Arcadia.

Though I have done my best to furnish pointers to the few distinctive qualities possessed by Caryll, Monckton, Rubens and Talbot, it must be admitted that stylistic differentiation can only be arbitrary. Indulging as they did in almost every possible permutation of mutual collaboration, their manner (derived from Sullivan rather than directly from French or Viennese sources) often displayed a uniformity that was more than superficial : only the shrewdest connoisseur, when hearing for the first time one of their composite productions with which he happened to be unfamiliar, could unerringly apportion each single item. It therefore comes as a relief to find that the remaining contemporary practitioner of comparable importance, LESLIE STUART (1866–1928, real name Thomas Barrett), had an individuality which sprang from a devotion to rhythmic idiosyncrasy. Many distinguished British musicians, among whom Sullivan and Stanford have been discussed in these pages, employed rhythmic devices as a normal means to appropriate accentuation in word-setting. Stuart's quirks, on the other hand, bore little relation to the rise, fall or stress of verbal phrases, and indeed were often inapposite in a metrical context. Rhythmic impulse was the sole motivation and rhythmic variety an end in itself; the outcome was often fortuitous. This is not to deny that Stuart wrote tunes which were capable of standing on their own merits — *e.g.* 'When I was a girl like you' from *The School Girl* (1903) and 'Decorate the room with roses red' from *The Belle of Mayfair* (1906). But preoccupation with the rhythmic aspect was everywhere apparent, and one feels that *these* melodies, even, were contrived rather than conceived. If freedom from conventional trammels often caused embarrassment in solo pieces it was very welcome in ensembles, where an occasional false accent was a venial offence. 'Tell me, pretty maiden' from *Florodora* (1899) is a case in point, and any superior person who does not promptly succumb to its enchantment should be made to copy it out bar by bar. Other examples, less well-known but equally bizarre, were 'Hunt the slipper' from *The Silver Slipper* (1901) and the brilliant opening choruses of *Havana* (1908) and of *Peggy* (1911). These were all models of their kind, but so dependent for effect on an elaborate pile of rhythmic contrasts that the quotation of a short extract would do no justice to the composer. However, condensation of a simpler choral passage from *Havana* will illustrate the delights — and the dangers — of Stuart's haphazard, almost *outré* approach.

Ex.141

Unfortunately rhythmic imagination, though fertile, was not inexhaustible; as time went on the artful dodges came to sound forced and could no longer disguise melodic insufficiency. Stuart's last few works were plagued by iterations ; one little figure that recurred constantly was an unsophisticated anticipation of elementary jazz. Had he so wished, he might have competed successfully in that corner of the building, but he retired from active participation in 1912, being content to remain in solitary occupation of the niche he had carved out for himself.

For the sake of completeness the names of Felix, Lehmann, Haines and Norton must be added to our list. The ubiquitous HUGO FELIX was born at Vienna in 1872. His first operetta *Die kleine Katze* (1890), was a teen-age trifle ; it was followed by *Husarenblut* (Vienna, 1894), *Madame Sherry* (Berlin, 1902) and *Les Merveilleuses* (Paris, 1903). The last two enjoyed considerable success in London, where Felix settled for several years and qualified for inclusion in this chapter — rather than elsewhere — by writing *Tantalizing Tommy* (1904), joining George Edwardes's team of resident composers at the Gaiety, and entering into fifty-fifty collaboration with Howard Talbot in *The Pearl Girl* (1913). Presently North America beckoned, and after *Lassie* and *The Sweetheart Shop* (both 1920) had been produced in New York, Felix made for Hollywood, where he remained until his death in 1934. Despite his origin, not all his waltz-tunes were specifically Viennese in character ; they relied to an unusual degree on simple chromatic contrasts. Smooth workmanship was apparent in many excellent ensembles (the bustle and excitement of a motley crowd was well caught in the opening scene of Act II from *Les Merveilleuses*) and there was some use of simple *Leitmotive* in the later Lehár manner. On the other hand Felix had little flair for melody ; a charming verse from *Lassie*, 'Oh, there's an echo in the wind', was exceptional.

An operetta by LIZA LEHMANN (1862–1918) — *Sergeant Brue* — did good business at the Strand Theatre in 1904 without showing her talents to best advantage ; it was overburdened with comic songs in 6/8 rhythm. Meanwhile the versatile Seymour Hicks joined forces with HERBERT HAINES (1880–1923) in a handful of 'musical plays' all dated between 1904 and 1907. Of these *The Catch of the Season* proved the most popular, though it was not noticeably better than the others. Nothing else in Haines's output led one to expect the accomplishment of the sprightly opening chorus from *The Beauty of Bath*. In this work he was assisted by three other composers, among them FREDERIC NORTON (1875–1946), who is inevitably remembered by his music for *Chu Chin Chow* (1916), which was crude in parts but adequately tuneful throughout. This 'Musical Tale of the East' set new standards both in spectacular *décor* and popular appeal; it provided momentary escape from realities for countless thousands during the anxious days of the first world war and proceeded on its unruffled way for the first three years of that long-awaited period of peace, when composers of operetta no less than politicians, found it necessary to adjust themselves to changed conditions.

XXIII

FORTY YEARS OF FRUSTRATION

IT has already been hinted that the later operettas of Monckton and his colleagues degenerated into something like musical comedies ; and indeed from about 1914 onwards the distinctive characteristics of the two genres gradually disappeared in a partial merger. The resultant hybrid was rarely imbued with either the uninhibited gaiety of Edwardian musical comedy or the artistic integrity observable in genuine operettas like *The Geisha, Merrie England, Miss Hook of Holland* and *The Quaker Girl*.

The more acceptable specimens of the new amorphous category featured 'music' rather than 'comedy', the 'romantic' aspect being tempered with only a small measure of humour. HAROLD FRASER SIMSON (1873–1944) — whose burlesque-operetta *Bonita* (1911) had been ruined by its libretto — struck this balance in *The Maid of the Mountains* (1917), which partly reconciled Edwardian traditions with war-time requirements. It was easily his best work as well as his most successful. The half-dozen which followed were more perfunctory, but they showed up well beside most of their type. Fraser Simson's melodies, though tiresomely conventional in pattern, were often very pretty, he rarely descended to vulgarity or cheap sentimentality and never fell a prey to jazz. Moreover he had learnt a lesson from *Bonita* and thereafter was careful in his choice of librettists ; they included Frederic Lonsdale (*The Maid of the Mountains*), Edward Knoblock (*Our Peg*, 1919), Seymour Hicks (*Head over Heels*, 1923), Hastings Turner (*Betty in Mayfair*, 1925) and A. A. Milne (*Toad of Toad Hall*, 1930).[1] In *A Southern Maid* (1920) and *The Street Singer* (1924), however, the composer subordinated his

---

[1] *Toad of Toad Hall*, based on Kenneth Grahame's *Wind in the Willows*, was not an operetta. Like Frederic Norton's charming *Pinkie and the Fairies* (1908), Roger Quilter's perennial *Where the Rainbow Ends* (1911) and Benjamin Britten's very original *Let's make an Opera* (1949), it provided Christmas fare for parents who disapproved of pantomime and children who were bored by it.

talent to meet the requirements of his leading ladies, José Collins and Phyllis Dare. MONTAGUE PHILLIPS (1885–   ) made a brave attempt to recapture the mood of *Merrie England* in *The Rebel Maid* (1921). He only succeeded in emulating the more questionable side of German's art, but now and again there was a welcome if rather self-conscious display of harmonic initiative (the occasional inconsequent shiftings of tonality were curiously suggestive of Prokofiev) and his instrumentation was skilful.

Meanwhile a few composers of greater distinction were spasmodically tackling the problem from a loftier standpoint, each in his or her individual manner ; their praiseworthy efforts demand a different standard of criticism. GUSTAV HOLST (1874–1934) had written an operetta at the age of eighteen — *Lansdowne Castle* — which is said to have owed much to both Sullivan and Grieg. In 1923 he startled opera-goers with the finely original *Perfect Fool*, marred only by some perfectly foolish parodies of Verdi and Wagner. *At the Boar's Head* (1925, drawn from Shakespeare) was an essay in the manner of his friend Vaughan Williams : it was founded on folk melodies which were painstakingly documented in the vocal score. *The Boatswain's Mate* (1916) by that sterling warrior ETHEL SMYTH (1858–1944) was based on a story by W. W. Jacobs which combined comedy and sentiment in just proportions, and much of the music was as apt as it was clever. But the construction was faulty and there were occasional lapses in taste. It was a confession of weakness to make a centre-piece of the lovely Somerset folk-song 'Lord Rendal', an indiscretion to cloud its purity with chromatic harmonisation. Nevertheless the merits of *The Boatswain's Mate* — which should perhaps rank as an *opéra comique* — were considerable. The shorter and attractive *Entente cordiale* (1925) — definitely an operetta — showed that Ethel Smyth was familiar with the methods of Arthur Sullivan. So too was CECIL ARMSTRONG GIBBS (1889–1960), though his operettas bore a personal stamp. *The Blue Peter* (1923, libretto by A. P. Herbert) had many of the qualities that go to make a good curtain-raiser — conciseness, consistency, humour and tunefulness.[1] This accomplished

---

[1] *Entente cordiale* and *The Blue Peter* were first played at the Royal College of Music ; neither has achieved deserved recognition away from South Kensington.

trifle had only four participants. The same restraint was exercised, more improbably, in the full-length *Midsummer Madness* (1924, libretto by Clifford Bax), which was carefully wrought but a little too 'intellectual' in conception to have a wide appeal. However, 'Put down your tray' and 'Come, will you dance me a measure' were unequivocally charming. Armstrong Gibbs was keenly interested in operetta but more at home when pursuing his bent as a miniaturist; in his stage works he did not pay sufficient attention to the problems of orchestration.

With all deference to Holst, Ethel Smyth and Armstrong Gibbs, the most attractive British operetta produced during this hesitant period was the simple and straightforward *Mr. Pepys* (1926), with words by J. B. Fagan and music by the organist and song-writer MARTIN SHAW (1875–1958). A purist might cavil at a seventeenth-century subject being treated in the manner of eighteenth-century ballad-opera (short numbers and few ambitious ensembles), but there was no spurious imitation of either period. Although reliance on 6/8 rhythms was rather too pronounced, almost every item was both artistic and tuneful.

Ex.142
Andante espressivo

You lov'd me once, I know. I did but turn my head And all your wits were fled— But that was long a-go.

All this was a labour of love, for so far as operetta was concerned the British public was quite content with the works of Lehár (see page 138 *et seq.*), Friml and Romberg (pages 246–7), an occasional novelty from Fraser Simson — and revivals of Gilbert-and-Sullivan. Consequently *The Boatswain's Mate, The Perfect Fool, Midsummer Madness* and *Mr. Pepys* aroused little interest outside musical circles and within them set no precedents. 'At the present time [1928] our theatres are content to import trash from America or dullness from Vienna or, alternatively, to employ native writers, who are frankly purveyors rather than artists, to stir the jazz-pot and ladle out the poisonous fluid in a tepid state to more or less apathetic audiences.' One need not concur with all the implied strictures to recognise that THOMAS DUNHILL (1877–1946) here expressed a contemporary point of view widely held by serious-minded musicians. Soon afterwards he himself tried to break the impasse with *Tantivy Towers* (1931). He had much in his favour, not least a libretto — which surprisingly included no dialogue — by A. P. Herbert, the Gilbert of his generation. And the music did indeed show good taste, sound technique, apt characterisation and adequate stage sense. What it lacked was the commensurate melodic spontaneity which might have been expected from a composer who in a portfolio of songs and piano pieces had proved himself uncommonly gifted in that respect. The second act ended with a rousing ensemble based on 'D'ye ken John Peel?' : despite the panache of the trio 'Two suitors wooed me in a dream last night' and the lyrical intensity of the tenor's 'Wear your white, my love, tonight' one left the theatre convinced that 'John Peel' had been the tune of the evening. For those who still hoped against hope that British operetta had a future, *Tantivy Towers* was both stimulating and frustrating ; stimulating because it was so much better than it might have been, frustrating because all the same it wasn't *quite* good enough. Author and composer strove mightily for a cause which both had much at heart ; one could not say that Dunhill let his colleague down, but he had less self-confidence and was perhaps overborne by the weight of his responsibilities. It was nine years before he wrote another adult operetta — *Something in the City* (1940). The choral sections showed signs of hurried workmanship, but several of the songs and duets were well worthy of this talented composer. A great deal more thought went into the detail of Ex. 143 than is apparent at first glance.

Q

Ex.143

Andante moderato

I am, I know, No-thing to you.   That be-ing so, ___ What can I do?

Midsummer Madness and Tantivy Towers were both produced at
the Lyric Theatre, Hammersmith, by that enterprising actor-
manager Nigel Playfair. In 1920 he had a flying start with Frederic
Austin's version of The Beggar's Opera (which enjoyed nearly
as long a run as Chu Chin Chow), and presently he followed
up with other eighteenth-century ballad-operas — e.g. Linley's
Duenna in 1924, Dibdin's Lionel and Clarissa in 1925 and Arne's
Love in a Village in 1928.[1]   They were revitalised by his clever
musical director ALFRED REYNOLDS (1884–   ), who added
selected items from various Italian intermezzi (of an earlier period)
and occasionally slipped in a creation of his own.   But Reynolds
had no real opportunity to demonstrate his quality until 1932, when
he set Derby Day, a full-length libretto by A. P. Herbert. (In 1926
they had collaborated in the one-act Policeman's Serenade which
lived up to its sub-title — A Grand Little Opera.)   Derby Day was a
commendable piece of work, all things considered the most generally
acceptable British operetta since The Arcadians, though musically not
the most distinguished.   The tunes did not everywhere match the
brilliance of the verses, but they were well above the average and
their treatment was appropriately — not obtrusively — up to date.
The music Reynolds wrote in 1934 for Reginald Arkell's stage
version of Sellar and Yeatman's classic 1066 and All That — despite
the quartet for the four Georges (an admirable piece of burlesque)
— was unoriginal ; perhaps Playfair's varied demands militated
against the development of stylistic individuality.

After recording so much suburban activity it is a pleasure to find

[1] For a comment on the Playfair Vie parisienne see page 28 footnote.

two British operettas which had their *premières* in the West End —
The Pride of the Regiment (1932) and *Jolly Roger* (1933). They were
the outcome of a collaboration between V. Clinton Baddeley and
WALTER LEIGH (1905–1942). Viewed in retrospect both works
look immature ; they relied too much on parodying conventions
most of which were already outworn. Of greater importance is
clear evidence that for the first time since 1875 two comparative
youngsters, both very talented, were meeting on equal terms in a
joint enterprise that seemed full of promise. Unfortunately, during
the next few years they drew in their horns and concentrated on
work which, while involving no lowering of artistic standards, was
of its nature ephemeral. Any hope that they might profitably
renew their association in operetta under more propitious circumstances was blown sky-high when the composer gave his life
for his country fighting the Germans in the Western Desert. Although *The Pride of the Regiment* courted cheap popularity by introducing a catchy 'theme song' ('Love calls as no-one supposes') there
were also signs of sensitive musicianship, and the admirable effect of an
overlapping rhythmic figure in Ex. 144 was particularly noteworthy.
Jolly Roger ranged from the braggadocio of 'Barratry, arson, rape
and slaughter' to the fluent charm of a ballad well-designed to catch
the public fancy without offending the susceptibilities of the most
exacting musician (Ex. 145).

While all this was going on, the Australian-born ARTHUR
BENJAMIN (1893–1960) had been at work on two short operettas —
The Devil take her (1931) and *Prima Donna* (1933) — which were
conceived in a modern idiom and inhabited the same sphere as
Roland-Manuel's *Isabelle et Pantalon* (see pages 102-3). Until he again
came to the fore some twenty years later with *A Tale of Two Cities*,
Benjamin's reputation in this country rested largely on *The Devil
take her* and *Prima Donna*. I have not had the good fortune to hear
performances, but to judge from the vocal scores the latter is the
better-fashioned of the two.

It is not with *Hugh the Drover* (1924) or *Sir John in Love* (1929)
that RALPH VAUGHAN WILLIAMS (1872–1958) makes a belated
and welcome appearance on the scene. Though the former was
designated a ballad-opera and the latter was tentatively put forward
as a companion-piece to Holst's *Boar's Head* rather than as a challenge
to Verdi's *Falstaff* (which was unthinkable), it would strain the
elasticity of our agreed definition to call either an operetta. On the
other hand, the less well-known *Poisoned Kiss* (Cambridge, 1936)
definitely *was* one, besides being a reminder that this illustrious
composer was always on the look-out for new worlds to conquer.
If *The Poisoned Kiss* conquered no new world it was none the less a
remarkable achievement for a young man of sixty-three. The
libretto by Evelyn Sharp (Mrs. H. W. Nevinson) was not so bad as
has sometimes been made out, and she played her part nobly with
deft satirical verses for the ensemble 'Today when all the world
behaves'. The wonted folk-strain, though perceptible, was less
thunderous than usual, and Vaughan Williams relished the chance
to write patter-songs and syncopated waltzes ; he also made at least
one good joke at his own expense (Ex. 146). (Or was it, after all,
not so much a joke as an acquiescence ? Simona Pakenham, a friend
of the composer and a most persuasive champion, has told me that
by his own boast a duet from *The Poisoned Kiss* was inspired by
'There grew a little flow'r' from Sullivan's *Ruddigore*.[1])

---

[1] James Day's *Vaughan Williams* (1961) was published too late for me to take
advantage of the author's erudition, but just in time for me to note briefly that his
penetrating appraisal of this 'romantic extravaganza' incorporates several specific
comparisons with Gilbert-and-Sullivan.

Ex.146

The Poisoned Kiss, along with Mr. Pepys, Tantivy Towers and the others, was soon driven back to the obscurity of the printed page — a sad commentary on the parlous state of British operetta. And the rest of the story is anti-climax, for several of the names that remain for inclusion in this chapter are unlikely to be found in any standard Dictionary of Musicians. IVOR NOVELLO (1893–1951, real name Ivor Davies) contributed to various musical comedies during and just after the first world war — The Golden Moth (1921) was almost entirely his own — but for many years he was better-known as an actor-manager and a playwright than as a composer. (His plays — notably I Lived with You — were well constructed and carefully written.) It was not until 1935 that he inaugurated an astonishingly successful series of operettas (one can call them nothing else) which followed one another at fairly regular intervals until 1949. Bearing glossy titles like Glamorous Night, Careless Rapture and Perchance to Dream, they surpassed The Maid of the Mountains in their concentration on Romance — with a capital R — and in their avoidance of humour. Novello wrote both dialogue and music (though not the lyrics); his gift of superficial melody, backed by rudimentary technique, furnished a repletion of senti-mental effusions which could be 'plugged' ad nauseam. What mattered still more was that he played all the leading rôles himself. Georges Edwardes had titillated the gilded Romeos of his day with a glorification of womanhood. In an age of female emancipation — and preponderance — Novello evolved a masterly antithesis : no wonder he was popular. Any intrinsic merit his operettas may have possessed has been inflated beyond reason in the panegyrics of undiscriminating eulogists ; it is high time the bubble was pricked.

His only challenger as a versatile man-of-the-theatre was NOEL
COWARD (1899–   ), whose approach has always been more
sophisticated. His literary work is a compound of sentiment, biting
satire and epigrammatic wit ; as a director he exploits a remarkable
instinct for 'theatre'; as an actor his timing is superb ; and though
he cannot sing he contrives a *parlante* croak which less polished
artists have tried to emulate with disastrous results. His knowledge
of music being *nil*, the elementary fabrications which he fits to
his own verses have to be written down, harmonised, jazzed-up and
orchestrated by a corps of *entrepreneurs*. He only concerns us here
because at one stage of his career he not only wrote, acted in
and directed a handful of operettas or what-you-will, but also insti-
gated their music. The cloying *Bitter-Sweet* (1929) and the more
characteristic *Conversation Piece* (1934) were the most successful ; a
share of the credit belongs to his anonymous confederates.

VIVIAN ELLIS (1904–   ), whatever his shortcomings, is at
least a *composer*. His musical comedies show awareness of classical
operetta, but even his post-war collaborations with A. P. Herbert —
e.g. Big Ben (1946) and *Bless the Bride* (1947) — are regrettably
tarnished with the harmonic clichés which riddled popular light
music during the thirties. He has a flair for rhythmic aptness in
word-setting, however, which raises his work above the level of
most contemporaries in the same field. The close of the 'theme
song' from *And so to bed* (1951, libretto by Ellis himself) illustrates
his weakness and strength simultaneously.

Ex.147 Allegretto

Substantival use of the word 'musical' is inartistic but convenient; the comprehensive umbrella covers both grandiose white elephants like *South Pacific* (see page 248) and frolicsome little lambs like *Salad Days* (1954), which must have earned a fortune for its unassuming young composer JULIAN SLADE (1929–   ). ANTONY HOPKINS (1921–   ) and LENNOX BERKELEY (1903–   ) have followed a (financially) less rewarding tradition, that of Holst and Benjamin. With the best will in the world it is difficult to believe that Hopkins's one-act *Three's Company* (1953) and Berkeley's one-act *Dinner Engagement* (1954), clever though they are, will find any more secure a place in the repertory than have *The Perfect Fool* or *The Devil take her*. (*A Dinner Engagement* is unusual in reverting to the *opera buffa* convention of separate arias, duets, etc., connected by *recitativo secco*.)[1]

That a discussion of British operetta has run to six chapters — while no other national school apart from the French has been accorded more than three — is only partly due to an expectation that British readers will have more interest in the native product; the disproportion is historically justified, and derives from the flood which ensued when *H.M.S. Pinafore* burst open the lock-gates in 1878. (Had this breach not been made, the stream might have dried up, as it did in Italy.) The triumphs of Gilbert and Sullivan proved a mixed blessing for their successors, for while audiences became operetta-conscious the high standard required from competitors was disconcertingly apparent. During Sullivan's lifetime that was fair enough, and all might have gone well if posterity could have come to regard him as a component part of a tidy chronological sequence — as it could Offenbach, Lecocq and Messager, or Suppé, Johann Strauss and Lehár. But Sidney Jones, for all his talent, was no Messager; Edward German no Lehár. Consequently Sullivan, whose reputation weathered all storms, remained the yardstick against which every British exponent from Alfred Cellier to Walter Leigh had to be measured; inevitably they all fell a long way short of the mark. Dunhill's complaint about managerial and public indifference was not wholly justified in so far as it applied to

---

[1] Benjamin Britten's *Albert Herring* (1947), though unquestionably a 'comic opera', has an amplitude which sets it beyond our present scope.

operetta *per se*. One understands his resentment, and it was certainly a bad thing that between the wars half a dozen clever composers, including himself, should have demonstrated an aptitude for the genre and then been obliged to desist for want of encouragement. But the explanation did not lie in apathy so much as in the perpetuation of a solitary gauge for comparison. Although Sullivan in his secret heart believed that the 'Savoy trifles' were beneath his dignity, he probably realised that they would help to keep British operetta alive for the next few years at least. He, no less than Gilbert, would be surprised to learn that their continued and deserved popularity had eventually helped to kill it.

§

FINALE

XXIV

THE TRANSATLANTIC SCENE [1]

DURING the early nineteenth century travelling opera companies
and symphony orchestras visited the North American continent
with increasing frequency. As time progressed so did appreciation
of good music — at any rate in the eastern States. But creative
art was slow a-growing. It is generally conceded that the first
'American' opera was William Henry Fry's *Leonora* (1845) and
the second George Bristow's *Rip van Winkle* (1855). Thereafter over
forty years elapsed before the production of Walter Damrosch's
Scarlet Letter in 1896, and it was not until 1910 that the Metropolitan Opera House in New York admitted a native composer —
Frederick Converse with his *Pipe of Desire*. Meanwhile, however,
operetta had established itself. The first example, so far as I can trace,
was Sousa's *Our Flirtation* (1881), which the composer later described
as a 'musical comedy' ; at the time of its presentation that term was
not yet in general currency.

JOHN PHILIP SOUSA (1854–1932) was born at Washington of
mixed Portuguese and Bavarian parentage. As a violinist he had the
invaluable experience of leading the orchestra which accompanied
Offenbach's triumphal tour in the mid-seventies (see page 39), and
presently he became a conductor ; among his assignments was the
New England trip of *The Contrabandista* mentioned on page 190.[2]
For ten years or so he was in charge of the United States Marine

---

[1] For biographical information on three or four comparatively obscure composers
mentioned in this chapter I am indebted to J. Walker McSpadden's *Operas and Musical
Comedies* (1946, revised 1951).

[2] This was not Sousa's only connection with a Sullivan operetta, for he
married, very happily, a charming young lady whom he first met when she
was understudying the soubrette part in one of the many pirated versions of
H.M.S. Pinafore.

Corps Band, and in 1892 he formed one of his own. Marches like *Liberty Bell* and *The Stars and Stripes for ever* are a worthy legacy, but Sousa also wrote six operettas — not counting his immature *Flirtation*. Except in *The Charlatan* (1897), which had a Slav setting and incorporated polkas and mazurkas, they were largely comprised of marches and Latin dance-measures. *El Capitán* (1896) was the most popular, but the opening chorus of *The Bride Elect* (1898) and a brilliant vocal scherzo ('This is my busy day') from *The Glass Blowers* (1912) deserve high commendation for their originality. (In the last-named work there was a lusty chorus for the girls with the verbal *motif* 'My love is a blower.') Another early exponent was WILLARD SPENSER (1852–1933) with *The little Tycoon* (1886), but he soon faded into obscurity; WOOLSON MORSE (1858–1897) died before he could fulfil the promise of his unpretentious *Wang* (1891) and *Panjandrum* (1893). It was left to REGINALD DE KOVEN (1859–1920) and VICTOR HERBERT (1859–1924) to establish a delayed and short-lived tradition.

De Koven was born in the State of Connecticut but was educated in England (he was an Oxford graduate) and in Germany. His *Begum* (1887) and *Don Quixote* (1889) attracted little attention, but the success in 1890 of *Robin Hood* (then called *Maid Marian*) enabled him to pay another extended visit to Europe where he met (among other notabilities) Johann Strauss, Sullivan and Messager; he returned to the United States in 1892. Victor Herbert, grandson of the Irish novelist Samuel Lover and a native of Dublin, was taken to Germany at the age of seven; as a youngster he emulated Offenbach's prowess on the cello. In 1885 he married the Viennese opera-singer Thérèse Foerster, and when she was engaged by the Metropolitan he accompanied her to New York. For several years he earned his keep as cellist and conductor, but he had the itch to compose, and his first operetta — *Prince Ananias* — came in 1894. From then on the careers of de Koven and Herbert marched side by side. In character they had little in common : de Koven was a frigid and aloof ascetic, Herbert a friendly and good-natured *bon viveur*. But for many years they shared the same librettist, and never can two promising aspirants have been worse served : I choose at random two typical examples of an amazing flair for ungram-

matical bathos. At a moment of dramatic intensity in Herbert's
Viceroy (1900), the heroine broke into an impassioned solo —

> Oh, what disgrace, what a fate for me,
> What would they say who await for me ?
> My parents dear at home,
> Who sent me forth to roam —
> You at least believe me,
> Your distrust would grieve me,
> Pray, oh ! say I'll not to jail be sent,
> For I'm innocent.

And in the opening scene of *The Fencing Master* (1902) de Koven
was faced with —

> PASQUINO. Oh, listen ! and in verse I will relate
> The sort of maid the Duke desires to mate.
> THERESA. The Duke desires to mate ? Is that my fate ?

Yet the author, whom I shall allow to remain anonymous, was not
insensitive to Gilbertian precedent. Here are two couplets from the
libretto of de Koven's *Highwayman* (1899).

> Dignified and stately — dignified and stately —
> Thus we trip a gavotte sedately.

> How the 'Froggies' quake with fear
> As we give a cheer and overhaul 'Mounseer'.

(It is just as well that Arthur Pougin — see pages 193-4 — was not
in New York at the time.)

De Koven was a lyric rather than a dramatic composer, and he
rarely handled a stage situation to best advantage. In *Rob Roy*
(1894) the lines — intended to be taken seriously —

> How dare ye, knaves, disturb me thus ?
> I'll shoot you with my blunderbuss —

were set to a tripping dance tune (perhaps it was all they deserved),
and the battle scene from *Maid Marian* (1901) was a travesty. (This
operetta was a sequel to the earlier *Maid Marian*, which thenceforth
was known as *Robin Hood*.) De Koven's style was old-fashioned,
and the music of his first few operettas, in which humour was

unobservable, was in many respects imitative of Balfe's *Bohemian Girl* and Wallace's *Maritana*, though solo cadences were often echoed by the chorus *à la* Sullivan. His second visit to Europe induced a little more enterprise, but he never threw off a regrettable tendency to sentimental balladry. Matters were not improved when the hero had to express admiration of his adored in such phrases as 'I love your nose's tip' (*The Red Feather*, 1903). De Koven's addiction to patriotic effusions of the rally-round-the-flag-boys type was moderated in *The Student King* (1906), where he tried with some success to catch a Slav atmosphere with mazurkas, polkas and — less appropriately — a csárdás. He was at his best in vocal ensembles, and it is worth noticing that the charming part-song 'Love may come and love may go' (*Maid Marian*) *preceded* Edward German's 'Love was meant to make us glad' (*Merrie England*). Another attractive *fa-la-la* was 'Come! sing a roundelay' from *The Red Feather*, and a few bars from 'Happy is the summer's day' — *Happyland* (1905) — will serve to illustrate his straightforward approach.

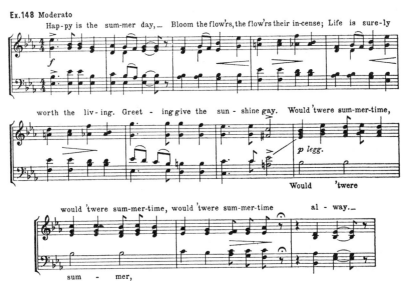

De Koven's choral writing lacked initiative : 'Come the bowmen in Lincoln green' from *Robin Hood* incorporated a colourful modulation

through the dim supertonic minor to the bright supertonic major, and the opening of the second act of *The Three Dragoons* (1899) was spirited in both harmony and rhythm, but these were exceptional efforts. If *Robin Hood* was his greatest popular success, *Foxy Quiller* (1900) must be rated his best achievement. It included four healthy tunes of over-average quality : 'We build the walls', 'If I go with thee', 'I've been to the East' and 'The king on his throne is not happy'. His later operettas were monotonous and repetitive. After the failure of *Her little Highness* (1913) he turned to 'grand opera' ; his *Canterbury Pilgrims* was played at the 'Met.' in 1917.

Victor Herbert's *Natoma* (1911) and his one-act *Madeleine* (1914) also achieved that honour, but it is operettas, of which he wrote about thirty-five, that are our present concern. His early ones were dubbed comic operas; later came 'musical comedies', 'musical farces, fantasies and extravaganzas' ; *When sweet sixteen* (1910) was a 'song-play', *The Enchantress* (1912) an 'opéra comique'. But there was little generic distinction except that from about 1913 onwards Herbert abandoned the 'operatic finales' which had hitherto been an agreeable feature, and as poor compensation introduced fox-trots and other modern dances. The character and calibre of his music was comparable with that of his Anglo-Belgian contemporary Ivan Caryll, whose proneness to 'dotted' rhythms he shared to the full, but he was a more versatile craftsman than de Koven and had a better sense of the stage. Among his more successful works were *The Wizard of the Nile* (1895), *The Serenade* (1897), *Babes in Toyland* (1903), *The Red Mill* (1906), *The Lady of the Slipper* (1912) and *The Princess Pat* (1916), but his most consistent productions were *Naughty Marietta* (1910) and *The Madcap Duchess* (1913). The former had an exceptionally accomplished opening chorus, where the 'Come, come, come' of a group of flower-sellers was gradually overwhelmed by the 'Clear the way, come out I say' of the passing street-sweepers ; far more attractive than the nostalgic 'Sweet mystery of life' was the concerted 'Taisez-vous', which had a rhythmic originality suggestive of Leslie Stuart (as had the opening chorus of *The Red Mill*), and the first-act finale was well constructed. The high-spot of *The Madcap Duchess* was an evocation of Watteau shepherds and shepherdesses in the duet 'Far up the hill', which

I find irresistible. (A technical point to note is that the vocal
canon is first at bar-length but presently catches up half the distance.)

The second act opened with an unaccompanied chorus, a
favourite manœuvre which Herbert also carried out in *Cyrano de
Bergerac* (1899), *The Only Girl* (1914) and *Hearts of Erin* (1917).
Elsewhere he showed his quality in a Viennese waltz, 'Love is a
tyrant to all', from *The Singing Girl* (1899) ; in a delicate sextet,
'The dreaming Princess', from *The Enchantress* ; in a 'pizzicato
polka' from *The Lady of the Slipper* (which was danced by Lydia
Lopokova) ; and in an excellent song in Hungarian style from
The Debutante (1914) —'When I played Carmen at the *Opéra-
Comique*'. It must be admitted, however, that evidence of an
individual talent needs searching for amid a welter of blaring
marches and commonplace ballads.

Commonplace ballads also figured prominently in the operettas
of JULIAN EDWARDS (1855–1910), who wrote two in his native
Manchester before taking himself to New York — where he wrote

seventeen more. Of these the most successful were *Brian Boru* (1896), *In the Palace of the King* (1900) and *Dolly Varden* (1901). *In the Palace* contained a few attractive pieces of pastiche (notably a bourrée and a pavane), but Edwards, who had a good knowledge of theatrical requirements, appeared to best advantage in concerted items, *e.g.* the vocal quintets 'Sweet the birds were singing' from *The Jolly Musketeer* (1898), 'I fear my dancing has its faults' from *When Johnny comes marching home* (1902) and 'There's my bird' from *Love's Lottery* (1904). The two last-named works reached a higher musical plane than most of his efforts, for in them he devoted more care than usual to accompanying detail. His tunes were often trivial to triteness, but lyrical artistry was discernible in a barcarolle from *Jupiter* (1892) and in the 'wood-nymph song' from *The Princess Chic* (1900). Edwards was blessed with a sense of proportion and therefore humour; in his last operetta *The Motor Girl* (1909) he added a neat touch of rudimentary ragtime rhythm to the burlesque chorus of Quakers 'That's why we behave just so — in Philadephia'.

Ludwig Engländer (1859–1914), Austrian by birth, arrived in the United States in 1882 and began to write operettas in the mid-nineties. His earlier specimens, though their workmanship was professional, were heavily encumbered with sentimentality; most of those which followed were not so much operettas as musical comedies or *vaudevilles* of little worth. In fairness one must mention an unexpected dab of local colour in the waltz 'Singing and dancing' from *The Monks of Malabar* (1899), which hovered intriguingly between D minor and E♭ minor, and the key-contrasts (D, B♭, G) in the 'prologue-duet' from *The Strollers* (1901), Engländer's only real success. Of the rest, the less said the better: the clever medley for countesses, maids-of-honour and pages in the second act of *A Madcap Princess* (1904) was an oasis in a desert of triviality.

Gustav Luders (1866–1913), who came from Germany at the age of twenty, was extremely fortunate to find a competent librettist in Frank Pixley; together they wrote seven operettas. Except for the whimsical *Woodland* (1904) and the pretentious *Gypsy* (1912) these were full of fun. But though Luders wrote some good hearty choruses his musical attainments were inadequate for his set purpose, and it was almost entirely due to Pixley's efforts that *The Burgo-*

R

master (1900), *King Dodo* and *The Prince of Pilsen* (both 1902) enjoyed popularity in their day.

Another immigrant from Germany was GUSTAV KERKER (1857–1923), whose family settled in Louisville in 1867. One would like to think that his *Belle of New York* (1898, libretto by Hugh Morton) was characteristic of American operetta, but it never aroused quite the same enthusiasm in its home town as it did in London. British audiences have always acclaimed it as a spirited piece of work, and nobody need be ashamed to enjoy the unsophisticated charm of 'Oh, teach me how to kiss, dear' and 'When we are married — why, what shall we do ?' Nor should a musician turn up his nose at the *più mosso* in the first-act finale where the waltz-tune 'For she is the Belle of New York' leaps joyously from the key of D♭ major to F major. 'The anti-cigarette society' and 'The ornamental purity brigade' introduced absurdity tinged with appropriate vulgarity, but they simultaneously pointed Kerker's weakness. His tunes were far too often based on rhythmical repetitions on or around a single note, followed after a bar or so by a sharp upward or downward curve. This mannerism became very noticeable in later operettas like *The Social Whirl* (1906, afterwards re-christened *The Whirl of the Town*) and *The Grass Widows* (1912), where *two* such melodies were combined in elementary counterpoint ('A boy — when but a whipper-snapper'). But as a rule rhythmic vitality saved the music from tedium ; there was a nice sense of originality in the 'gnomes' chorus' from *The Social Whirl* and of humour in the finale of the one-act *Burning to Sing* (1904), a preposterous and amusing skit on grand opera. Like most of his colleagues Kerker jibbed at the word 'operetta' and searched precariously for a satisfactory alternative. One of his weaker works — *Winsome Winnie* (1903) — was a 'comedy opera' on the cover of the vocal score, a 'musical comedy' on the title-page, and a 'comic opera' on the first page of the music.

RUDOLF FRIML (1879–   ), native of Prague, pupil of Dvořák, and for many years accompanist to the illustrious violinist Jan Kubelík, had no etymological inhibitions. He wrote a vast quantity of piano music and — after reaching America — about two dozen unashamed operettas. One would like to be able to record that they profited from his impeccable background and sound musicianship — but most of them didn't. There was restraint in *Firefly* (1912), *Katinka* (1915) and *You're in Love* (1916), but presently Friml became a naturalised citizen of the United States and identified himself whole-heartedly with a national characteristic by expressing a determination to write the 'biggest' operetta yet. And so he did — *Rose Marie* (1923).[1] Almost equally 'big' were *The Vagabond King* (1925) and *The Three Musketeers* (1928), which were musically more satisfying. From the former the 'Song of the Vagabonds' can still stir the blood, and *The Three Musketeers* was perhaps his *chef d'œuvre* ; the genial trio 'Love is the sun' and — in different mood — the sombre 'Here in the night alone I stand' were worth a dozen of *Rose Marie's* Indian love-calls.

Often associated with Friml in the public mind is the Hungarian Jew SIGMUND ROMBERG (1887–1951), who wrote *The Student Prince* (1924), *The Desert Song* (1926) and over fifty other operettas (nearly all of which are forgotten). He came to the United States about the same time as Friml and proved himself far more prolific, though he was a less accomplished musician and relied almost entirely on instinct. Much of his music was negligible, but the duet 'Of love I've often heard' from *The Student Prince* was pleasantly inspired, and to the composer's credit the subsequent waltz-refrain ('Deep in my heart, dear'), instead of being 'plugged', was kept firmly in place and only recurred twice. The popular 'Riff song' from *The Desert Song* emulated Friml's vigour, but when in *The New Moon* (1928) Romberg attempted a résumé of Viennese music from the *Ländler* to the 'Slowfox' his shortcomings were apparent. (This item was omitted when *The New Moon* was played in London.) The extrovert and prophetic 'Polo Rag' from *A World of Pleasure* (1915) and a 'chromatic tango' from *Nina Rosa* (1934) held more attention.

JEROME KERN (1885–1945) was a child of his time. Between 1912 and 1926 he wrote eight or nine conventional musical comedies (the libretti were usually by Guy Bolton and P. G. Wodehouse). Several are still remembered because of detached numbers which have retained popularity, *e.g.* 'You can't keep a good girl

---

[1] This is the date given in the 1960–61 edition of *Who's Who in America*, presumably by the composer himself. It certainly looks likelier than 1916 (*Grove* and *Thompson*), for *Rose Marie* was not played in New York till 1924.

down' from *Sally* (1920) and 'Two little blue birds' from *Sunny* (1925). In 1927 he came right to the fore with *Show Boat* (after Edna Ferber). Negro melody and rhythm had long been part and parcel of dance-music, but this was the first time that negro idiom had been the *primum mobile* of a stage production. Kern tackled the job seriously, and one regrets that he admitted a few stylistic incongruities like 'Only make-believe'. One may tire quickly of 'Old Man River' and 'Can't help lovin' dat man', but not so soon of such invigorating expositions as 'Niggers all work on de Mississippi'. Wisely, perhaps, Kern never attempted to repeat *Show Boat*; instead he showed his versatility in *The Cat and the Fiddle* (1931), an up-to-date affair set in the artistic quarter of Brussels, which lightly stressed romance without eschewing comedy and was better than most of its kind. Thereafter his work deteriorated; one is sorry to have to debit him with that last desperate resort of the dismal crooner — 'Smoke gets in your eyes' (*Roberta*, 1933).[1] Everything that Kern did GEORGE GERSHWIN (1898–1937) did just a little bit better. He capped *Sally* with the more sophisticated sallies of *Lady, be good* (1924); *Sunny* with the sunnier *Oh! Kay* (1926); the conventionally unconventional *Cat and Fiddle* with the bitingly satirical *Of thee I sing* (1931, libretto by George R. Kaufmann); *Show Boat*, even, with *Porgy and Bess* (1935) — but that was no operetta.

The last twenty years have seen a vast number of spectacular American 'musicals', of a type for which *Rose Marie* and *White Horse Inn* (see page 152) had set the precedents. Outstanding collaborators have been Oscar Hammerstein II (the librettist), RICHARD RODGERS (1904–   ) who provides the tunes, and the less well publicised Albert Sirmay who 'edits' them. The Rodgers-Sirmay share has been inconsistent in taste and quality. There was plenty to enjoy in *Oklahoma!* (1943), not quite so much in *South Pacific* (1949), less still in *The King and I* (1951).[2] Outside the

---

[1] According to McSpadden (*op. cit.* page 239 footnote) 'the stage manager vigorously balked at the inclusion of this song, and it was only at Kern's insistence that it was retained'.

[2] Rodgers also played his part in *Pal Joey* (1940, revised 1952) which bewitched nobody; British audiences, at least, were left bothered and bewildered. Hammerstein has died since this chapter was written; his last joint-productions with Rodgers were *Flower Drum Song* (1958) and *The Sound of Music* (1960).

Hammerstein-Rodgers series *Guys and Dolls* (1950), which was *The Belle of New York* brought up to date, probably owed its success mainly to public familiarity with Damon Runyon's tough Broadway citizens and their inimitable vernacular, but one and all were gratified more than somewhat at the spiel of FRANK LOESSER (1910–   ), who has recently shown his true quality in *The Most Happy Fella* (1956), which includes some very accomplished concerted numbers.   FREDERICK LOEWE (1902–   ), who was born in Vienna and emigrated to the United States in 1923, set himself on the high road with *Brigadoon* (1947), and has had no need to worry since 1955, when he wrote the music for *My Fair Lady* (adapted from Shaw's *Pygmalion* by A. J. Lerner) ; here he did less than justice to his tunes by hammering them home the way he did.   Though most American musicians would rate far higher the contributions of the Italian-born Carlo Menotti (see page 167), Loewe's success has been no less deserved than that of LEONARD BERNSTEIN (1918–   ), the versatile conductor of the New York Philharmonic Orchestra, whose *Trouble in Tahiti* (written in 1949, produced 1953) fore-shadowed rock-and-roll, and whose *West Side Story* (1957) was its musicianly apotheosis.   *Candide* (1956) was less violent in impact, although Voltaire's views on prosody (see page 42 footnote) might have been shaken by the characteristic cross-accents of Ex. 150.

Ex.150 Allegro molto

This is   the heart of   the best of   all poss - i - ble worlds.

Pangloss's philosophic outlook, however, is no longer applicable to operetta, for the garden is now so overgrown that traditional methods of cultivation are seemingly impracticable.

XXV

CURTAIN CALL

BECAUSE Albert Lortzing wrote some 'unassuming little operas', and because his maturity (of which *Zar und Zimmermann* may be taken as representative) roughly coincided with that of Adolphe Adam and Louis Clapisson, he must definitely be regarded as a Composer of Operetta, and his youthful *Ali Pascha von Janina*, dated as early as 1824, has therefore qualified for discussion under our terms of reference. But Lortzing's praiseworthy efforts led to little in the end, since operetta never really took root in Germany, and for practical purposes Adam's *Chalet*, which did not come till 1834, must be reckoned as the earliest significant example. A quarter of a century later operetta (sometimes in the guise of *opéra bouffe*) was accepted in Paris as a distinctive genre, whereas it had hardly been heard of in Prague, meant little in Berlin (despite Lortzing), and in London and Vienna was still in the chrysalis stage. So French operetta, first in the field, inevitably exercised a profound influence on the growth of the other national schools when the time came. Hence the lay-out of this book in 'geographical' sections, with a full review of French operetta to begin with. To conclude it, a brief chronological résumé on an *inter*national basis may help to put the whole picture in perspective.

During the fifteen years or so which followed *Le Chalet*, when Adam and Clapisson had things more or less their own way in Paris (since as yet Jacques Offenbach had acquired little repute as a composer), there were few signs of activity outside France except in Spain, where the inception of nineteenth-century *zarzuela* was something apart.[1] It is true that in Germany Lortzing went on writing *Singspiele* and Otto Nicolai produced his unique *Merry Wives of*

---

[1] *Zarzuela*, as such, had no eventual impact north of the Pyrenees.

Windsor, while in Austria Franz von Suppé was tentatively adapting Italian *opera buffa* to Viennese requirements ; but none of this seemed to be leading anywhere and the all-round prospect was bleak. When the eighteen-fifties were well under way, however, there were some important happenings. The opening of Hervé's Folies-Nouvelles in 1853 and Offenbach's Bouffes-Parisiens in 1855 consolidated the establishment of French operetta on firm ground ; the people of Paris soon acquired the taste, and many composers in the wake of Hervé and Offenbach seized every opportunity to indulge it. It was this period that saw the emergence of Émile Jonas, Ferdinand Poise, Léo Delibes and a host of others. The year 1858 had especial importance. At the Bouffes-Parisiens Offenbach, freed from some vexatious licensing restrictions, produced his first full-length operetta *Orphée aux enfers*. A month or two later he paid the first of his several visits to Vienna and stimulated the inauguration of a native school under the initial guidance of Suppé. It was in 1858, too, that Thomas German Reed took over the lease of the Gallery of Illustration, which was to be the breeding ground of Frederic Clay and Alfred Cellier, the first recognisable exponents of *British* operetta. Things were beginning to move.

Throughout the sixties, however, Offenbach was still in full command of the situation. This was the decade of *La Belle Hélène*, *Barbe-bleue*, *La Vie parisienne*, *The Grand Duchess of Gerolstein* and *La Périchole*, which were played with great success not only in Paris but almost all over Europe. His main rival in popularity was Hervé, though the latter's artistic standards were in no way comparable with those of Delibes or of Charles Lecocq who, after a slow start, came near the fore in 1868 with *Fleur de thé* and *Les Jumeaux de Bergame* without yet aspiring to leadership. Offenbach also dominated (from behind the scenes) in Vienna and London. He provided the impulse for Suppé's *Schöne Galathe*, and his influence was even more pronounced in the early works of Karl Millöcker and in Arthur Sullivan's first operetta *Cox and Box*. Nor should one overlook Bedřich Smetana's comment on his own *Bartered Bride*, quoted on page 153.

The Franco-Prussian war marked the termination of Offenbach's hitherto unquestioned pre-eminence ; his subsequent productions, with a few exceptions, added nothing to his reputation. Hervé presently had further success, and Robert Planquette came into the limelight with *Les Cloches de Corneville* ; but maintenance of the tradition during the early years of the Third Republic devolved largely upon Lecocq. Right nobly he did his job, with a fine series of operettas which included *La Fille de Madame Angot*, *La Petite mariée*, *Le Pompon* and *Kosiki*. And there were important developments elsewhere. In Vienna Suppé's *Fatinitza* and *Boccaccio* displayed increased initiative and Franz Genée's *Nanon* did nearly as well ; above all, the more accomplished Johann Strauss the younger, also inspired by Offenbach, turned his attention to operetta and brought the Viennese variety to perfection with *Die Fledermaus*. Meanwhile Antonín Dvořák entered the field with *King and Collier*, and in *The Peasant a Rogue* demonstrated a supreme aptitude for the genre. The same year (1878) witnessed the first unequivocal triumph of Gilbert and Sullivan — *H.M.S. Pinafore* — which quickly conquered the New World as well as its own small corner of the Old.

Faced at last with serious foreign competition French operetta had to look to its laurels. In the eighties it was obliged to retire to a back seat, for the main interest shifted from the Bouffes-Parisiens to the Savoy Theatre, London, where from 1881 (*Patience*) until 1889 (*The Gondoliers*) Sullivan, having escaped from Offenbach shackles, put all others in the shade. His luminence need not blind one altogether to Alfred Cellier and Edward Solomon, who were at least as talented as the majority of their contemporaries in Paris. Here Lecocq and Planquette had become repetitive, and Gaston Serpette was ineffectual ; a more hopeful sign was that Edmond Audran, after achieving a *succès fou* with a commonplace triviality, was beginning to show awareness of a composer's responsibilities in such works as *La Cigale et la fourmi*. The early operettas of André Messager also looked extremely promising, but for the moment that was merely an augury for the future. The Viennese front was relatively quiet ; Suppé, Strauss and Millöcker were carrying on as before, with *Die Afrikareise*, *The Gipsy Baron* and *Der Feldprediger* as their respective high-spots.

That French operetta recovered its pristine glory during the nineties was due to Messager, who set a high standard with *La Basoche* and *Madame Chrysanthème*. Audran surpassed himself in

La Poupée and Planquette came back into the picture with *Mam'zelle Quat'sous*, but it was Messager again who capped them both with *Les P'tites Michu* and *Véronique*. Britain provided one bright flash in the pan — Charles Villiers Stanford's *Shamus O'Brien* — as well as the first few operettas of Sidney Jones and Leslie Stuart ; among them were *The Geisha* and *Florodora* which were especially note-worthy since Sullivan was by now in decline. So too were Strauss and Millöcker : Vienna had little of importance to offer beyond Karl Zeller's *Obersteiger* and Richard Heuberger's *Opernball*, deservedly remembered for its overture. At the turn of the century, therefore, the order of precedence was Paris — London — Vienna ; it was soon to be put in reverse.

For the next two decades Messager, busied with administrative commitments, did not find much time for writing operettas, and his French contemporaries in the same field proved broken reeds except for Maurice Ravel whose *Heure espagnole* stands by itself. In Britain Sidney Jones and the less prolific Edward German, with spasmodic assistance from Lionel Monckton and Paul Rubens, did something to keep the spirit of Offenbach and Sullivan in evidence, but operetta soon yielded right of way to a type of musical comedy which at its best was inoffensively entertaining without laying claim to artistic integrity. In Vienna, on the other hand, genuine operetta was given a new lease of life by Franz Lehár, Oscar Straus, Emmerich Kálmán and Leo Fall, who kept the flame alight until the upheaval of 1914. After the war they found themselves obliged, in varying degree, to lower their standards in order to conform with contem-porary demands ; during this period the only truly civilised operettas to achieve popular success were those of the naturalised Frenchman Reynaldo Hahn. As regards more recent develop-ments, which have only in small measure been directly concerned with operetta in its normal connotation, nothing can profitably be added to what has been recorded in previous chapters.

So many operettas are musically uneven in quality, and so many others have been ruined by poor libretti, that it would be unfair to blame those 'adapters' who have attempted pasticcios, comprised of selected items from different works by a single composer — say Offenbach, Johann Strauss or Millöcker. (Lehár sometimes performed the same operation on himself.) There can be no valid objection to this method of keeping attractive music alive rather than allowing it to disappear for ever, so long as it is presented in a manner that accords with the intentions of the composer. What should not be condoned in such 'operettas' is spurious modernisation, let alone the interpolation of extraneous and incongruous 'theme songs'. This sort of commercial exploitation is unfair to the memory of even a modest Millöcker ; to subject to the same treatment a handful of shrewdly-picked snippets from the works of great composers like Schubert (in *Lilac Time*) or Borodin (in *Kismet*) is an artistic outrage. In any case a pasticcio, however competently contrived, can rarely be a satisfactory substitute for a straightforward *revision*. What should the formula be ? Briefly : rewrite dated dialogue, furbish up trumpery lyrics, cut out the worst trivialities without shirking healthy vulgarity, speed up the action ; but unless the plot has to be twisted out of recognition retain the bulk of the music as originally conceived, since that will help to preserve a sense of unity. Yet on the last point one should not be too dogmatic, lest the approach lack proportion ; no operetta should be regarded as hallowed by reason of the music any more than by reason of the words. By all means let there be pruning and carpentry in order to ensure continuity in a new dramatic framework ; this may result, incidentally, in a higher level of consistency. But let the work be done by experienced and conscientious craftsmen in tune with the spirit of the original. Much has already been accomplished along these lines, notably for recent Sadler's Wells revivals of well-known works by Viennese, French and British composers. It is to be hoped that this will prove to have been the thin end of a wedge, for of the thousand or so operettas which have found mention in these pages there are many which, if judiciously edited without being brought self-consciously up to date, might still have the power to attract audiences looking for something more than a period-piece. Admittedly selection would need to be discriminating, for otherwise there might be an unwitting public endorsement of Francis Hueffer's unkind judgment that operetta was 'the miry slough which swamped the sweetest growth of French national art' — i.e. *opéra comique*. I have made no attempt to disguise the fact that some of the works which I have passed under review were utterly paltry, and Hueffer's opinion need not necessarily be ascribed to narrow-mindedness (though it was far too sweeping as a generalisation).   Even those who share his views, however, may regret the form of words in which it found expression and be glad to recall that at the formal opening of the *Conservatoire américain* at Fontainebleau on 26th June 1921 the eighty-five-year-old Camille Saint-Saëns chose a more gracious metaphor :

L'opérette est une fille de l'opéra comique, une fille qui a mal tourné ; mais les filles qui tournent mal ne sont pas toujours sans agrément.

BIBLIOGRAPHY

THE works of reference, criticism and biography to which I have most frequently had recourse for factual information are all named, once each at least, at appropriate points in the main text or in footnotes, but two of them deserve more specific acknowledgment. They are *The Origin and Development of Light Opera* by Sterling Mackinlay (1927, not to be confused with his earlier book simply entitled *Light Opera*) and *Die Operette in ihrer geschichtlichen Entwicklung* by Otto Keller (Vienna, 1926). Mackinlay was a tireless enthusiast who viewed operetta from the standpoint of a stage-producer ; his canvas was overcrowded and he did not always get the details quite right, but the chapters dealing with *Origin* are a mine of historical interest and some of his researches — notably on the Scandinavian derivatives of *Singspiel* — broke virtually new ground. Keller's is the only work I have come across (in any language) which makes some pretence of dealing with the *musical* aspect of operetta on an international basis. He ignored Scandinavia, Czechoslovakia and Spain, but granted a chapter to France and a few pages to Britain ; he even brought in Italy (*La Rondine*) and the United States (*The Belle of New York*). His well-documented review of operetta in his own country was admirably comprehensive, but not all his judgments were surely founded : to set the Viennese picture in perspective *Die Operette* needs to be read in conjunction with Anton Bauer's *150 Jahre Theater an der Wien* (Vienna, 1952).

I append a list of works which contain well-informed critical comment on the operettas of individual composers.

BIZET
  Winton Dean, *Bizet* (1948), pp. 129-33.
DELIBES
  Henri Parent de Curzon, *Léo Delibes, sa vie et ses œuvres* (Paris, 1926, in French).
DVOŘÁK
  Otakar Šourek, *Dvořák : Leben und Werk* (Vienna and Leipzig, 1935, a shortened version in German of his monumental *Život a dílo*

Antonína Dvořáka in four volumes, published complete only in Czech), pp. 43-8, 67-71, 223-8.

Otakar Šourek, *Antonín Dvořák : his Life and Works* (Prague, 1952, a separate book written in English), pp. 98-102, 108-9.

LEHÁR

Ernst Decsey, *Franz Lehár* (Vienna, 1924, in German).

OFFENBACH

Anton Henseler, *Jakob Offenbach* (Berlin, 1930, in German).

SMETANA

Zdeněk Nejedlý, *Smetana, the Great Master* (1924, an English translation), pp. 33-7, 42-4, 49-51.

STRAUSS

Ernst Decsey, *Johann Strauss : ein Wiener Buch* (Berlin, 1922, in German).

SULLIVAN

Thomas F. Dunhill, *Sullivan's Comic Operas* (1929).

Arthur Jacobs, *Gilbert and Sullivan* (1951).

INDEX OF OPERETTAS, 1824-1960

S

GENERAL INDEX